Story of My Life

VLADIMIR JABOTINSKY'S
Story of My Life

EDITED BY
Brian Horowitz and Leonid Katsis

WAYNE STATE UNIVERSITY PRESS
DETROIT

© 2016 by Wayne State University Press, Detroit, Michigan 48201. All rights reserved. No part of this book may be reproduced without formal permission. Manufactured in the United States of America.

20 19 18 17 16   5 4 3 2 1

ISBN 978-0-8143-4138-4; ISBN 978-0-8143-4139-1
Library of Congress Control Number: 2015934525

∞

Designed by Bryce Schimanski
Typeset by Keata Brewer, E.T. Lowe Publishing Co.
Composed in Adobe Caslon Pro

The author gives special thanks to the Imre Kertész College at the University of Jena and the Frankel Center at the University of Michigan.

CONTENTS

A Note on the Text   vii

Introduction. Muse and Muscle: *Story of My Life* and the Invention of Vladimir Jabotinsky   1
Brian Horowitz

Story of My Life by Vladimir Jabotinsky   33

   My Origins   35

   Between Childhood and Youth   41

   Bern and Rome   48

   Journalist   56

   Kishinev   64

   The Congress   68

   St. Petersburg   72

   Wanderer   76

   Through the Storms of the Russian "Spring"   79

   Helsingfors   88

   Elections, Marriage, Vienna   92

   Constantinople   95

   Crossroads   101

   When the Volcano Erupted   107

   Lust for a Fight?   112

CONTENTS

Around the Front 119

The Jewish Accent 123

Notes 125

Index 157

A NOTE ON THE TEXT

This volume presents the first publication in English of *Story of My Life* (originally published in Hebrew as *Sippur yamai* [1936]), one of three major autobiographical writings by Vladimir (Ze'ev) Jabotinsky. The other works are *Story of the Jewish Legion* (originally published in Russian as *Slovo o polku: Istoriia evreiskogo legiona* [1928] and *The Five* (published in Russian as *Piatero* [1936]), the autobiographical novel that portrays Jabotinsky in the revolutionary year of 1905.

The present text of *Story of My Life* is based on the rough draft of an English translation discovered by Professor Leonid Katsis in the Vladimir Jabotinsky archive of the Jabotinsky Institute in Tel Aviv. We have been unable to identify the original translator.

It must be acknowledged at the outset that it is hard to define with full certainty the length of *Story of My Life* because no canonical text exists, and publications of *Sippur yamai* in Hebrew and Russian do not correspond exactly to one another. The major problem is that *Story of My Life* and *Story of the Jewish Legion* have been published several times in different languages, before and after Jabotinsky's death.[1] Therefore we are unable to say with absolute confidence that one or another text represents the canonical version.

We have opted to depart from two variant texts: the first version that appeared in 1936 and the version that appeared after Jabotinsky's death, in 1946–47, and edited by Eri Jabotinsky in the volume *Avtobiografiyah,* in Vladimir Jabotinsky's *Ketavim (Collected Works)*. The reasons motivating our decision are connected with a desire to present the most complete book possible without repeating *Story of the Jewish Legion* (1928; English translation 1945).

We could have adopted the 1936 version, since it is the last text to appear in Jabotinsky's lifetime, but we feel this version leaves out too much. It ends with the closing of part 1 of the 1946–47 edition:

> Here ends the first part of the story of my life, because the thread became interrupted on its own; it was a period that had no continuation. If I

wanted to live, I had to be reborn anew. But I was thirty-four, long past my youth and half into middle age, and I had wasted both. I do not know what I would have done if the whole world had not turned upside down and thrown me into unforeseen paths. Perhaps I would have gone to Eretz Yisrael, perhaps to Rome; maybe I would have created a political party, but that summer the world war broke out.

The 1936 version ends with the chapter "Crossroads" and does not include descriptions of events connected with the outbreak and first years of World War I—events that are treated in short-hand in the first chapter of *Story of the Jewish Legion* ("Birth of the Legion Idea"). The four additional chapters included here ("When the Volcano Erupted"; "Lust for a Fight?"; "Around the Front"; "The Jewish Accent") appeared in the 1946–47 version of *Story of My Life*. These chapters seem to form a coherent part of the text of *Story of My Life*, and we follow Eri Jabotinsky's lead in publishing them in this volume.

However, it is also important to note that Eri Jabotinsky took several other chapters from *Story of the Jewish Legion* and placed them under the title *Story of My Life*. His Hebrew version of *Story of the Jewish Legion* in *Avtobiografiyah* begins with the chapter "Between the Barracks and the War Office," which was published as the fifth chapter in the original Russian and English versions of *Story of the Jewish Legion*. We do not understand the need to lengthen *Story of My Life* at the expense of *Story of the Jewish Legion*, and therefore have rejected adding to our text entire blocks that have already appeared in print in English. It should be noted, however, that in the case of the 1946–47 Hebrew edition, Eri Jabotinsky's editorial decision had no real consequences for the reader; because *Story of the Jewish Legion* followed immediately on the heels of *Story of My Life*, no text was lost.

In sum, in our English edition of *Story of My Life*, we wanted to present a text that was complete yet distinct from *Story of the Jewish Legion*. Therefore we included the additional materials about World War I that appear in the 1946–47 edition but stopped at the point where *Story of the Jewish Legion* begins. To that end, the text in this volume concludes with the chapter "The Jewish Accent" ("*Ha'dagesh ha'yehudi*").

On a different issue, we also note that Jabotinsky's language choice—Hebrew—is curious. The editors of the 1936 volume underscore this fact, remarking that *Story of My Life* "was written by the author's hand in Hebrew. The essays that follow were written for the most part in Russian and translated into Hebrew by others."[2] Shlomo Zal'tsman—the publisher of *Exile and Assimilation*, the 1936 book that contains the first version of *Story of My Life*—makes a mystifying statement about Jabotinsky's Hebrew: "As is known, the author of this book has a particular approach to Hebrew writing, and for that reason we adapted the translations to correspond with the author's approach."[3] The editors are referring to Jabotinsky's theories of Hebrew translation, which he published in 1923.[4] Among these is his idea that conveying meaning has primary importance in translation. Jabotinsky also specified that translations should be conveyed in colloquial Hebrew (rather than biblical or literary Hebrew), and should use the Sephardic pronunciation. Additionally, he advised adding letters for vowels (instead of *nikkudot*), although he did not insist on the practice.[5]

To emphasize the rigor and accuracy of the Hebrew text, the editors underscored the participation of Yehoshua Ravnitzky, the well-known Hebrew writer, in preparing the 1936 volume, noting that it was Ravnitzky's "fate to be Z. Jabotinsky's first teacher of Hebrew, and he now helped us with useful and trustworthy advice in Hebrew in the first edition of Ze'ev Jabotinsky's selected works."[6]

As we have mentioned, the English text that appears here was found in the Jabotinsky archive located in the Jabotinsky Institute in Tel Aviv. It is hard for us to say when the translation was made or whether there were plans to publish this translation. Additionally, the identity of the translator is a mystery. Was it Samuel Katz, the translator of *Story of the Jewish Legion* and later Jabotinsky's biographer? Or was it someone else whose identity is hidden? At this point we do not know. The editors here can only speculate that, although the translator had an excellent command of English, English was likely not his native language, due to certain nonidiomatic usages.

Unable to resolve these mysteries at this time, we prefer to turn to Ze'ev Jabotinsky, Vladimir Jabotinsky's grandson, with gratitude. Mr. Jabotinsky has given us the opportunity to make this text available to the English-speaking reader.

INTRODUCTION

Muse and Muscle

Story of My Life and the Invention of Vladimir Jabotinsky

BRIAN HOROWITZ

Vladimir Jabotinsky's autobiography, *Story of My Life* (1936), was written with a political purpose: to provide the reader with a portrait of a charismatic leader who has acquired his right to lead by virtue of his biography—his family, spiritual origins, and practical experiences.[1] In the book Jabotinsky describes his personal development during his childhood and early adult years in Odessa, Rome, St. Petersburg, Vienna, and Istanbul, during Russia's Silver Age, a period known for individuals' spiritual searching and at the same time characterized by political violence, radicalism, and pogroms. Producing a self-image radically different from those of his supporters in the 1930s, Jabotinsky offers few signs of the militarist leader, the hostile enemy of socialism, or the angry critic of Chaim Weizmann that he would become. Jabotinsky emphasizes his softer qualities and depicts himself as an easygoing youth for whom school was secondary. His true learning took place through active, real-life encounters and by way of stringent self-criticism.

He offers us a self-portrait from his birth in 1880 to the period just after the outbreak of World War I. He tells us about his childhood in Odessa, his escape to Rome as a youth, and then his return to Odessa. He gives us important interpretations (if not certifiable facts—more on that later) about his adoption of Zionism, and about his struggles with rivals and colleagues in politics and journalism. At the same time he refuses to write about his personal life; he explains that he has placed a "high fence" between his professional and personal lives. Nonetheless, we gain some information about that as well.

The translation appearing here is important not only because it is the first English-language publication of *Story of My Life* (*Sippur yamai*), an event in and of itself, but also because the text spotlights a new trend in the study of Jabotinsky. Removed from the passions unleashed against him during his lifetime and the fury ignited by debates in Israel during the last sixty years, a new image is emerging.[2] There is room to recover other Jabotinskys—not merely an enemy of the left and a hero of the right but the Russian-Jewish intellectual, the talented fiction writer, journalist, and playwright, and the translator of poetry into Russian and Hebrew. Although these new images will not displace those of the militarist and political fighter who, more than anyone else in the Jewish world, trumpeted the idea that Israel would be born from violent struggle, they certainly complicate the picture.

One wants to ask with regard to Jabotinsky's image: How do we connect the Hebrew translator of Dante with the organizer of Betar, the militaristic youth movement that was especially popular in Eastern Europe? What is the connection between the Odessa writer of humorous and sometimes erotic stories and the head of Revisionist Zionism or the Irgun Zvai Leumi, the underground military group that valorized terror in the 1930s?[3] It is also worthwhile to compare his novel, *Samson the Nazarite* (*Samson Nazorei*, 1927), or his fictionalized memoir, *The Five* (*Piatero*, 1936), with the life and ideas of the politician, although contradictions multiply.[4] In fact, one of the central themes of *Story of My Life* pivots around the differences between two images: the militarist and the writer; the representative of a Jewish radical right and the idealist and liberal theoretician of a better world. Although Jabotinsky tried to diminish the poisonous image of the militarist in *Story of My Life*, boldly promoting the portrait of a liberal nationalist, the reader (even today's reader) knows and remembers that Jabotinsky was regarded by many, including David Ben-Gurion, as a fascist. Mapai members in the 1930s called him "Vladimir Hitler."[5]

But what do these conflicts of the 1920s and 1930s mean for us today? Although they might appear harmless—since for the first time in Israel's history the country seems to lack a competitive Labor Party—it is worth recalling that part of Israeli political history was shaped by the passionate conflicts between Labor and Herut, Ben-Gurion and Menachem Begin.[6] Now, more than seventy years after Jabotinsky's death, one might consider as his most lasting achievement the establishment of a Zionist rightwing political orientation that has served as a permanent alternative to the Israeli left.[7] Despite the fluctuation of his image according to the needs of his followers, many of his ideas have been adopted into the program of the Israeli right in general and the present-day Likud Party in particular. Despite its weakness, the Israeli left has made Jabotinsky an emblem of everything they regard as wrong with the political right: militarism, anti-Arab provocation, the idea of a Greater Israel, settlement-building, and the inequality of wealth.[8]

Chronologically *Story of My Life* ends with the onset of World War I and blends into *Story of the Jewish Legion* (1928).[9] It is possible that Jabotinsky wrote *Story of My Life* with the legion book in mind. However, the origins of *Story of My Life* are complicated, because various parts were written and published in different versions at different times. For example, Jabotinsky published articles in 1907–8 titled "Sketches without a Title" ("Nabroski bez zaglaviia"), in which he described aspects of his biography, such as his arrest when he was found with an Italian translation of Sergei Witte and his experiences in an Odessa prison.[10] Furthermore, from 1932 to 1934 Jabotinsky published a number of sketches in Yiddish with the title "Zichronos fun meinem a ben dor" ("Reminiscences from My Generation") and "Fun mein tagbuch" ("From My Diary") in the New York periodical *Der Morgen Journal* and in the Warsaw daily newspaper *Haynt*.[11] These works closely resemble in content and narrative voice the language of *Story of My Life*.[12]

The various components were reworked and formed the basis of the longer, stand-alone autobiography, *Sippur yamai* (*Story of My Life*). Written in Hebrew, it was published in Tel Aviv in 1936 in a volume of collected pieces titled *Golah ve-hitbolelut* (*Exile and Assimilation*), and was later reprinted by his son, Eri, in the late 1940s, in a volume of Jabotinsky's collected works with the title *Autobiography*. This volume included *Story of My Life*, *Story of the Jewish Legion*, and Jabotinsky's Acre prison memoir.[13] Yet questions about the original text remain unanswered, such as whether it was initially written in Russian or whether the original language should be considered Yiddish or Hebrew.[14] It might be noted as well that *Story of the Jewish Legion* (1928) was written in Russian, Jabotinsky's first language, as were *Samson the Nazarite* and *The Five*, his main literary texts of the period.

In *Story of My Life* Jabotinsky mixes true events with myths, a real biography with a fabricated one. In his book *Autobiographical Jews* (2004), Michael Stanislawski challenges the formerly conventional view of the book as a confession of fact and nothing but fact:

> I was working on my last book, on Zionism and the fin de siècle, and discovered that one of my most important sources, Vladimir Jabotinsky's wonderful and indeed stirring autobiography, entitled in its original Hebrew *Sippur yamai* (The story of my life), was all but invented

Vladimir "Ze'ev" Jabotinsky in the early 1930s. Courtesy of the Jabotinsky Institute, Tel Aviv.

out of whole cloth—i.e., it contradicted the massive data, in black and white, in Russian, Hebrew, German, Yiddish, and Italian, that I had gathered on three continents by and about Jabotinsky, on matters both small and grand. [. . .] In due course I realized that far more interesting than debunking Jabotinsky's own retelling of events in his life was deciphering the ways in which he had retroactively created his own mythologized, and to a large extent, mythological, life-story, constructing a supremely controlled and controlling narrative in which truth-telling necessarily gave way to the overarching purposes and goals of the work: a brilliant, but highly fictionalized, self-fashioning.[15]

Although there is a great deal of truth in what Stanislawski writes, he has perhaps overstated the case. Certainly many of the details have been embellished and modified. But to say that everything is invention is also a stretch.[16] In fact *Story of My Life* follows the basic biography of Jabotinsky's life as reflected in his bibliography and in documents about him (his collection of letters and the body of writings about him). For example, Jabotinsky writes that in Rome he published an article about Anton Chekhov and Maxim Gorky. Indeed, one can find the article in the bibliography. If one wonders whether Jabotinsky was really in Istanbul in 1909 and 1910, one can check his letters to see that he was there, and that indeed he did edit a half-dozen journals, as he claims in *Story of My Life*. He did complain about the situation there to David Wolfsohn, the president of the World Zionist organization, and he did resign his position.[17] So the case is even more complex than Stanislawski imagined. *Story of My Life*, like other fictionalized autobiographies, is neither entirely nonfactual nor entirely truthful. In each situation one has to know the body of biographical materials in order to check Jabotinsky's narrative against a more accurate context that exists only as the sum total of the factual materials, many of which are themselves questionable because they reflect ideological tendencies.

Nonetheless one has to wonder about Jabotinsky's loose attitude toward facts: Why is he an unreliable narrator? What did he hope to achieve by inventing scenes that likely never happened? Although one might want to consider Jabotinsky a kind of modernist who plays with expectations and leaves readers uncertain about truth, it is unlikely that his intent was purely aesthetic. Thus Stanislawski makes a strong case: Rather than trying to show where and how Jabotinsky strays from the facts, one may interpret *Story of My Life* more productively by examining Jabotinsky's self-fashioning. I have already stated that Jabotinsky had a political agenda. Let us turn now to that agenda.

What did Jabotinsky in the mid-1930s want to say about his childhood and youth? To answer that question we need to know about his situation at the time he was writing the book. In the 1930s Jabotinsky was engaged in a number of severe internal and external battles that were taking a toll on his Revisionist Zionist Party. In 1933, in opposition to Jabotinsky's threat to take the Revisionists out of the World Zionist Congress, Meir Grossman, previously his closest friend, mounted a takeover at the World Congress of the Revisionist Movement in Katowice. In response Jabotinsky summarily fired the entire executive committee and took total control of the party. After a few months he held a referendum and won more than 90 percent of the votes cast.[18]

The rank-and-file vindicated his coup d'état, but his old friends among the Russian émigrés left to form the Jewish State Party, which sought to harmonize their Revisionist goals with participation in the World Zionist Organization (WZO). In 1934 Jabotinsky took his Revisionists out of the WZO. Arguing against the futility of serving as a permanent opposition, Jabotinsky claimed that only by creating its own organization could Revisionism fulfill its potential. His New Zionist Organization (NZO) held its first international congress in 1935.

Jabotinsky was a figure of opprobrium for reasons other than simply his purging of the party. In 1933 Jabotinsky played a major role in the defense of Abraham Stavsky, a Revisionist youth, against charges that he had assassinated Haim Arlosorov, the well-known Labor Zionist leader who was killed in Tel Aviv.[19] Jabotinsky, comparing the Arlosorov affair to the Mendel Beilis blood libel of tsarist times, objected to the political motivation to "hang a Revisionist." He solicited support from important quarters, including Rav Kook (Abraham Yitzhak ha-Cohen), the chief rabbi of Palestine, who counseled acquittal.[20] In time Stavsky was released due to a lack of evidence.

The perception was widespread among Jabotinsky's critics that the Revisionists were a group of violent hoodlums and their leader was a Jewish tyrant. The boiled-up anger over Arlosorov's assassination prevented Mapai members from ratifying an agreement for cooperation between Mapai and the Revisionists, which had been negotiated in private by Ben-Gurion and Jabotinsky in 1934. With Hitler now in power in Germany, there was also a strong backlash against Revisionism because some Revisionists, such as Abba Achimeir, had lauded the Nazis. Even the memory of Jabotinsky's role as the founder of the Jewish Legion was not sufficient to stave off such poisonous criticism. Publishing an autobiography offered Jabotinsky opportunities to promote a different image.

An autobiography that showed his selfless commitment to Zionism and which linked him to the Jewish people would be helpful. However, as he and everyone who knew his history understood, Jabotinsky was weak precisely on the point of his Jewish background. He had been born and raised in Odessa, the city on the Black Sea famous for tolerance and its multinational, multilinguistic population. He did not receive a Jewish education, nor did he master Yiddish or Hebrew as a child. Moreover, until he "discovered" Zionism in 1902, he did not pay attention to happenings in the Zionist movement. His indifference or ignorance had to be explained.

Jabotinsky depicted the history of a Zionist leader that was very different from more conventional models. For example, instead of denying his lack of Jewish education, Jabotinsky emphasized his handicaps. But he compensated in ways calculated to redeem his flaws. For example, at age seventeen, during his first travels westward to Bern, he passed through Ukraine. He expressed surprise and alienation at seeing a railway car full of traditional Jews. From his negative reaction the reader understands that the author is removed from traditional Jewish life. That impression is deepened by a confession that he once denied being Jewish. In *Story of My Life* he admits:

> Once, in the gay company of young girls and boys, when their conversation touched (half-respectfully, half-ironically) on the rites of the Catholic Church, one of the girls sitting beside me asked, "And do you belong to the Greek Church?" I answered yes. I do not know why I answered yes. There is no doubt that my prestige would in no way have been impaired in their eyes if I had told the truth. Perhaps I was afraid of losing prestige in my own eyes by admitting in front of these free people that I was a slave.

Of course the explicit purpose of this confession is to shock the reader. But he contrasts it with other recollections. He sentimentalizes about his mother, "One more decisive thing I learned from her brief answers: I was about seven years old or even younger when I asked her: 'Shall we Jews also have a kingdom in the future?' And she replied: 'Of course, we shall—you silly boy!' From then until today I did not ask anymore; I already knew." Although this interchange seems fatuous, it is intended to show that he imbibed his Zionism with his mother's milk, and that Zionism was part of the air he breathed. Similarly Jabotinsky tells the reader that at the time of his bar mitzvah he studied Hebrew with Yehoshua Ravnitzky, one of the greatest Hebrew writers of the day, who happened to be a neighbor. And in another instance he describes his first public speech, at a meeting in Bern, Switzerland, years before he became a Zionist. There he tells his reader that he spoke ardently in favor of radical Zionism, along the lines that all the Jews of Russia must make *aliyah* or face certain death. These and other examples display how Jabotinsky divorced Zionism from Judaism, giving himself a Zionist pedigree in the absence of a traditional Jewish education.

Jabotinsky's recounting of the intellectual origins of his Zionism deserves scrutiny. He acknowledges that in his youth he was a cosmopolitan, a citizen of the world who became a "Roman in Rome" and did not give much thought to the "Jewish problem." Instead of his arriving at Zionism as the result of experiencing anti-Semitism or out of a populist love for "the people," Jabotinsky attributes his nationalism to cosmopolitanism. Jabotinsky puts forward the intriguing argument, seemingly paradoxical, that cosmopolitanism was not an obstacle to nationalism, or even a contradiction, but could serve as its very source, as the *fin de siècle* mentality urged a transformation of the individual and a discontent with life as it was. Thus "decadence"—usually associated with physical and spiritual decline—turned out to stimulate spiritual growth. In *Story of My Life* Jabotinsky writes of his friend Vsevolod Lebedintsev that he "divided his time and his enthusiasm among his three ideals: the study of astronomy at the university, evenings at the Italian opera, and also lovemaking with the young singer Armanda degli Abbati.[21] He was also an active member of the SR party. To my question, 'How does all of this harmonize in one soul?' he answered, 'Don't you understand that these are all the same things?' Now I do not 'understand,' but then I did."

His confession—"Now I do not 'understand,' but then I did"—does not need to be taken seriously. But he is serious about bending life to his will. Decadence signifies an appeal to transform life in the Nietzschean sense. Theodor Herzl's dictum—"Wenn ihr wollt, ist es kein Märchen" ("If you will it, it is no dream")—has a similar significance. Jabotinsky conveys that Zionism is the Jewish version of striving for the transformation of reality.

Another of Jabotinsky's central goals in *Story of My Life* is to refute the claim that he is a fascist. In several places he reiterates that he is a liberal and that people have misunderstood him. For example, he describes his love for liberalism in *fin de siècle* Italy. "[It was a great] concept because of its very broadness: a dream of order and justice without compulsion, a vision embracing all mankind, composed of compassion, patience, faith in the fundamental goodness and justice of the human race. At that time there was not yet even the slightest hint in the atmosphere of that worship of 'discipline' that later found its expression in fascism."

In spite of his praise for liberalism, Jabotinsky kept Revisionism relatively free of it. Indeed Jabotinsky established the Zionist Revisionist Party in 1925 as a reaction against liberals such as Chaim Weizmann (who favored compromising with the British government) and the leftists of Mapai. Jabotinsky's political positions were distinctly more conservative. Although he discouraged the worship of authority, he expected discipline and conformity. He promoted a cult of personality and demanded that others show obedience to him as their leader. Jabotinsky spoke of there being room for any and all nationalities in Palestine, but insisted that the Jews have a majority and political dominance. He advocated using military force—an iron wall—if needed to attain these goals.[22] Jabotinsky's praise for liberalism was not a lie, but it was contradictory, and it is impossible to ignore the inherent chauvinism of Revisionist Zionism or Betar ideology.[23]

The question of liberalism in Jabotinsky's worldview is especially problematic and needs to be interpreted according to the timeline of Jabotinsky's intellectual biography. In Russia in 1905 to 1907, Jabotinsky adopted a position that mixed civic and ethnic liberalism (democracy with equality for all and additional national rights for Jews and other minorities). Turning his attention to Palestine in the 1920s, he advocated various political set-ups that provided priority to the rights of the Jews in Palestine (by virtue of their future majority) and offered the Palestinian Arabs civic rights. He never wavered regarding his defense of Arabs in the civic polity, but he insisted on the dominance of the ethnic principle, the rights of Jews to decide the direction of Palestine's future. His goal was a Jewish state on both sides of the Jordan River with a Jewish majority and Jewish government and culture, but with an Arab minority that had security of person and property, as well as voting rights.[24] So, generalizing overall, one would have to be circumspect regarding Jabotinsky's liberalism and define specifically what liberalism in this context entails.

Similarly, the issue of violence in Jabotinsky's politics needs unpacking. In the 1920s, the period of realistic state construction, the conflict with the Arabs became one of the central impediments to Zionist achievements. Threats of violence with the Arabs was one option, as were negotiation or collaboration. What was unique was not Jabotinsky's advocacy of paramilitary preparation, but as the historian of Zionism Yosef Gorny writes, the order, the turn to violence as a precondition for state-building. The Revisionists "reversed the order of Zionist priorities by arguing that military force took precedence over the constructive effort, rather than growing organically out of the building of society. Jabotinsky also called on Great Britain to demonstrate its support for Zionism and its respect for the Balfour Declaration by establishing a Jewish Legion to guard the Yishuv. This extreme demand was intended to exert pressure on British politicians to arrive at positive decisions regarding Zionism."[25] In other words, militarism emerged as a strategy for dealing with a particular historical moment in Zionist history.[26]

At the same time, Jabotinsky called for a major colonization effort in which Jews from around the world would be invited to Palestine to exploit state-owned lands, engage in industry and the crafts, and invest in the country. In part, his radical approach was conceived out of frustration that in the early 1920s the Jews were not coming. It was possible that a Jewish majority would never be created and that the once-in-a-lifetime opportunity offered by the Balfour Declaration would be lost. Jabotinsky began to use his political proclamations of a Jewish majority in order "to exert pressure on the opponent so as to force him, in turn, to clarify his own aims and to be clearly aware of what lay ahead. Such pressure might not change the opinions of opponents nor persuade those who were vacillating, but it would force the Jews to open their eyes to facts and to prepare the instruments for confrontation with reality."[27] Jabotinsky's appeals enraged Weizmann and enraged England but helped create a new camp of followers who wanted to exploit the rare historical opportunity.

Although his subject is the past, his attitudes in the present emerge in the autobiography. In particular, Jabotinsky polemicizes through the book with the Zionist leadership. For example, he writes, "With the exception of the Sixth Congress (my first), I did not like them; I always used to 'wander' like a stranger, and now it is real mortal torture for me to think that I may be compelled to participate once more. But the conferences of Ha-Tsohar and Betar—those I like very much."[28]

Another feature of Jabotinsky's autobiography is his depiction of himself as a Betarist *avant la lettre*.[29] He portrays himself as a young man who respects the values of chivalry, honesty, integrity, loyalty, and decorum—qualities he would formulate later as those of the ideal Betarist. For example, he describes his first meeting with Jeanne (Johanna) Galperin, who later became his wife:

> I was fifteen years old, and it was my first year in the Richelieu Lyceum, when one of the Jewish pupils invited me to his home and introduced me to his sisters. One of them was playing the piano at the moment I passed through the room; afterward she confessed bursting into laughter behind my back, so strange was the impression made by my Ethiopian profile.[30] [. . .] Nevertheless that very same first evening I won her favor by calling her "Mademoiselle"—the first to do so among all her acquaintances.

He continues:

> I am no admirer of Japheth and his descendants (nor of Shem or his Semites . . .), but there is one characteristic trait of the Nordic peoples that I have and of which I am proud: the worship of women.[31] I am certain that every average woman is an archangel without exception. If she hasn't yet shown her qualities, it only means that she was not forced to do so, but wait till the opportunity arises and you will see. Life brought me close to three [women], and in all three I found the same nature.

Jabotinsky's praise of women in general reflects a patriarchal viewpoint that parallels the principles of *hadar betari*, the values of a Betar disciple. The list of obligations for boys encompasses chivalry, along with good manners, personal hygiene, and respect for discipline.[32] Betar girls are given the no less important but nonetheless traditional tasks of cooking, bearing children, and raising a family.[33] Jabotinsky's self-portrait is supposed to provide an example worthy of emulation. If you were a boy or girl reading *Story of My Life* in the 1930s, you would have a model in the young Jabotinsky, who already in his youth embodied, albeit anachronistically, the Revisionist values he acclaimed as an adult.

As *Story of My Life* deals with Jabotinsky's Russian period, an examination of his attitudes toward Russia is in order. The Russia of this period is the tsarist empire, a country that included Congress Poland and Finland in the west and which reached the Pacific Ocean in the east. It was governed by a tsar (a king), who was supported by various ministers and bureaucracies. Jews in Russia occupied a paradoxical position: On the one hand, Jews there compared their existence with that of their forebears in Pharaoh's Egypt; especially during the period of Jabotinsky's youth, numerous economic liabilities and limitations in educational opportunities affected Jews exclusively. But on the other hand, enforcement of such exclusionary rules was chaotic. There were true horrors, such as pogroms, the expulsion of Jews from Moscow in 1891, and blood-libel trials, but in many nongovernmental domains—such as the revolutionary movement, journalism, the arts, and business—some Jews thrived.

It is essential to recall that Russia at this time was home to 5,500,000 Jews, the world's largest Jewish population; and, despite mass emigration from the country, the number of Jewish inhabitants did not diminish, as the population's birthrate remained high. In several cities in the Pale of Settlement, Jews made up 50 percent or more of the population. Although overall the average Jew was relatively poor, there were pockets of Jewish wealth, and a small but growing Jewish professional class was establishing itself.

Zionists found little to praise about tsarist Russia. Zionist thinkers—from Leon Pinsker and Ahad Ha'am to Weizmann and Berl Katznelson—have emphasized the government's anti-Semitism as it was manifested in the May Laws, pogroms, blood-libel trials, and the Black Hundreds.[34] These and other episodes in Russian history symbolize more than a century of misery that became known as the *Judennot* (Jewish distress), a term coined by Max Nordau in his speech to the Second Zionist Congress. Certainly Russia could be praised as the home of early Zionists—the Bilu and Hibbat Zion—but these examples confirm only that Russia was a place to leave, not a place in which to build a future.³⁵ However, one cannot help but detect a certain tension in this attitude, since many Jews expressed an undeniable sentimentality toward their country of origin: Russia was their birthplace, the land in which their parents lived and in which they grew up.³⁶

Jabotinsky praises many things about Russia. He is proud of his father's professional success. Although he did not get to know his father well before his untimely death, the stories he heard conveyed an image of Yevgeny Jabotinsky as a top administrator of ROPIT, the Russian grain export company. His father had deep roots along the Dnieper River in Ukraine, and close relations with the region's farmers and business elite. In these recollections one gets a sense of a timeless utopian relationship among Jews and non-Jews, the grain buyers and the farmers.

Jabotinsky deepens the impression of harmony with his assertion that he did not encounter anti-Semitism at school or from neighbors. How can this be? Certainly he acknowledges instances of government anti-Semitism, as when he wanted to enroll in school, for example. However he also notes his close friendships with non-Jews, such as Vsevolod Lebedintsev, a schoolmate, and Kornei Chukovsky, the famous writer.³⁷ Odessa appears unique among cities for its multicultural and multiconfessional character. The Greeks, Ukrainians, and Jews who comprised the majority of the population were themselves minorities in the empire. Odessa was far from the capitals of Moscow and St. Petersburg, as well as from older Ukrainian centers such as Kiev or Lviv (Lvov). Conquered from the Turks near the end of the eighteenth century, Odessa, with its economic wealth, invited new peoples to it. Ethnic and religious discrimination was not deeply rooted in its history, although there were pogroms in Odessa in 1871, 1881, and 1905. The absence of widespread anti-Semitism in Jabotinsky's life can perhaps be explained by the circles in which he moved and perhaps also by the population's anger at the incompetent government that scapegoated Jews instead of effectively running the country.

Jabotinsky had his own vision of Odessa, although it corresponds to one of the classic myths of Odessa as a beacon of freedom.³⁸ He loved his hometown because it did not stultify its sons with book learning but liberated a person with its *joi de vivre*. He describes getting his "education" in the city park, where he played games with the local boys. As he portrayed it, Odessa of the *fin de siècle* inculcated the values of creativity, imagination, limitless energy, and a courageous stance against hypocrisy, falseness, and bourgeois satisfaction.

In his professional life Jabotinsky was a journalist. His writing sustained him during his Rome years (1898–1900), and he earned his living from it for most of his life. He became well-known thanks to his feuilletons, especially for *Odesskie Novosti*, from 1900 to 1906. His pseudonym, Altalena (Italian for seesaw), became a household name among the city's readers, who enjoyed his acerbic wit, exuberance, and critical judgment. Nonetheless between 1902 and 1904, Jabotinsky, the happy-go-lucky intellectual scamp, became a committed Zionist to such a degree that he devoted his entire life to the cause. How that transformation occurred is the subject of much controversy. In *Story of My Life* Jabotinsky presents his version of this evolution as one that centers on the awakening of latent feelings within him that Jews absolutely must head for Palestine. Yet a study of his biography suggests a more gradual development.

Jabotinsky surprised many people in the city when he began to insert a strong defense of Zionism in his newspaper columns. In 1902 he became a ubiquitous figure in Jewish self-defense in Odessa, and in 1903 he was sent to Kishinev to aid victims of the pogrom there. In Kishinev he met Hayim Nachman Bialik, the poet about whom Jabotinsky admits he had never heard up to that time. Before long Jabotinsky had translated Bialik's masterpiece "*Ir ha-Harega*" ("City of Slaughter") into Russian ("Skazanie o Nemirove").[39] Introduced to a group of Odessa businessmen by his mentor, the Zionist and publisher Shlomo Zal'tsman, Jabotinsky is invited to represent them at the Sixth Zionist Congress.[40] Despite his use of literary estrangement to describe the congress in *Story of My Life* (similar to that of Natasha at the ball in Leo Tolstoy's *War and Peace*), it is clear that the congress in Basel taught Jabotinsky a great deal; namely that Zionism has a real organizational platform to achieve its ends.

Russian experiences continued to shape Jabotinsky's political outlook. His participation in *Rassvet* (also known as *Evreiskaia Zhizn'*), the first Zionist monthly newspaper in the Russian language, played an essential role in his education. There he met Avram Idel'son, the Zionist theorist and editor, who articulated a blend of Marxism and Zionism.[41] Idel'son became known for inventing the term "synthetic Zionism" (a mixture of theoretical and practical Zionism) and for *Gegenwartsarbeit*—the idea that Jews in Russia should participate in local politics and demand national rights in addition to civil rights. Jabotinsky wrote, "I am sure that it would not be an exaggeration if I say that the word 'talent' is inadequate to describe Idel'son. That man stood on the threshold of genius."

Jabotinsky was very impressed by the Helsingfors Conference (the Third Conference of Russian Zionists in 1906), where representatives decided to modify the "negation of the *galut*" in order to devote themselves to political activity in Russia.[42] Although the long-term goal of a Jewish home in Palestine remained unchanged, the theory went that Jews in the Diaspora had to devote themselves to self-realization. They had to learn Hebrew, study farming or business, and build up experience in their host societies to prepare for a future in Palestine. Certainly the theory was paradoxical, since it encouraged the development of the Diaspora only to quicken its demise. Jabotinsky explained:

> Our ideal consisted in preserving only what is alive in Judaism, the energy that at one time was transferred into our workshops; i.e., they shook the dust of the Diaspora from their feet. That [ideal] is still true. But now we bend down and pick up from the ground the clumps of this "dust" and try to analyze them. We immediately see that it is full of valuable organic ingredients that turn out to be productive when used properly. Let us analyze the ghetto. A terrible institution that has poisoned us physically and morally—but at its base is found the healthy principle of estrangement, and it is worth cultivating this principle [albeit] in a different form. At the same time, take assimilation: an indisputable illness, moral gangrene—but it put into our hands the whole cultural arsenal of modernity without which we would not even be able to dream of any building. Take the Jew's cowardliness and physical passivity, his response to a pogrom, "the dark cellar." It is shameful and an invitation to other pogromists, but in certain conditions it is precisely the very best method for a weak minority's self-defense.[43]

Jabotinsky remained loyal to the idealism of Helsingfors and especially the theory of minority rights articulated there. Throughout his life Jabotinsky claimed that the state was only a frame for the development of the nation; the nation was the living body that needed to grow.[44] Loyal to this principle, Jabotinsky did not insist on a Jewish nation-state in Palestine. He was satisfied with a multinational, multiethnic, and multiconfessional state under the condition that Jews comprised a majority and would have political dominance. Arabs, although constituting an ethnic minority, would enjoy full civil and even national rights.[45] His willingness to negotiate with members of Brit Shalom (the group favoring a binational state with the Arabs) with regard to a federalist project in the Levant in the late 1920s reflects his commitment to full Arab rights within a Jewish state.[46]

What becomes clear in *Story of My Life* is that Jabotinsky is offering a different version of the development of Zionism. In contrast to the conventional perspective that sees Zionism as catapulted forward in the post-Herzl era—thanks to the political left in general and the members of the Second Aliyah in particular—Jabotinsky locates another source in Russia. He valorizes individuals involved in *Rassvet* (Israel Trivus, Arnold Seideman, Nikolai Sorin, Julius Brutzkus, Isaac Naiditsch, and Vladimir Tiomkin), who gave voice to issues of national culture in the Diaspora—Hebrew language and modern Jewish education, minority rights, and armed self-defense.

The *Rassvet* team was composed of men who were similar in age. They were born in the mid-1870s (Jabotinsky was the youngest) but diverse in geographic origins—the whole Pale of Settlement was represented.[47] Although most had studied in a Russian university and had participated in the radical student movement, they had all come to respect liberalism, albeit a liberalism that linked the rights of citizens with additional national rights. Such rights included access to Jewish schools, cultural institutions, and even an internal Jewish parliament with representatives elected through a democratic process. Such national rights were among the dreams of 1905.[48]

Jabotinsky writes about that spirited time when freedom was in the air. He and the others would turn more pessimistic after the October pogroms of 1905, the dispersal of the first two Dumas, summary hangings by Pyotr Stolypin, and the blood-libel trial of Mendel Beilis (1911–13). But the government was only one source of disappointment. The official Zionist leadership was another. In *Story of My Life* Jabotinsky lambasts David Wolfsohn, Menachem Ussishkin, Efim Tchlenov, and Chaim Weizmann. Jabotinsky desired a more rigorous commitment to Zionism than his colleagues. He imagined fostering a new kind of Jewish and Hebraic culture based in Hebrew but of world significance. In the years before World War I, he traveled across the Pale, giving lectures on the importance of the Hebrew language, Hebrew schools, and Hebrew literature. But he received pushback: people thought he was utopian and irresponsible; who really needs schools in Hebrew in tsarist Russia?[49]

Although Jabotinsky's experiences between 1904 and 1914 do not entirely predict the development of Revisionism, with its emphasis on individualism and hostility to socialism, a line can be drawn across the Russian and post-Russian years. Although socialism appealed to Jabotinsky, because in Russia the "best" people were involved in it (those who rejected the corrupt government), he learned to distrust leftists—socialists and liberals—because of their betrayals of the Jews. Jabotinsky did not appear surprised that Russian socialists did little to defend Jews in the State Dumas or that liberal leaders, such as Pyotr Struve, abandoned the goal of Jewish equality.[50] Although he had already left Russia in 1915, nonetheless he too was frightened by the stories of Red Terror that came from friends who left Bolshevik Russia and joined him in European emigration. One could hardly predict that Jabotinsky would come to abhor socialism, but retrospectively it does not seem out of character.

Just as there is a Russian theme in *Story of My Life,* so too is there also a vital Polish theme, albeit less developed. At the time Jabotinsky was writing his autobiography, he was negotiating with the Polish government for aid in evacuating Jews to Palestine, and thus he was careful with his comments. He twice mentions Roman Dmowski, the leader of the nationalist party, Endecja. The second time he cuts himself off:

> In 1911 a controversy between me and the Warsaw press emerged. Endecja circles even now have not forgiven me, and neither have I them, but free Poland is now the slogan of Piłsudski, not of the ND [Narodowa Domokracja], and I hope and pray that the government of this noble nation never again falls into the hands of men such as those who then, in the time of Dmowski, betrayed the tradition of nobility. And this is enough—I shall not write any more about it.

However, earlier in the narrative he describes his meeting with Eliza Orzeszkowa, the progressive writer, and criticizes Dmowski more openly, describing his preference for a multinational Poland. Nonetheless, he acknowledges sensitivity to Polish national aspirations, while noting, however, that there was nothing special about it, since generations of Russian intellectuals had opposed Russian oppression of Poland.

Jabotinsky is especially respectful of Polish sensitivities. He describes how he favored refraining from giving any speech if it had to be in Russian (or "Moskal," a derogatory term Poles used for the Russian language). Similarly, he underscores his love for Polish literature, especially that of Adam Mickiewicz. Finally, he emphasizes the superiority of Polish Zionists by virtue of their being Polish:

> We considered the Zionist youth in Warsaw the very elite of the new Zionist generation; and we were right. A particular depth and refinement, a sort of echo of the *neshama ha-yetera,* were perceptible in their whole being, in their approach to the problems of national existence, and in the modes of reaction to every decisive event. Perhaps this was due to their proximity to the West; perhaps to the atmosphere of the country, saturated with Polish tragedy and romanticism.

As noted earlier, Jabotinsky had reasons to seek good relations with Polish authorities, the Polish public, and Polish Jewry: Polish Zionists made up a large percentage of Revisionist supporters in Europe and formed the basis of Jabotinsky's electoral and financial strength. Furthermore he (and almost every other Zionist leader) viewed the Eastern European diaspora as a potential population pool for the future Jewish state.

Since the autobiography is one of the most plastic and ubiquitous genres in Western literature, it seems appropriate to ask about Jabotinsky's sources for *Story of My Life*. Is there a Zionist antecedent? Herzl and Nordau offer precedents for Jabotinsky's politics, but I cannot locate a similar mythologized autobiography from them. The best Zionist memoirs—those by Chaim Weizmann, Shmarya Levin, and Ben-Gurion—were written with the intention of providing an accurate depiction of the writer's own life.[51] Theirs is not the same kind of self-conscious or aesthetic self-fashioning that one finds in *Story of My Life*.

An obvious source for Jabotinsky's *Story of My Life* is the Russian literary tradition where leading writers developed a genre that mixed fiction, memoir, and autobiography. Such examples are Leo Tolstoy's *Childhood, Boyhood and Youth;* Maxim Gorky's *Childhood;* Boris Pasternak's *Safe Conduct;* and the works of émigré writers such as Ivan Bunin's *The Life of Arseniev* and Vladimir Nabokov's *Speak, Memory*. Russian fictional memoirs are characterized by a loose and playful attitude toward biographical fact in the hope of getting closer to the "truth" of how people actually live and feel. *Story of My Life* resembles these and similar Russian texts with which Jabotinsky was familiar.[52]

One should also turn one's attention to Vladimir Korolenko and his five-volume memoir, *History of My Contemporary* (*Istoriia moego sovremennika*), because there are generic and idiosyncratic parallels between the two works.[53] In the beginning of *Story of My Life,* Jabotinsky makes a self-conscious and surprising confession: He has left out of his narrative everything concerning his private life.

> This story is condensed and fragmentary in many respects. First of all, I did not even attempt (except in one or two instances) to describe people with whom my life has brought me in contact, not even people who played an eminent role in the life of my generation and nation. Because of this, of course, I reduced the scope and the interest of my story, since

what is valuable in every autobiography is not the description of the narrator himself but that of his contemporaries. But what could I do? My present does not allow me to recover the rich material that lives in my memory; and besides I do not like to pass judgment on people, whether alive or dead. At the same time one cannot draw a true-to-life picture of flesh and blood without some personal "judgment."

But even with regard to my personal memories I have told only one half: the life of the writer and the public figure, not the private life of the man. These two zones are separated in my life by a very high fence; all my life I have refrained as much as possible from allowing them to interfere with one another. As a private person, I have had and have friends, connections, experiences, memories, traditions, whose influence has never encroached and never will encroach on my public activity, even though in my real inner life this half outweighs all the other impressions, and my private romance is deeper and richer in deeds and contents than the public one—you will not find it here.

If these assertions were true, it would surely hurt the book. But they are not true; in fact, we learn about Jabotinsky's family—his mother, sister, and wife. We learn about his friends, among them Shlomo Zal'tsman, Vsevolod Lebedintsev, Israel Trivus, Apolinari Hartglass, and Avram Idel'son. So why the false denial?

Although there may be other reasons, our hypothesis is that Jabotinsky's mystifying confession winks at Vladimir Korolenko, a writer who influenced him in many ways, including in providing a model for *Story of My Life*.[54] Jabotinsky's title, *Sippur yamai* (literally *Story of My Days*), parallels the title of Korolenko's memoirs, *The History of My Contemporary;* both emphasize the epoch rather than the writer himself. In his introduction Korolenko denies writing an autobiography and self-consciously distinguishes between his own life and the life of his epoch. "I write the history not of my time, but merely the history of one life at that time, and I would like it if the reader became acquainted beforehand with the prism with which it [the time] was reflected."[55] Korolenko continues by problematizing his book's genre. This sounds as if Jabotinsky could have written it:

> These sketches are not a biography because I didn't worry much about the validity of the biographical facts; not a confession because I do not believe in the possibility or effectiveness of public confession; not a portrait because it is difficult to draw one's own portrait with any assurance of accuracy. [...] And therefore I repeat. I am not trying to give my

own portrait. The reader here will find only the traits of "the history of my contemporary," a person known to me and closer to me than all the other people of my time.[56]

Following Korolenko's model, Jabotinsky makes a similar statement, guarding his own life from the reader. In fact both authors actually offer a great deal of information about themselves. However, by deflecting interest from themselves, they widen their scopes and give us fuller understandings of the larger epochs in which they lived.

The reader is invited to analyze *Story of My Life* in comparison with *Story of the Jewish Legion*, since the two are connected chronologically. (*Story of My Life* ends where the *Legion* book begins.) Specifically, *Story of the Jewish Legion* details Jabotinsky's role in establishing the Jewish Legion, the first distinctively Jewish military unit in nearly two thousand years. Jabotinsky depicted the legion as the shock troops for the conquest of Palestine. Consequently their struggles and sacrifices entitled Zionists to a place at the Paris Peace Conference and justified claims to a Jewish Palestine. The problem was that the Jewish Legion consisted of around five thousand soldiers who arrived in Palestine only during General Allenby's final assault. Despite the historical weakness of his case, Jabotinsky insisted on taking credit for the Balfour Declaration. He explains in *Story of the Jewish Legion:*

> I say with the deep and cold conviction of an observer—speaking only of the short war period: half the Balfour Declaration belongs to the Legion. For the world is not an irresponsible organism; Balfour Declarations are not given to individuals. They can be given only to Movements. And how could the Zionist Movement express itself in those war years? It was broken and paralyzed, and was, by its nature, completely outside the narrow horizons of a warring world with its war governments. Only one manifestation of the Zionist will was able to break through to this horizon, to show that Zionism was alive and prepared for sacrifice; to compel ministers, ambassadors, and—most important of all—journalists, to treat the striving of the Jewish people for its country as a matter of urgent reality, as something which could not be postponed, which had to be given an immediate yes or no—and that was the Legion Movement.[57]

The phrase, "Balfour Declarations are not given to individuals," is a barb directed at Chaim Weizmann. In fact, Jabotinsky repeatedly tried to delegitimize his rival. For the most part in *Story of the Jewish Legion,* Jabotinsky ignored his colleague, although Weizmann's disappearance from the text is strange, considering that Jabotinsky stayed with Weizmann and his wife in London during part of World War I. The one time Weizmann does appear, Jabotinsky portrays him as a coward: Weizmann says that he would like to help Jabotinsky with the legion but cannot do so publicly out of fear of criticism; nonetheless he will give secret support.[58] In contrast, Jabotinsky enumerates his own sacrifices. He joins the British army as a private. How else could he convince others to join the legion if he avoided service? He emphasizes the unpleasantness of serving in any army, even the British army, and admits to cutting a silly figure, a middle-aged volunteer among teenaged conscripts. One of his jobs is to wipe clean the officers' tables. He gets his share of abuse, too. For example, he describes receiving the first copy of his new book, *Turkey and the War,* and just at that moment a young corporal enters the mess hall and shouts, "Open it." "Open what?" asks Jabotinsky. "The bloody windows, you fool."

Although he is considered an oddity, because he gets summoned to visit Whitehall and the top military brass almost daily, he gets along well with everyone, especially the low-ranking privates for whom he is known as "Jug-O-Whiskey."[59] About his service Jabotinsky readily tells us that he saw action at the end of the war; and with the other members of the legion, he experienced harrowing moments under fire, in the desert heat and amid the discomforts of life in the Levant.

Jabotinsky published *Story of the Jewish Legion* in 1928 in order to legitimize his leadership role in the new Revisionist political party. But just as writing *Story of My Life* presented opportunities and limitations, so too did the legion book offer possibilities. To solidify his reputation as a major leader, he developed certain techniques of metonymy—linking himself to other, more illustrious, individuals. He also used this method for the same effect later, in *Story of My Life.*

Already in the 1920s, he saw the need among Revisionists for a military hero and martyr. Revisionism was new, and the party was still small and undeveloped. The hero could not be Jabotinsky himself, because he was alive and his biography still unwritten. Therefore, in *Story of the Jewish Legion,* he placed his spotlight on Joseph Trumpeldor, the military hero, and tried to connect himself and Revisionism to Trumpeldor.

Early in the book Jabotinsky introduces us to Trumpeldor with a thumbnail sketch:

> He was born in the Caucasus in the year 1880. His father was one of those men of iron endurance who went through the hell of Nicholas I's barracks—twenty-five years' service—losing neither their health nor their Jewishness. Joseph was not admitted into the university, on account of the numerus clausus; so he became a dentist. Then came military service and the Russo-Japanese War. Trumpeldor's regiment was sent to Port Arthur, and there he lived through eleven terrible months of siege. There he lost his left arm, almost to the shoulder. But no sooner had he come out of hospital than he demanded to be sent back to the front. After the fall of Port Arthur, he was taken prisoner by the Japanese, together with the rest of General Stoessel's Army. In captivity he organized Zionist societies and collected money for the Jewish National Fund.[60]

In telling us that Trumpeldor was tsarist Russia's only Jewish soldier with an officer's rank, Jabotinsky emphasizes his talents but also his sufferings and self-sacrifice. (He would give his arm and if necessary even his life for the anti-Semitic tsar—that's dedication!) A tireless fighter for Zionism, Trumpeldor immediately understood the value of the legion project. He makes an appropriate foil to the hot-headed Jabotinsky, purportedly because Trumpeldor judged things by their proper weight—"like a Goy," Jabotinsky notes, alluding to the legend of Jewish anxiety. The antidote to panic is Trumpeldor's life philosophy, one that Jabotinsky fully endorses as well.

> In Hebrew his favorite expression was *en davar* (Never mind); and they say it was with these words on his lips that he died, five years later, at Tel Hai. There was a complete philosophy contained in this *en davar*: do not exaggerate; do not see danger where none exists; do not regard a man who does his duty as a hero—for history is long, the Jewish people everlasting, and truth is sacred, but everything else, trouble and care and pain and death, *en davar*.[61]

Jabotinsky inserts the philosophy of *en davar* into his text at several key points, especially when discussing the dangers of facing death. He calls life a game that should be played skillfully, in which one should not exaggerate one's own personal significance. Trumpeldor convinced others to accept England's offer of a Zion Mule Corps in 1915, when some, Jabotinsky included, were hesitant, because mules seemed undignified. When Colonel Patterson was injured, Trumpeldor commanded the troops at Gallipoli; and with Jabotinsky, he went from office to office to promote a Jewish legion. Once permission was given, he taught the soldiers to march and shoot.

In *Story of the Jewish Legion*, Jabotinsky praises the volunteers, the miraculous Jewish "tailors" who do their duty until the last moment, despite the fact that they had no interest in making history and dreamt only of returning to their homes, wives, and children in London's East End.[62] They too represent the ethic of *en davar*, which balances individual will and collective duty, and advises one to overcome adversity by seeing the big picture rather than concentrating on the present moment. It is not a coincidence that *en davar* resembles Jabotinsky's Betar credo of *hadar*, with its emphasis on stoicism, chivalry, and quiet dignity.

Trumpeldor's death at the hands of Arab marauders at Tel Hai in 1920 shaped his status as a martyr; since then his image has been used in myriad ways by different groups.[63] For Jabotinsky, Trumpeldor transmits Jewish patriotism and national identity; there are things in life that are worth dying for. (His final words purportedly were: "It is good to die for our country.") In 1930, on the tenth anniversary of Tel Hai, Jabotinsky notes that Trumpeldor's death signified a new departure for Jews who, in contrast to other nations, always abandoned their position under fire. Trumpeldor showed that now, when attacked by fire, Jews hold their ground and return fire.[64]

Jabotinsky manipulated Trumpeldor's reputation to make it fit his needs, because Trumpeldor had been involved in the leftist kibbutz movement and followed the ideas of A. D. Gordon, the advocate of Jewish collective farming in Palestine. Jabotinsky transformed the legacy by revamping the meaning of Tel Hai from involvement with agriculture to armed defense. He named the Revisionist national fund "Tel Hai," and saw to it that "Tel Hai" was employed as a Betarist greeting.[65]

In *Story of the Jewish Legion*, Jabotinsky also connects himself to Max Nordau, the great leader of the Zionist movement. In 1915 Jabotinsky came to Spain to find Nordau, once the no. 2 Zionist official after Herzl and now an elder statesman. Nordau had been rudely ejected from France as an enemy noncombatant. Jabotinsky tells Nordau about his legion idea. The latter answers with an adage about Jewish logic: A Jew hesitates to buy an umbrella until he's soaking wet.⁶⁶ The allusion is to the Jews' rejection of their self-interests generally, but one can hear in it an echo of regret for the rejection of Nordau's plan for mass immigration to Palestine. (Nordau wanted one million Jews to immigrate immediately.) The lack of *olim* in the early 1920s bothered Jabotinsky a great deal, and it was this that led him to establish the Revisionist Party in the first place. Jabotinsky was convinced that Jews would immigrate only if economic conditions were propitious; he did not believe that socialism or philanthropy could produce a thriving economy. Only private enterprise and private capital could do that.

Nordau ultimately had a powerful influence on Jabotinsky.⁶⁷ Jabotinsky embraced Nordau's idea of the muscular Jew who could defend himself through physical strength. Later in the 1930s Jabotinsky adopted an expanded version of Nordau's plan, proposing that ten million Jews immigrate to Palestine in ten years.⁶⁸ This vision was not as unrealistic as one might think. Jabotinsky had the support of the Polish government, which had its own reasons for wishing to see Jews leave Eastern Europe.⁶⁹

Just as Jabotinsky linked himself to Trumpeldor and Nordau, he also accentuates his relationships with leading Zionist leaders in *Story of My Life*. For example, he links himself with Herzl numerous times, both in a serious and also in a jocular mode. He mockingly describes his one and only meeting with the father of Zionism at the Sixth Congress (Herzl's last), in 1903. In his version of the incident, Jabotinsky describes how Herzl cut him off in the middle of a speech and had him removed from the stage. As one might expect, Weizmann played a nefarious role in this drama. In response to the commotion in the hall, Herzl comes out from behind the podium and asks what the young Russian is saying. Weizmann responds, "Quatsch." Herzl announces, "Ihre Zeit ist um" ("Your time is up").

Michael Stanislawski's hypothesis, that this scene of Herzl chasing Jabotinsky from the stage was fabricated, is likely correct. For one thing, the protocols indicate that Herzl was busy in another meeting during Jabotinsky's speech.⁷⁰ If this description is a fabrication, it offers another paradigmatic example of Jabotinsky's myth-making.

But Jabotinsky did not end his narrative about Herzl there. He switches immediately into a laudatory ode. In *Story of My Life*, he continues:

Herzl made a colossal impression on me—this word is no exaggeration, no other description would fit: colossal—I am not one of those who will easily bow to a personality. In general I do not remember, out of all the experiences I have had in my life, one man who made any impression on me whatsoever either before Herzl or after him. I felt that truly there stands before me a man of destiny, a prophet and leader by the grace of God, deserving to be followed even through error. [...] And even today it seems to me that I hear his voice ringing in my ears, as he swore to all of us, "*Im eshkahech Yerushalayim....*"[71]

Theodor Herzl serves as a bridge from Jabotinsky's adulthood to his youth; indeed Jabotinsky had already tried to link himself to Herzl at the time of the latter's death, when he wrote an article in 1905 titled "Sitting on the Floor..." ("Sidia na polu...")—the allusion here is to sitting *shiva*. In the article Jabotinsky threatens suicide:

> We became different people, became alive from touching the ground that he placed under our feet. Only recently have I felt the ground entirely under myself, and I only understood from that minute what it means to live and breathe. If tomorrow I would awaken and suddenly see that it had all been a dream, that my former self and the ground under my feet did not exist and never had existed, I would kill myself, because one who has breathed the air of the mountaintop cannot return in resignation and sit beside the ditch.[72]

Jabotinsky also wrote his poem "Hespêd" at the time, a solemn dirge and farewell to Herzl.[73]

Although admitting that he voted against Herzl's project of settlement outside Palestine, Jabotinsky never stopped trying to acquire Herzl's mantle. For example, he often repeated that only he retained a commitment to Herzl's politics.[74] Jabotinsky underscored the connection, calling his new party Ha-Tsohar (Zionist Revisionist Party). In the 1926 policy statement *What Do Revisionists Want*, Jabotinsky was entirely clear about how he viewed Herzl's legacy: "In this firm belief we call on the Zionist public to renew Herzl's tradition—to the energetic, systematic, and peaceful political struggle to attain our demands."[75] And what are these demands? He enumerates: "The first goal of Zionism is the creation of a Jewish majority in Palestine, east and west of the Jordan [River]. That is not the last, final goal of the Zionist movement, which has several broader ideals, such as the solution of the Jewish Question in the whole world, and the creation of a new Jewish culture."[76]

In *Story of My Life* Jabotinsky's also emphasizes his closeness to Hayim Nachman Bialik, the so-called Jewish national poet. In 1911 Bialik's verses appeared in Jabotinsky's Russian translation, accompanied by a long introductory essay. Echoing the theme of shame so famously expressed in the poem "City of Slaughter," Jabotinsky drew attention to the Jewish self-defense in which he had participated in Odessa: "Then Bialik threw 'The Tale of the Pogrom' ['The City of Slaughter'] in the face of his dishonored brothers and revealed to them a feeling that they did not know what to name. The name was shame. More than a day of grief, it was a day of shame: the basic idea of this strike with a hammer is the form of the poem."[77] But, he continues, "Kishinev's shame was the last shame. Homel happened in 1904; several hundred pogroms broke out across Russia in 1905: Jewish grief was repeated even more mercilessly than previously, but shame did not return."[78] Pride in the ability to defend oneself physically became for Jabotinsky a *sine qua non* for Jewish national consciousness. It connected Jabotinsky to Bialik, Kishinev, and Jewish self-defense.

As I noted earlier, Jabotinsky's poetry and fiction are receiving increased critical attention. Dan Miron published a monograph on Jabotinsky as a poet and translator of poetry.[79] He observed that Jabotinsky was influenced as much by classic poets such as Dante, Shakespeare, and Pushkin as by the Decadents of the nineteenth century, Edgar Allan Poe and Stéphane Marllamé. Clearly Jabotinsky was also influenced by the Russian Symbolists, especially, from among the older group, Valery Bryusov, Konstantin Balmont, and Dmitry Merezhkovsky. Recently a number of scholars have begun to study Jabotinsky's fiction, analyzing its distinctive features, plot elements, characters, and use of narrative voice.[80]

Jabotinsky's fiction work is associated closely with "Russia Abroad," the literature of Russia in exile.[81] Although some of his early stories were published in Russia, the collection *Razskazy (Stories)* appeared in Berlin in 1931. The novels *Samson the Nazarite* and *The Five* were written in Russian and published in Western Europe. It is easy to connect Jabotinsky to such brilliant émigré writers as Vladimir Nabokov, Ivan Bunin, Marina Tsvetaeva, Vladislav Khodasevich, Teffi (Nadezhda Lokhvitskaya), and Nina Berberova. Their immediate readers consisted of the relatively small group of Russians in Europe, sales to whom could hardly provide an income for any of them. Undoubtedly the dream of all these writers was to reach their natural audience among the millions of book-buyers in Russia. But that was unlikely to happen until the end of Bolshevik rule, and when that would happen nobody knew.

Jabotinsky's first volume of fiction includes stories written over a long period. Some were written by a mature writer and have a decadent tonality, such as the story "Edmée," where one can perceive the influence of European modernism; while others, such as "Belka," reflect the anecdotal and naive quality of the early journalist.[82] Most of the stories revolve around a simple anecdote or portray the psychology of the young Jabotinsky. Such is the setting for "Diana," a story of a love triangle in Rome, with Jabotinsky in the role of third wheel, hopelessly and unrequitedly in love with Diana. The most striking feature of these works is the appearance of an author-narrator who inserts his own autobiography into the plot construction. These experiments with autobiography helped shape a style that he would put to use later in his longer fiction.

One can see Jabotinsky transfigure his own experience in the novel *Samson the Nazarite* (*Samson Nazorei*, 1927), in which Samson, the main hero, faces questions about politics, love, self-identity, and relations to other tribes. Because Samson speaks of the need to emulate the Philistines and make weapons of iron, some readers have considered Jabotinsky's novel as propaganda for Jewish self-defense. However, a close reading shows parallels to other aspects of Jabotinsky's life.[83] Like Samson, Jabotinsky had to choose sides between two cultures and peoples (in his case, Jewish and Russian). In the novel Samson is invited to lead the more populous and powerful Philistines, but he decides to side with the tribe of Dan. Although the story takes place at the time of the biblical judges, Jabotinsky presents the issue of national identity and culture as an existential problem. In a scene from the novel, Jabotinsky explores Samson's inexplicable rejection of the Philistines, which mimics Jabotinsky's biography: his own "official" rejection of Russian culture, invoked at the time of the Cherikov Affair, which occurred in 1908, when Russia's leading writers expressed their preference for Jews staying out of Russian culture.[84]

> "To Love," "Not to love,"—Samson answered with contempt. You are a wiseman, but with me you speak the language of women. Really is one's own and not one's own perceived through love? Do you really love the work of a Saran [accountant], do you love to count taxes and judge crooks? I have heard a lot about you: you love scrolls from papyrus, the stars in the heavens, and sailor stories. Nevertheless you are a Saran.
>
> —My father was a Saran, and all my grandfathers,—his voice from the darkness registered.

In Samson's answer anger already appeared.

—I understand your hint. Let's leave it. Even if the truth came down to you from your journey to Tsorait, what of it? Let's say that one of my two ancestors played the lute and wore a multicolored cap. But the other, like an ant, crawled through slavery, through the desert, like an ant bore a path in the dry earth of this damned region; and everything he met he gnawed to the bone and swallowed. Maybe they met face to face at the hour of my conception; but, if that is so, then the ant in me would long ago have eaten your colorful cap. Your blood is a goblet of wine; that blood is a cup of poison; if they mix—what will remain of the wine? I am not yours. Call me to your drinking parties, Philistine, I will come and entertain you . . . even if the drinking will take place around my execution. Love to drink and joke with you. But build? You said, "Build"? With you? From you? I do not trust you.[85]

In this conversation with the Philistine taxman, the author (through Samson) explains that identification does not depend on preference or pleasure. Rather, genealogy is physical; Samson knows to whom he belongs and cannot change allegiance. Jabotinsky the Zionist loved world culture and acknowledged that Hebrew must learn from Shakespeare and Dante, but he also maintained that Hebrew culture is his, even if the affiliation means he must reject Russian culture.[86]

The biggest question for scholars of Jabotinsky has been how to unite the two dimensions of Jabotinsky the creative writer and Jabotinsky the politician. The two autobiographical texts, *Story of My Life* and *Story of the Jewish Legion*, seem to define clearly who Jabotinsky was and what he stood for; yet in the same year in which Jabotinsky finished *Story of My Life* he also published the autobiographical novel *The Five* (*Piatero*, 1936), a book that presents a very different portrait.[87] Although it is difficult to interpret the author's position, it appears that Jabotinsky portrays himself in *The Five* as being ambivalent toward assimilation, which in ideological terms is the antithesis of Zionism.

In terms of genre, *The Five* is an autobiographical novel that plays with the relationship between *Dichtung* and *Wahrheit*, artistic license and actual fact. The book is written as though it were nonfiction, but the story is surely fictional or at least partly fictional; some or none of the characters are real, and some or none of the events really happened. One can compare it to Jabotinsky's *Story of My*

Life, since the latter purports to be factually accurate but contains many factual inconsistencies.

The first difference between *The Five* and *Story of My Life* is Jabotinsky's geographical presence: Where was Jabotinsky during the Revolution of 1905? In *Story of My Life* the author curtly informs the reader that he was with friends in Italy when he saw a newspaper that informed him of the Russian defeat at Port Arthur. Later he says that he was in the south of France when he heard of the tsar's pronouncement regarding the establishment of a legislative Duma. He tells us that at that point he returned to St. Petersburg rather than Odessa. In this account he spent the summer of 1905 in St. Petersburg and Warsaw; he does not mention Odessa. He relates visiting Odessa in 1906, during a speaking tour around the Pale of Settlement to promote Zionist candidates to the Duma.

Insofar as we can tell from the letters collected in volume 1 of Jabotinsky's published correspondence, he was in St. Petersburg from the end of 1904 until April 11, 1905.[88] After that, he was in Elisavetgrad, and then he arrived in Odessa at latest by June 2. He remained in Odessa until July 7. The next letter, from October 17, has a return address in Geneva. The following letter, written nearly six months later, locates him in Vilna on April 6, 1906. Clearly some of the letters did not appear in the volume or were lost.

The Five portrays Jabotinsky squarely in Odessa during the entire year of 1905.[89] The novel portrays the Milgroms, an assimilated Jewish family, and features a narrator named Vladimir Jabotinsky, who has characteristics of the author but cannot be identified entirely with him. The narrator focuses on the five children, who represent five different paths for a Jew in modern Russia; none takes the path of Zionism. Each child is shown as having a moral flaw that leads to a tragedy. Within a few years, Marusya and Marko are dead, and Serezha is maimed by a jealous husband; Lika becomes the lover of a spy in the pay of the tsar, and Torik converts to Christianity for the sake of his career. The parents, having witnessed their children's ruin, are emotionally broken. The father turns to the Book of Job for consolation.

Some readers have interpreted the novel as a castigation of assimilation, because Jabotinsky indeed appears to use the plot to make that point. Alice Nakhimovsky, for example, has written, "The novel may have a message congruent with Jabotinsky's teachings—that assimilation is a form of death."[90]

Yet there is a problem with this point of view. To begin with, there is no character in the novel who serves as an ideological counterweight to assimilation. Contrary to one's expectations, the narrator is not hostile to the Milgroms.

Rather he is full of deep and elegiac love; he cares for them as though they were his own family. The narrator emphasizes that he himself is an assimilated Jew who fully shares the Milgrom's modern, secular interests (opera, books, music, current events, and gossip). Surprisingly, the narrator does not vigorously advocate a Zionist position, so that neither the narrator nor any other character serves as an example of what Jewish nationalism or traditional Judaism would look like. In fact, in this circle of Odessa Jews, assimilation is the unmarked characteristic; everyone is assimilated.

An examination of some formal aspects of the novel/memoir can help us to see the fundamental paradox. Purposely playing with the problem of *Dichtung und Wahrheit,* the author invites the reader to identify the person of Jabotinsky with the narrator. For example, the narrator has the same characteristics as Jabotinsky: he is a young journalist famous for his witty feuilletons and is known for his pro-Jewish national views. By joining the identity of the author and narrator, Jabotinsky patently wants the reader to interpret the text as reality. Nakhimovsky argues that the novel has a broad autobiographical subtext and features Jabotinsky's own self-identity, his "emotional essence," as she calls it.[91]

Nonetheless, the actual truth-value of the portrait becomes less important than the author's image as fashioned for the readers' perception. In this portrayal of Odessa in 1905, assimilation appears as a road leading to a higher level of reality. The narrator ruminates, "Torik [one of the Milgrom children] said 'disintegration.' Maybe he is right. The lawyer [...] spoke about decadence, but he added that epochs of decadence are sometimes the most fascinating times. Who knows? Perhaps not only fascinating, but also superior in their own way? Of course I am in the camp that struggles against disintegration. I do not want neighbors; I want all people to live on their own islands. But who knows?"[92]

That question—"Who knows?"—marks the narrator's ambivalence. In spite of the Milgroms' sad fates, the narrator acknowledges that ethnic, religious, and ideological difference served to enrich the people of Odessa. Assimilation seems to symbolize the start of something new, beautiful, and ideal. Attracted to the dreams of universal brotherhood, the narrator announces a utopian vision:

> One thing is already a proven historical truth: one has to pass through disintegration to reach renewal. This means that disintegration is like a fog before the birth of the sun or like a predawn dream. Marusya said that the most wonderful dreams are predawn ones. Whose poem

is this? "The prophesy of dawn is still imperceptible, emerald and cornelian, lilac and azure: the unsung words drift into my mind, perhaps, of an unborn poet, the singer of a country still not created by the creator, where invisible visions are silent like music and whose shroud for a moment, the moment before awakening, elevates predawn dreams to us." I am afraid that these verses are my own. Getting old, I quote myself more and more often. I quote (for the second time) the following: "I am a child of my time, I love all its stains, love its full poison."[93]

The last part of his speech—I am a child of my time—is entirely comprehensible, and his confession of love for the poison of his culture also makes sense. But what are we to make of the predawn dreams, the reaching beyond to a better world? What is the higher stage that should emerge from assimilation?

Certainly the allusion to predawn dreams, the use of synesthesia—silent music—and such paradoxical language as "unborn poet" and "a country still not created by the creator" recall concepts of Russia's Silver Age, with its emphasis on the intangible, ideal, and spiritual aspects of being. This last quote, a confession of sorts, serves as a perfect example of the complicated and contradictory quality of Jabotinsky's "emotional essence." For the author, assimilation appears as wonderful and dangerous, ideal and unattainable.

Although it is typical of Jabotinsky to place in doubt the essential premises of his own worldview, in *The Five* the author intimates that assimilation has an unmistakable beauty, especially at a time of decadence. More important, *The Five* intimates that art, literature, beauty, and love are foundational stones for the creation of Vladimir Jabotinsky, the man who perhaps in his deepest heart knew of another ideal besides Zionism.

To this day I have yet to find a clear explanation as to why Jabotinsky would write a novel in 1936 that does not promote Zionism but which seems equally to valorize assimilation and decadence. Although any answer must be speculative, one may take Jabotinsky at his word: he was contradictory, attracted to different ideals that were logically true and aesthetically beautiful within their own times and value systems. As hard as one tries to find reconciliation between Zionism and assimilation, Palestine and Odessa, history and eternity—the opposing poles cannot be reconciled. It is perhaps only within Jabotinsky himself, in the realm of the imagination, and in the confessional mode of a novel, that these opposites can find a synthesis.

Is Jabotinsky's *Story of My Life* significant in the Zionist literary canon? Is it as important to Zionism as Lev Pinsker's *Auto-Emancipation*, Herzl's *The Jewish*

State, or Ahad Ha'am's or Max Nordau's essays? To answer, one can say that *Story of My Life* is one of the most intriguing books written about Zionism in Russia from 1900 to 1914, an epoch when the movement shifted its strategy from ideology to practical politics. It is intriguing at once because one cannot be sure whether all the facts are correct, but also because Jabotinsky offers sketches of little-known yet vital political fixtures and heroes in the Russian Zionist camp. But that is not all. Jabotinsky's autobiography has a certain literary flair; he has an eye for details, paradoxical ideas, and the logic of the big picture—"Why I am a Zionist?"

If one can, it makes sense to read *Story of My Life* in conjunction with the other long autobiographical texts, *Story of the Jewish Legion* and *The Five*. The three work in tandem by confirming and contradicting each other, and in subtle ways give aesthetic pleasure from the uncertainty over whether one is reading fact or fiction. Moreover, one can gain insight into multiple Jabotinskys, into his dreams and fancies as well as his ironclad logic. By realizing Jabotinsky's multi-faceted dimensions—the presence of a writer and dreamer next to the politician and militant—one gains a deeper understanding of Jabotinsky and, paradoxically, greater uncertainty about him as well.

Although *Story of My Life* can be viewed as a generational portrait of "other" Zionists who have been somehow left out of the history's glory, it is also a personal book, in which Jabotinsky paradoxically remembered the past for the sake of a present that was unfolding. But for Jabotinsky there was no paradox. He assumed that his situation in the mid-1930s could be helped by recalling the years before World War I. He viewed the two periods as connected by a beginning in Russia and an end that would culminate in a Jewish state in Israel.

STORY OF MY LIFE

VLADIMIR JABOTINSKY

This story is condensed and fragmentary in many respects. First of all, I did not even attempt (except in one or two instances) to describe people with whom my life has brought me in contact, not even people who played a prominent role in the lives of my generation and nation. Because of this, of course, I reduced the scope and the interest of my story, since what is valuable in every autobiography is not the description of the narrator himself but that of his contemporaries. But what could I do? At this time I am restrained from describing the rich material that lives in my memory; and besides I do not like to pass judgment on people, whether alive or dead. At the same time one cannot draw a true-to-life picture of flesh and blood without some personal "judgment."

But even with regard to my personal memories I have told only one half: the life of the writer and the public figure, not the private life of the man. These two zones are separated in my life by a very high fence; all my life I have refrained as much as possible from allowing them to interfere with one another. As a private person, I have had and have friends, connections, experiences, memories, traditions, whose influences have never encroached and never will encroach on my public activity; even though in my real inner life this half outweighs all the other impressions, and my private romance is deeper and richer in deeds and contents than the public one—you will not find it here.

My Origins

My mother was born in Berdichev, about one hundred years ago, the daughter of Meir Zak from a merchant family.¹ So far as I know, there are no rabbis or other "spiritual dignitaries" in the history of my family; my sole possible consolation may be that at least my wife's family is connected to the Maggid of Dubno.² I never heard any details about my mother's childhood, but from what little she told us, I got the impression that her family was considered among the best in town.

Several images from among those she recounted remain stuck in my memory, especially the splendor of the rituals of Shabbat, and the Passover seder at her father's house. I visited Berdichev at the beginning of this century, and even then at the railway station I still found Christian porters who spoke Yiddish much better than me, and even in their Russian speech you could perceive Yiddish song. At that time Berdichev was still the most Jewish of all the cities of Ukraine, and it was much more so in the days of Mother's childhood.³ There is no doubt that my grandfather was a progressive *maskil*, perhaps even an *apikores* according to his milieu, since Mother was sent to a modernized *heder* to learn German and Western manners.⁴ The latter had to be memorized in verse. For instance, if you were introduced to an important lady, you were to say:

"Bonjour Madame charmante,"
And right away kiss her hand.

My mother spoke German; she made mistakes, but you could tell by the expressions she used that she had learned the literary language. The favorite authors of her youth were Schiller and another fellow who is now forgotten even in Germany—Zschokke.⁵ On the other hand, she learned the Russian language only after her marriage, apparently because of the need to talk to the servants. Although she spoke in Russian with my sister and me all her life, she wrought havoc on Russian grammar. She understood Hebrew, the language of the bible and of the prayers, liked to study, and was very strict about religious customs.

I once asked my mother: "What are we, Hasidim?" and she answered, almost angrily: "And what do you think—*Mitnagdim*?"[6] From then to this very day I consider myself a born "Hasid."—One more decisive thing I learned from her brief answers: I was about seven years old or even younger when I asked her: "Shall we Jews also have a kingdom in the future?" And she replied: "Of course, we shall—you silly boy!" From then until today I did not ask anymore; I already knew.

Besides my sister, Tamar, I also had a brother, Miron or "Mitya," the oldest, but I do not remember him at all, as he died when I was still a little boy.[7]

We were well off as long as father lived, but he died when I was six and left us penniless; this continued until my sister grew up and began from the age of sixteen to give lessons and thus saved us from poverty. My recollections are of a life of want. We lived in a mansard, and the parents of my rich comrades, with whom I used to play in the backyard, did not permit their children to visit me lest they get contaminated by the spirit of poverty, nor did my mother allow me to cross the thresholds of their homes.

My mother was generally considered "proud." After my father's death, when she returned to Odessa with her two orphans, a family council was convened at the house of her brother Abraham Zak to discuss what to do with us.[8] One of his sons, a successful lawyer, voiced his opinion: "We have enough 'scholars'; send the girl to learn sewing, and let the boy learn to be a carpenter." Sound advice perhaps, but in those days the idea of *Umsichtung* [changing classes] had not yet penetrated into the hearts of the middle class—and from then on never again would we come to the lawyer's house and neither did he come to ours. If I were to meet his wife and children in the street, I wouldn't be able to recognize them, and they are my closest relatives. Some twenty years after the consultation, my cousin tried to speak to my mother in the courtyard in front of the synagogue. He begged her pardon, explaining that she had misunderstood him. She answered, "I am not angry, goodbye," and proceeded up the stairs to the *ezrat-nashim*.[9]

I am no admirer of Japheth and his descendants (nor of Shem or his Semites ...), but there is one characteristic trait of the Nordic peoples that I have and of which I am proud: the worship of women.[10] I am certain that every average woman is an archangel without exception. If she hasn't yet shown her qualities, it only means that she was not forced to do so, but wait till the opportunity arises and you will see. Life brought me close to three [women], and in all three I found the same nature. Regarding the first—my mother—I cannot remember even one single day in her life when she was not compelled to struggle, push, and overcome obstacles. I know about the years of my father's illness episodically, but those episodes are an epic; I do not mean an extraordinary event; on the contrary, it is a chapter similar to thousands of chapters from the stories of thousands of women whose lives are feats of heroism day in and day out. Born rich, lived rich. Only yesterday she had a home full of every refinement; her husband, a nobleman, king, and ruler in his own milieu, and she, his queen. And then, in one day, everything wiped out: position, money, future, and on her shoulders a wreck of an invalid, grown old overnight, and already doomed to die. She gathered us all, took us to Berlin, summoned the best physicians; they examined my father, shook their bald heads, whispered Latin words to each other, and then said in plain German: the cure will take a long time. She left us for two months, returned to Odessa, sold or pawned the furniture and the jewels, and came back to fight for Father's life. For about two years the professors tried to delude themselves that cancer was no cancer. Finally they bowed their heads hopelessly. Mother did not give up: in Russia too there are famous surgeons—who knows? She brought us to Kiev, and then to Kharkov. The police wanted to expel us from Kharkov because my father had stopped paying his fees as a member of the merchant guild, and he no longer had the right to reside in that city. Mother appeared before the governor of the state and obtained an extension of our stay until after the operation. But it did not help. I don't know why we moved from there to of all places Alexandrovsk, a small town on the Dnieper.[11] Perhaps my father wished to die in his native countryside, on the shores of "Ole Man River," who fostered his childhood and witnessed his past glory.

After his death we returned to Odessa. I remember the small rooms, and the fresh bread Mother gave to my sister and me every morning, while she herself ate only yesterday's. But she rejected my cousin's advice out of hand: she sent both my sister and me to high school.

I don't remember my father at all, or very little, but I heard many tales and even legends about him. In those days the commercial wealth of Odessa was made in the grain capital for the whole of Ukraine, and my father seems to have been foremost among those who "made" her. The Russian Steamship & Trade Co. (known by its Russian initials as ROPIT) led the grain market, and my father was one of its leading agents—some say the leading agent—for the purchase of wheat from the entire territory around the Dnieper, a region that in those days supplied food for the whole of Europe.[12] A long novel could be written, and it would be worthwhile (but there is no danger of that—I don't have the time), about my father's trips aboard the ROPIT steamers, on the mighty river from Kherson until the waterfalls amid the rocks they call *porogi* (thresholds) in Russian and *hirlo* (throat) in Ukrainian. He was accompanied by a huge retinue of attendants, aides, experts—perhaps loafers or bums. Apparently my father was very highly esteemed by the management of the ROPIT, because many years after his death, in our mother's apartment, I used to see one of the directors who came to visit every time he was in Odessa. I even remember his name, Pchelnikov. He used to drink a cup of tea and praise Father profusely.

Jews called my father "Yona"; Russians, "Yevgeny." He was born in Nikopol, a small town on the shore of the Dnieper.[13] His father had owned some seven relay stations on one of the large highways; at the time the railroads had not yet reached that part of the Ukraine. These stations combined the attributes of an inn, a tavern, a post office, and a horse stable for mail coaches. One of my friends discovered the name of my grandfather on the list of the first subscribers to the first Hebrew newspaper published in Russia, *Ha-Melits*, if I am not mistaken.[14]

Admiral Chikhachev, ROPIT's director, once told my father: "Your name is Yevgeny, and you are a 'geny' (genius in Russian)."[15] Perhaps he exaggerated, perhaps he was right. Every time I visited the Dnieper regions, I heard the same thing from many people. Once, in Alexandrovsk, a dozen old men, from among the veterans of the grain trade, gathered around me and tried until midnight to explain to me the essence of my father's charm. I did not understand, but I took away a powerful impression of the intricate combination of connections, relations, and networks of influence uniting Argentina with the Ukraine, the Black Sea with the three oceans, the Ballhausplatz in Vienna, seat of the foreign office of Austria-Hungary, to the café Robinat, where grain dealers in Odessa used to meet. One thing I understood: They told me that my father used to make his calculations mentally—"up to one eighth of a penny." (This gift I did not inherit from him. For me even the multiplication table is a mystery.) Also this: Many a time was he warned that his helpers "rob" him—and he always answered: "One who robs me is poorer than me, and perhaps he is right." This philosophy I did perhaps inherit from him.

Father seems to have inherited his talents from his mother, about whom I also heard many legends, but this is not the place to recount them. A spiritual inheritance from Grandfather's side had another character—a drop of nervousness, bordering on hysteria, symptoms of which I found in many of those who bear my family name. One of them, the youngest of my uncles on Father's side—a member of that strange race of pleasant rascals, endowed with an inborn genius for lying—possessed a musical gift of a very peculiar kind. He could warble like a nightingale, and half the population of the small town of Nikopol used to gather before the window of his house to listen to his trills. When he grew old he lost his wits, and sent me letters signed "Jesus-the-Second." But Father liked him more than his many other brothers.

Once Father gave him a responsible post—put him in charge of sending grain abroad—while he himself went away for two weeks. When he came back to Odessa, he found havoc in the business and sulky faces in ROPIT's administrative offices. A couple days after this discovery, Father felt a suspicious pain inside; doctors pronounced it "cancer" and sent him to Germany. We spent two years there, in Berlin during winter and Bad Ems on the Rhine during summer. In Berlin I attended a German kindergarten, and in Ems I once saw old Kaiser Wilhelm take off his hat in reply to my bow; at that time there still was such a thing as courtesy in the world, even in that part of the world.[16] Father did not recover.

The third of the factors that left an imprint on my childhood is Odessa. I never saw a city as light-natured as she, and I do not say that as an old man who believes that the sun has vanished from the horizon because it does not warm him as it did before. I spent the best days of my youth in Rome. I also lived in Vienna when I was young, and I can compare the spiritual climate with the same yardstick. No city could match Odessa—I mean Odessa of that generation— with the spirit of jolly buoyancy and the light intoxication floating in the air, without a shade or hint of mental complication or moral drama. I do not claim, God forbid, that I found a great deal of profundity and nobility in that atmosphere, since its very lightness lay in the absence of all tradition. The city sprang up out of nothing about one hundred years before me; her inhabitants chatted in a dozen languages, none of which they knew perfectly. Of all my numerous acquaintances there was only one whose father was also born in Odessa. (Of course without tradition and drama there can be no nobility.)

The city was like the gourd of Jonah the prophet, and every plant that grew in it—material, moral, social—was also like a gourd, a passing accident, joke, or adventure. Honor the truth of course, but lying is no crime either, as the person who listens to you also has a boiling imagination, supple and bubbling. On top of all these he also has a greedy curiosity toward what the rising morning may bring: every bit of news, however trifling, or a momentous event excites the crowd; hands are moving rapidly through the air, the walls of the stock exchange and the tables in the cafes shake with clamor all around. Kisses too are cheap, and even more than that—free. (And nevertheless, so far as I remember, these girls, all of them, were married later, to nice men, and each one became a model wife.)

Such an environment can exert a bad as well as a good influence on the child. It depends not on the milieu but on the character of the child himself. One will absorb the cheapness (the Russian poet Polonsky wrote a novel about Odessa, which he called *The Cheap City*); another, on the contrary, may absorb the clamor, curiosity, spirit of adventure, the eternal freshness for which every new morning is a miracle, along with that attitude of forgiving and a tolerant smile toward grief as well as toward happiness.[17] Strange, it is in the writings of an English poet, a man raised on the lap of the most powerful tradition in the world, and who all his life defended that tradition, that I found an echo of this mentality. Kipling has written (I do not recall the exact words): "Victory or defeat: learn to accept both with equanimity since both are deceptions." And in his old days he summed up the experiences of his life by saying to his creator: "Lord, I explored your whole land, and I saw nothing profane on its face; all I saw—was wondrous."[18]—Perhaps do I belong to the latter category.

Between Childhood and Youth

My birth certificate says: "On October 9th 1880, a son was born to the resident (*meshchanin*) of Nikopol Yevgeny Jabotinsky, and his wife, Yeva, and was given the name Vladimir." Three errors: my father's name is Yona, son of Tzevi; my mother's, Chava, daughter of Meir; and I was born on the fifth of October, corresponding to the eighteenth according to the Western calendar, verse "Va yar," according to my mother's system of counting.[19] Until age seventeen I lived in Odessa. At home and outside of it, we spoke only Russian. Mother spoke Yiddish with my old aunts: my sister and I learned to understand the language, but it never came into our mind to address Mother in Yiddish, or anybody else either. My sister taught me to read Russian. I was eight years old when one of our neighbors volunteered to teach us both Hebrew; this kind man was Mr. Yehoshua Ravnitzky.[20] I enjoyed his teaching for several years, until we moved to another house, and I protest the myth that I did not know the words "*Bereshit bara*" [the first lines of Torah] until I actively joined the Zionist camp. My mother would never have tolerated that! Later I had another teacher, whose name I forgot; he prepared me for my portion of the bar mitzvah, and with him I also read Yehuda Leib Gordon's poetry.[21] One of my cousins who spent about a year at our home taught me French, and my sister, who learned English at high school, gave me lessons in that language, too.

Aside from the Hebrew lessons, I had at that time no internal contact with Judaism. After Father's death I went three times a day to the small synagogue of the goldsmiths, not far from our house, until the end of the year. But I did not get used to it, and I did not take part in the prayers except the Kaddish. In our home we kept strictly kosher. Mother used to light the candles on every Shabbat eve, and prayed morning and evening; she taught us also the "*Mode ani*" and the "*Shema*," but all these customs did not "catch" in my heart.[22] In the library of Jewish shop clerks, where I hurried every day to exchange the volume I had "swallowed" the day before, there were many Jewish books, but I did not read them. Once or twice I tried—but there was no movement, no action in them, only sadness and dullness: not interesting. I had no convictions regarding Judaism in those days, nor later for that matter, perhaps not until the age of twenty or even after that; nor did I have any attitude regarding social or political problems in general. Had a Christian boy questioned me then what my attitude to Jews was, I would have told him that I liked them, but if a Jew had asked me I would have given him a different answer—and a more candid one. Of course, I knew that ultimately we would have a kingdom, and that I too would go to live there—my mother knew that too, as did all my aunts, and Ravnitzky; yet this was not a conviction but so to speak just a natural thing, such as washing one's hands in the morning and eating a bowl of soup at noon.

Pardon my mistake: One conviction did crystallize in me already from my early childhood, and until today it still rules over my whole attitude to society, although there are people who say that it is not a conviction but just a crazy notion. It is true: I am crazy as far as the notion of equality is concerned. In those years this tendency of mine was expressed in vehement protest against all who dared address me as "thou" instead of "you"—that is, against the entire adult world.[23] To this crazy notion I have remained true until now. In all those languages that possess this distinction, I shall never address even a three-year-old other than as "you," and even if I wanted to do otherwise I simply could not. I hate, with an intense, organic hate, stronger than any motivation, more powerful than reason, and even than the individual self, every notion that contains even the slight hint of discrimination between human beings. Perhaps this is not democracy, but its reverse: I believe that every man is a king, and if it were in my power, I would create a new social doctrine, that of "Pan Basileia."[24]

When I was about seven, Mother sent me to a private school founded by two young Jewish ladies, Miss Lev and Miss Zussmen. It had two classes—one of the ladies taught in the first, the other in the second; the pupils, boys and girls, learned together, a rare thing in those days. I described this school *en passant* in a story called "Squirrel," and also a modest love affair that occurred in a women's bath (*mikvah*).[25] That was the whole truth and nothing but the truth. I only want to add that I do not remember whether we learned anything "Jewish"—such as Jewish history or prayers—but the very fact that I do not remember is characteristic of my national indifference, as mentioned above.

I tried about four times to pass the entrance examination to the *gymnasium*, the so-called real or commercial high school, but failed. From 1888, a law had been enacted that only one Jew out of every ten candidates was to be admitted to the official educational institutions (government schools), and the competition among the candidates of the Mosaic religion was very acute.[26] To succeed one had to either be an undisputed genius or else have parents who could give a decent bribe to the teachers, and I could afford neither. Finally, through I do not know what miracle, I was admitted to the preparatory class of the Second Pro-Gymnasium. I graduated from it when I was fourteen and a half, and entered the fifth class of high school (*lyceum*). I hated both these institutions as much as any pupil. Even now, when I hear my younger friends say that they like their school, I feel surprised. During the whole time of my studies, I was an absolute idler on principle, disliked by most of the teachers, and I had countless scandals and waged war with the representatives of Russian pedagogy.

From these adventures I might perhaps mention just this one: I was expelled from the final examination at the *gymnasium*. I passed a note with the translation of a Latin fragment to my neighbor. The teacher intercepted the note, and we were both sent home. It was not until after the vacation that we were allowed to be reexamined. I had never heard of such punishment for this crime; but the hostile feelings between me and the teachers were mutual.

It is nevertheless my duty to acknowledge that the spirit of anti-Semitism was almost entirely absent from these government schools: perhaps because in those days public opinion generally was dormant in Russia, left-wing as well as right; that is why the entire period up to the last years of the nineteenth century is referred to in Russian as "Bezvremennye"—a faceless epoch.[27] We Jewish students suffered no persecution on the part of either the teachers or our classmates. The most astonishing thing about it was that, all this notwithstanding, we always kept apart from our Christian environment. There were about ten Jews in our class; we sat together, and if we met in a private house to play or to read or just to chat, all this was always and strictly among ourselves. At the same time several of us also had friends in the Russian camp. For example, I was bound by faithful friendship to Vsevolod Lebedintsev, a very fine fellow, whose name will still appear in the course of this story.[28] I visited him many times at his home, and he also came to mine, but it never occurred to me to introduce him to our separate circle, and neither did he introduce me to his group; I do not even know if he had a group. Stranger still was the fact that even inside our Jewish circle there was no Jewish spirit. When we read together, it was foreign literature, and discussions were concerned with Nietzsche and moral problems, morals in general or sexual morals—not the fate of Jewry, not even the Jewish situation in Russia, which was bothering every one of us.

Besides, with the exception of fragmentary knowledge of Latin and ancient Greek (and this I do value highly even now), everything I learned in childhood

I did not learn in school. Of course, I read a lot; without direction or supervision, I happened by chance to choose good books. First of all, we had a bookcase, left over from the time of my father's prosperity, in which I found the complete works of Shakespeare in Russian translation, as well as Pushkin and Lermontov.[29] These three I knew from A to Z. When I was not yet fourteen, and even today, it would be difficult to find a verse of Pushkin that I would not know, and could not complete. But even then I did not particularly like Russian literature (with the possible exception of poetry), and now it is foreign to my spirit. I have no interest in dabbling in unfathomable psychological depths; my heart yearns for action. The favorites of my childhood were the most famous among the writers of adventure stories of my generation, and I regret that the younger generation feels cold to them, so I've heard: Mayne Reid, Bret Harte, Walter Scott and "Père" Dumas, and all the rest of them.[30]

This choice, unoriginal and average, saved me from a premature maturity, an illness of vision afflicting the youth of the generation following mine. Even when there were no more books of this kind for me in that library, and I was compelled to switch over to "serious" literature, I preferred foreign authors, such as Dickens and Zola, Spielhagen and George Elliot, to the great Russian novelists, out of my aversion to psychology.[31] I must recognize nevertheless that the book that made the strongest impression on me was a Russian book—*The Precipice* by Goncharov.[32] This book marks something like a spiritual boundary between my childhood and my adolescence without my knowing why. In contrast to this paradox, the four poems of the world's poetical treasury which I liked more than any others (then as well as now) prove decisively the superficial simplicity of my taste: *Cyrano* by Rostand, "Frithjof's Saga" by the Swedish poet Tegnér, *Konrad Wallenrod* by Mickiewicz (a Polish classmate at the *gymnasium* taught me his language), and more than these, Edgar Allan Poe's "The Raven."[33] If I were rich, I would make myself a present: these four, bound together, each of them in its original language, monuments to the worship of the exalted gesture and the beautiful word that I failed to find in life.

Do not imagine, God forbid, that in those days I spent time at home. I read in the evenings, but every free hour until dusk I spent in the city park (the size of Odessa's Alexandrov Park corresponds to a sizeable part of the city itself) or at the seashore.[34] It also happened that I went to the *gymnasium* in the morning, but the smiling sun and the acacia shrubs in full bloom after awakening from their sleep proved too much for me, and I left my book bag at the shop near our house and hastened away to the harbor, to catch fish for crabs from the huge rocks known in Odessa as the "massive ones." I played a game called Cossacks and Robbers with a gang of loafers like myself in the park and returned home proud of scratches and black-and-blue marks on my face and body, traces left by the contact of a stick, ball, or stone.³⁵ Once, two friends and I swam out so far into the sea that the guard in charge of the bathing cabins got alarmed and caught us in his boat, brandishing a cab driver's whip in this hand. And many a moonlit and moonless night we spent in a hired fisherman's boat (sometimes without his knowledge), far away beyond the lighthouse, singing Russian sea songs or whispering sweet secrets into girls' ears.

I was fifteen years old, and it was my first year in the Richelieu Lyceum, when one of the Jewish pupils invited me to his home and introduced me to his sisters. One of them was playing the piano at the moment I passed through the room; afterward she confessed bursting into laughter behind my back, so strange was the impression made by my Ethiopian profile under my unruly hair. Nevertheless that very same first evening I won her favor by calling her "Mademoiselle"—the first to do so among all her acquaintances. She was ten, and her name was Anya—Jeanne Galperin—and she is my wife.³⁶

I also chose my occupation when I was still a boy: I began to write poetry when I was ten years old. I "printed" them in a publication written by hand, edited by two boys who studied at another school (one of them is now the Soviet ambassador to Mexico, if I am not mistaken). Later, in the sixth grade, we also founded a secret newspaper in our own school, and we now printed it on a hectograph. I was one of the editors. I say "secret" because publishing was prohibited by Russian laws in general and by the rules of our school in particular. But in our newspaper there were no "political allusions," not because we were afraid, but out of that indifference to political matters described above. However, the name of the newspaper was *Truth* (*Pravda*), and the chief editor was a Christian boy from a Montenegrin family who fell in love that year with two girls at one time, one of them called Lida, the other Lena. The former ultimately won, and he chose to sign his articles with the name "Lidin." Had Lena been the victor, he would have signed "Lenin"!³⁷

I translated the *Song of Songs* and "In the Depths of the Sea," by Yehudah Leib Gordon, into Russian, and sent them to *Voskhod*—but they did not print them.³⁸ I translated "The Raven" by Edgar Allan Poe and sent it to *Northern Messenger*, a Russian monthly in St. Petersburg—but they did not print it either.³⁹ I also wrote a novel, the name and contents of which I do not remember, and sent it to the Russian writer Korolenko; he answered politely and advised me to "carry on." Countless were the manuscripts I sent to editors and received back (and those that I did not receive back) between the ages of thirteen and sixteen.

I already despaired of my future, and was afraid that there was a sentence pronounced in heaven dooming me to be a lawyer or an engineer. Once, by chance, I opened an Odessa daily and found an article bearing the title "A Remark on Pedagogy"—mine! I present the coming generations even with the date—the twenty-second of August 1897—and also its contents: a sharp critique against the system of marks in schools, as this custom is liable to provoke feelings of jealousy in the tender hearts of pupils.[40]

In those days the well-known Russian poet Alexander Fedorov lived in Odessa. He saw my translation of "The Raven" and introduced me to the editor of the newspaper *Odesskii Listok*.[41] I asked, "Will you print my correspondence from abroad?" and he answered, "Perhaps—on two conditions: that you write from a capital in which we have no other correspondent, and provided you do not write nonsense."

He had correspondents in all the European capitals except Bern and Rome. Mother begged me, since I was leaving the *gymnasium*, "Don't go to Rome! Go to Bern, since at least there are students whose parents we know."

By the way, among the other beautiful legends about my origins that have been embellished without so to speak any participation on my part, I have also heard this one: that I was "expelled" from the *gymnasium*. I hope that if I had not left it then they would in the end actually have expelled me. However, I happened to leave of my own free will before this inevitable event.

I had long since become disgusted by the atmosphere of the *gymnasium* and intended to leave it at the first opportunity, even before finishing my studies. I had to fight hard for this decision with members of my family and friends. My young readers will not understand the value of the *gymnasium* for a Jewish boy forty years ago. A graduation diploma meant enrollment in the university, the right of residence outside the Pale of Settlement: in short, a human life instead of a dog's.[42] And I was already in the seventh class—one more year and a half, and I would be entitled to wear the blue cap and the black *tuzhurka* (uniform) of a student. What kind of a crazy notion was it to sacrifice and ruin prospects such as these; for God's sake—what for?

Honestly, I did not know "what for." "Just so," and perhaps there is no explanation of the will's mysteries more precise than this: "Just so."

The famous French political leader and friend of Zionism de Monzie once told me: "I understand everything about Zionism except the matter of language."[43] And he listed before me, with considerable analytical subtlety and excellent logic, a large number of convincing arguments against Hebrew language that severs every bridge between world culture and the people who created this culture. I sought a satisfactory answer but couldn't find any, so I replied: "And nevertheless, Hebrew it will be; why? Just so." De Monzie raised both his hands and said: "Now I understand. You Zionists are right. An aspiration that has no explanation is beyond and above explanation."

Of course, there is no need to invoke transcendent speculations about the essence of a nation—when I simply wanted to describe how a young boy ran away from school. But this was not the only case in my life when I submitted to that formula—"Just so"—and I don't regret it.

I had an uncle in Odessa, Mother's eldest brother, Uncle Abraham, a wealthy merchant, a Hebrew scholar, and a clean-shaven *maskil*, a clever man with great experience. He was the only one among my relatives who didn't ask me even once, "What for?"; but on the last day before I went away, when I came to take leave of him, he told me something most sensible and useful: "I heard that you intend to be a writer, and that you have chosen a strange way. This is not any business of mine. But you should remember this: If you are successful everyone will say that you are a clever fellow and that they knew it beforehand, but if you fail they will say: 'An idiot—we always knew that he was a fool.'"

In spring 1898, I left the *gymnasium* and went to Switzerland. This was the end of my early youth. I was seventeen, not very popular because of a tendency to paradox and striking poses and an exaggerated self-esteem. I had as yet no plan or goal in life except the desire to live.

Bern and Rome

I journeyed by way of Podolia and Galicia in third class, of course, in a train that crept forward very slowly, stopping at every station.[44] Day and night, Jews came into the car. Between Razdelnaya and Vienna I heard more Yiddish than I had ever heard before in my life.[45] I didn't understand all of it, but the impression was powerful and painful. In that train I got my first contact with the ghetto; I saw with my own eyes its degeneracy and decay, heard that slavish humor that was content with "ridiculing" the powerful enemy instead of fighting him. Now that I have grown old, I know how to detect, beneath the mask of ingratiation and mockery, also the echoes of pride and fortitude. At that time I did not know, and I bent my head and asked myself silently: Is this our people?

At Bern University (which I found located in the same building as the central police headquarters), I registered for the faculty of law. I must confess to my confusion: I do not even remember the names of the professors, except the Jew, Reichsberg, from whom I heard, for the first time, the doctrine of Karl Marx.[46] I was much more interested in the life of the "Russian colony" [the community of Russian émigrés in Bern]: they numbered about three hundred, the majority of whom were Jewish men and women, and I was the youngest of them all. At first I kept somewhat apart from them, as I had decided to become a vegetarian and would not go to their communal restaurant. But my own culinary experiments were not successful. Until this day I still remember the "cocoa" I personally manufactured—brown, solidified particles of matter floating on the surface of the milk, which more often than not would overflow and dribble down to the floor before I took the pot off the boiler. After a couple weeks of this regime, hungry as a wolf pack in winter, I renounced my vegetarian faith and became a regular guest of the restaurant "Colony."

I shall not attempt to describe the life of the students—it has already been described many times—as well as the inebriating and overwhelming impression caused by my sudden passage from the silence of Russia of forty years ago into [the colony's] seething agitation. All those words that were forbidden in Russia were as ordinary here as "good morning," "thank you," or "don't mention it." Revolutionary literature—which only a month before we mentioned only among ourselves, through hints and whispering—was complete in the library's bookcase, at everybody's disposal. There was freedom of speech and discussion, but not of action. The students lived in the shadow of the Alps and saw a dream on the Volga; they were like a wheel revolving with extraordinary speed because it revolves in the air, unconnected from a machine, and without moving anything.

Twice a week there were meetings in the colony, mostly discussions between Lenin's and Plekhanov's groups, or between the members of the SD and the SR. (My contemporaries remember the difference; it is not worthwhile to explain it to others.)[47] Sometimes a "social mixer" was organized where Russian songs were sung; but Zhitlovsky—I don't even remember if he also studied at the University of Bern or only joined us temporarily—saw to it that Yiddish songs were there too.[48] Once the colony also received a visit from Nahum Sirkin, who spoke in favor of a synthesis of Zionism and socialism; he did not find many followers, since there were few Zionists in that milieu.[49] But I remember well that discussion, because I gave the first speech of my life then, and it was a "Zionist" speech. I spoke in Russian, and the gist of it was as follows: I do not know whether I am a socialist—I didn't know that doctrine well enough—but I am a Zionist, no doubt about that, because the situation of the Jewish people is very bad. Their neighbors hate them, and the neighbors are right: in the end the Jews in the Diaspora are bound to experience a general Bartholomew's Night, and their only salvation is mass immigration to Eretz Yisrael. The chairman of the meeting, young Lichtenstein (toward the end of his life, he was a respected leader in Palestine, and he died there some years ago) translated my speech into German, condensing it to the extreme: "The speaker" is not a socialist, as he does not know what socialism is, but he is a convinced anti-Semite, and he advises us to hide in Palestine lest we all be slaughtered.[50] Apparently the impression made on me by that trip across Galicia had sunk deep into my heart! When the meeting was over, Hayim Rappoport (he is now one of the communist leaders in France) came over to me and said with a tolerant smile: "I did not expect that a zoological kind of anti-Jew still exists among the Russian youth!"—I answered, "But I am not Russian!"[51] He refused to believe me.

That summer I also began to write Zionist literature, although in a more dignified manner. The monthly review, *Voskhod*, in Petersburg, printed my poem "*Ir Shalom.*"[52] I am afraid that I forgot the teaching of Ravnitzky, that the letter "ayin" is in "*Ir*," and believed in my naive way that the meaning of *Yerushalayim*

(Jerusalem) was *Ir Shalom* ("City of Peace"). Now of course I already know that this is not so either literally or otherwise.

In the fall of that year I moved to Rome to continue my studies, and I stayed there for three years. If I have a spiritual homeland, it is Italy rather than Russia. In Rome there was no "Russian colony" whatsoever. From the day I arrived, I became absorbed in the world of Italy's youth, and I shared their life until the day I left. My whole attitude toward the problems of nationality, state, and society took shape during those years under Italy's influence. I learned to appreciate the art of the architect, the sculptor, and the painter, and also the Latin manner of singing, ridiculed in those days by Wagner's admirers and nowadays by those of Stravinsky and Debussy.[53] My professors at the university were Antonio Labriola and Enrico Ferri, and they planted in my heart a belief in the justice of socialism that I preserved as something self-evident until it was utterly annihilated by the spectacle of the Red Experiment in Russia.[54] The story of Garibaldi, the writings of Mazzini, the poetry of Leopardi and Giusti, enriched and deepened my superficial Zionism, and developed it as a tangible concept evolving from an instinctive feeling.[55] In the theater Salvini, Rossi, Adelaide Ristori had already left the scene; D'Annunzio was writing his best plays for Eleanora Duse; Ermete Novelli gave new life to the classical tragedy from Shakespeare to Alfieri; Ermete Zacconi was implanting in the souls of the southern public the bitter charm of Ibsen, Tolstoy, and Hauptmann; and the price of a seat on a wooden bench in the upper story of the theater was from forty centimes to one lira, in addition to the four hours of standing in line until the doors opened.[56] I felt at home in most of the museums; there was no forlorn corner in the narrow streets of the sections of Borgo or by the Tiber River that I did not know.[57] In most of these sections I also lived a month here, two months there, because invariably, after the first week's experience, the landladies, wives of respectable merchants or officials, protested the unceasing tumult in my room—the sounds of visits, songs, drinking glasses, the clamor of discussions and quarrels—and in the end they always suggested that I look for some other place to pitch my tent.

Italy was a delightful country in those days, on the threshold of the twentieth century. If I had to find a word to describe fully the common foundation of all the currents of political thought which competed there, I would choose that old-fashioned term that was already used by everybody ironically, and which has now become loathsome and "treyf" for the youth in Italy as well as throughout the world: "liberalism." A great concept because of its very broadness: a dream of order and justice without compulsion, a vision embracing all mankind, composed of compassion, patience, faith in the fundamental goodness and justice of the human race. At that time there was not yet even the slightest hint in the atmosphere of that worship of "discipline" that later found its expression in fascism. If my memory has retained signs that already then foretold some psychological change, they did not yet announce Mussolini, but Marinetti: that literary and philosophical tendency that only several years later went by the name of "futurism"—a tendency whose historical mission consisted perhaps in paving the road for Mussolini's movement.[58]

Among my fellow students I knew already a few who protested with bitter wrath against foreign tourists who insisted that Italy was a museum that contained mere relics of past beauty, a memorial to past glory, and treated the modern Italian as if he were only part of the *paysage* (landscape): a respectable part if it is the *lazzarone*, clad in patched rags and playing the mandolin; an unnecessary and troublesome one if he tries to erect factories damaging the impression of the *pittoresco* of the ancient ruins. From these few people I already heard: "The day will come when we shall send those tourists to hell. Yes, precisely our new life, precisely the smoking chimneys—this is the real Italy. It is perhaps better that we burn all the paintings from Botticelli to Leonardo, smash all the statues, and instead of the Colosseum build a factory to produce sausages!" In these days, one can hear a sort of anticipated echo of Marinetti's theories: the humming of the airplane is more beautiful than the modulations of a Neapolitan melody; the future is more beautiful than the past; Italy is a country of industry, the land of automobiles and electricity; she isn't at all a walking ground for the world's loafers searching for aesthetic pleasure. Modern Italian is an efficient organizer, strict in the keeping of account books; a builder and conqueror, obstinate and cruel. This is fascism's first source. But in my time we did not even know Marinetti.

Because of my duty as a journalist (I had become a correspondent for the newspaper *Odesskie Novosti*, and it remained "my newspaper" permanently almost until the end of World War I), and also due to an internal urge, I followed with particular attention the life of Montecitorio—the building of the Italian parliament.[59] Its general aspect was similar to that of most parliaments in that naive period: a right-wing government with a left-wing opposition—and how very moderate were both of them in their right and left tendencies, compared with the extremism exhibited today by both sides! The left wing was headed of course by the socialist group, and my sympathies, too, were with it, although I never joined it officially either in Italy or in Russia. Its final aim—the nationalization of the means of production—I considered a natural and desirable consequence of the evolution of society. I also believed that the working class was simply the flag-bearer for all the paupers, whether hired labor or shopkeepers or lawyers without clients. The egoistic dimension of the notion of class was not revealed in all its comprehensive display until after Lenin's victory in Russia; it had not yet received a definite and exact formulation.

Antonio Labriola, the principal proponent of Marxist theories in Italy, not only advocated them from his chair at the university but also used to meet with his disciples every evening in the café Aragno on the Corso. Now this avenue is called Corso Umberto, and I too was among Labriola's followers. There he spoke about the events of the day in Italy and abroad, on the war in Transvaal, the revolt of the Boxers in China, about the past and the future.[60] His attitude toward us was that of an educator and advisor. He once ordered me to accompany him at night, and on the way he scolded me because the day before he had met me in the company of several young men suspected of anarchistic leanings.

I did not know Enrico Ferri personally, but his influence on me was still more powerful than Labriola's. His official specialty at the university was criminal law, the theory of crime and punishment. But his lectures were a kind of encyclopedia, encompassing the near and the remote, the obvious and the hidden—society, personality, and the laws of physical and spiritual heredity; the world and its culture—literature, art, and music. He dominated us by virtue of his talent as an orator. If I am not mistaken, he was considered one of the best orators of that generation in Europe; his genius in this respect could be compared with that of Jaurès—but I was not privileged to hear Jaurès speak.[61]

The strange thing was, there was no problem in the world that we did not touch, either in Labriola's circle or among ourselves, in the students' milieu, from the situation of the blacks in America to the poetry of the Decadents—with the exception of one problem, which we did not touch even once: the Jewish question.[62] One evening—I remember it was precisely during a discussion on the Decadents—Labriola severely criticized Max Nordau's book *Decadence*, mentioning on that occasion several other of the author's offenses, but even then he passed over in silence the greatest of Nordau's crimes: his Zionism.[63] Not purposely—he just forgot, as we all did, even me. Not only was anti-Semitism absent in Italy then, but in general there was no specific, clear attitude toward Jews, as there was no definite attitude toward bearded people. Years later I came to know that among the members of my most intimate circle there were also two or three Jews. At the time of my studies in Rome, it did not occur to me to ask who they were, and neither did they ask me.

Perhaps it was a mistake when I just wrote: "I also forgot." On each of my return trips from Odessa to Rome after vacation, I traveled three times not only across Galicia but also through parts of former Hungary between Munkatch and

Kaschau (now they are called Mukachevo and Košice, in Czechoslovakia), where there is a dense Jewish population, and I felt the same depressing impression as earlier, perhaps even stronger. I did not "forget"; perhaps even then I had already in my heart taken the oath that after my school years I would devote myself to Zionist work, and everything I have already mentioned that I read about the history of the Italian revival became linked in my mind, perhaps unconsciously, with the idea of a Hebrew state. However, this oath was a passive one. I did not think about it; I was not interested in the congresses that assembled every year in Basel; and after a single visit, touristlike, to the ghetto of Rome (and even that was only because of the historical palazzo belonging to the family of Beatrice Cenci), I did not return there anymore.[64]

I must also confess with shame an even greater crime than this: Once, in the gay company of young girls and boys, when their conversation touched (half-respectfully, half-ironically) on the rites of the Catholic Church, one of the girls sitting beside me asked, "And do you belong to the Greek Church?"[65] I answered yes. I do not know why I answered yes. There is no doubt that my prestige would in no way have been impaired in their eyes if I had told the truth. Perhaps I was afraid of losing prestige in my own eyes by admitting in front of these free people that I was a slave.

However, all this is only one aspect of my memories of Rome and not the most important, either. The main thing in my life in Rome was life itself, the life of a healthy young man who assimilated to this milieu so completely that he became indiscernible in it. This was the one and only period in my whole life when I really lived among another people along with the native inhabitants. I practically never lived among the Russians in Russia; now I have been living in Paris for more than ten years as though I were on an island in the company of victims of a shipwreck, with no other inhabitants in the place, and I am gradually forgetting my French. Even now the Italian language is still my language, perhaps even more than Russian, although I stutter now, and in conversation search for forgotten words. When I was young, I spoke Italian as one of them. Romans thought I was from Milan, Sicilians mistook me for a Roman, but nobody thought of me as a foreigner. My thoughts, reactions, my joy and sorrow, as well as all my daily habits were not distinct from theirs.

No doubt many will call this way of life a waste of time and energy; nevertheless I do not regret it. Did he who has known the joys of drinking, pulling pranks, and all kinds of light and frivolous craziness really waste his life? It is only paying youth what is due to youth. And did he who walked that corridor pass onto the threshold of maturity absorbed in all its cares? I saw the life of the

Russian colony in Bern; later I saw the life of my generation in Russia, which fomented three revolutions, and I read the words of Bialik's bitter and condemning judgment: "My soul was scorched by fire."[66] My soul was not burnt at any rate, even if it was singed sometimes; it was not the inner, dry fire, but the fire of life, "real" life—contact with people and things outside myself. It is better this way, and I have no regrets.

I narrated selected parts of my life, certainly with embellishment, in the columns of *Novosti*.[67] When there was no other subject, or if the censor had slaughtered my article, I wrote an Italian story. Most of them are impossible to salvage, and it would not be worthwhile for the reader; but for my private self, personally, I would perhaps enjoy quickly skimming through these chapters of my youth. Did I describe the commune of crazy youngsters like me? Did I relate the incident with Fernanda, the bride of my friend Ugo, who we "redeemed" from a brothel and took out in a solemn procession with mandolins and torches? And about the quarrel that broke out between me and Ugo, this same friend of mine, and how I dispatched two seconds to summon him to a duel, and how a certain morning had already been chosen for our encounter at the Villa Borghese, pistols were purchased, and a special committee of our fellow students spent the entire night studying the code of chivalry (there is such a book, it is printed, and sold—*Il Codice Cavalleresco*) until they found in it the provision, or the tiny quibble, under whose rules there was no ground for a duel in such a case?[68] And what was the case? I have already forgotten. Have I told you how I performed the official part of a *shadchan* [marriage broker], dressed in black with yellow gloves, and appeared before Signora Emilia, the laundress and wife of the cab driver, asking for, on behalf of my friend Goffredo, the hand of her elder daughter, Diana?

I wrote a lot. Twice a week my letters appeared in *Novosti*, signed "Altalena."[69] (I have to confess that I chose this name through an amusing mistake. At the time I did not yet know Italian well enough, and I thought it meant "fan"—only later did I find out that it actually meant "seesaw.") During this time my articles also appeared in *Severnyi Kurier* in St. Petersburg, the liberal newspaper of Prince Bariatinsky.[70] I also published several articles in Italian in the socialist *Avanti* and one article, a more lengthy one, in a Rome monthly—the name of which I do not remember—on the "literature of moods" in Russia, Chekhov, and his school.[71] I also placed Gorky in this group.[72] At that time we knew only Gorky's short stories that echoed Nietzsche's theories in Russian attire: eulogies for the strong men of will and action, and shame on the slaves of "reflection," sterile men who impede every risk and adventure. I introduced Chekhov and Gorky to the readers of that review as two extremes of the same logical chain:

the former expresses the tedium, the longing, the thirst for change, no matter whether leading to construction or to destruction, and the other echoing back: "Throw yourself on the scales, make your life dynamic whatever the consequences!" I mention here the contents of this article because I later found these "extremes of the chain" in Bialik's poetry, first in "Forlorn Star" and later in the "Dead of the Desert."[73]

In the spring of 1899, I went to Odessa to take the graduation examination along with my fellow classmates. But I failed a very important subject, ancient Greek.[74] I returned to Rome and continued my studies there, outside the university more than inside. In the summer of 1901, I returned again to Odessa, intending to go back to Italy and finish my studies in law. But I was greatly astonished to find that in the interim I had gained a reputation with the public as a writer, and Mr. [I. M.] Heifetz, editor of *Novosti*, offered me a job writing a daily feuilleton at the fabulous salary of 120 rubles a month.[75] I did not resist such a temptation. I gave up the diploma, the career of a lawyer, my beloved Italy, and I stayed in Odessa, to start a new chapter in the story of my youth.

Journalist

This new chapter lasted two years, and it was the last transition that led me to Zionist work.

I found that Russia had a new face. Instead of "tedium and longing," there was a nervous unrest, a general expectancy of something, a mood of spring. During my stay abroad, important events had taken place—the revolutionary parties had come out of the basement, and one or two ministers were killed; here and there disorders broke out among workers or farmers; and in particular there was excitement in the student milieu. It is not an easy thing to explain to the young reader the social and political functions played by the university in those days. The educational function of the institution was altogether neglected, as universities became the front in the struggle for liberation. If someone asked us, "Who will be the leaders when the Day of Liberation arrives?" our unanimous response would have been, "The Student Assemblies, of course." And so it was in Odessa when the time came. When the first revolution, in 1905, broke out, the electrical workers actually came to the Student Assemblies and asked for an order: Should they put out the lanterns in the streets or not?[76]

In government circles, signs of panic could already be observed. The reins had slackened, and despite preliminary censorship (we had to show the censor each and every line before printing, even the social calendar and advertisements!), politically risky articles appeared in every newspaper; dangerous words, such as "constitution" and "socialism," were also heard in public lectures. Every Thursday, at the Literary Artistic Club in Odessa, people would meet to discuss a new book or a show in the city theater—but in the lecturer's every word you could hear hints of "liberation"; in discussions about *The Sunken Bell* by Hauptmann (how—I do not know), the principles of Marx collided with those of Narodnaya Volya.[77] Vsevolod Lebedintsev, that Russian friend of mine who I mentioned in earlier pages, divided his time and his enthusiasm among his three ideals: the study of astronomy at the university, evenings at the Italian opera, and also lovemaking with the young singer Armanda degli Abbati.[78] He was also an active member of the SR party. To my question, "How does all of this harmonize in one soul?" he answered, "Don't you understand that these are all the same things?" Now I do not "understand," but then I did.

I myself wrote in the same style. Several years ago I happened to see some fragments of the articles by Altalena from those days: silly twaddle, in my calm and sober opinion—my opinion today. But then this twaddle apparently possessed something hidden that connected it with the fundamental matter of the period. I found proof not only in the number of my followers and admirers but likewise, and more perhaps, in opponents' indignation. Opponents appeared from the start of my work as a feuilletonist. They did not belong to the conservative circle but were progressive-minded like me; yet they happened to be brethren in Israel. Some of them were also on the editorial board of *Novosti*, and Heifetz, our poor editor-in-chief, had a hard time because my articles "were in contradiction to the newspaper's policy." I met with the same opposition in the Literary Artistic Club, where I was invited to give a lecture, and I chose as my subject the fate of literary criticism. I attempted to prove that this profession—a famous and important one in the history of Russian literature, whose aim had always been to reveal the idea or the tendency hidden beneath every artistic image—had already fulfilled its function and that its time was up: "There are periods of thought and periods of action—and ours is a period of action."[79] To my great surprise, my lecture was received with indignation from all quarters; one orator after another reviled me, and finally, when my turn to answer came, the chairman—he was a calm and polite gentleman, one of the notables of the Greek community—declared that he would not grant me the floor because the applause that greeted the last speeches was a sufficient conclusion to the debate.

I do not think that this was prompted by an anti-Semitic feeling: Many Jewish lecturers spoke from the same stage, and the attitude of the public was either approving or indifferent. Among my attackers there were Jews as well as Christians, and the only one who defended me was Christian. Therefore, it was not anti-Semitism but something else—something in me, apparently, some feature or particular quality—that incited the anger. After this experience I had many occasions to observe that things that were forgiven others were not forgiven me. Even my friends told me: "You sharpen the edges, exaggerate the points." Perhaps I shall have the opportunity in the course of this story to point out this disturbing "talent," which often helped to complicate and obstruct my public activity.

Nevertheless, I enjoyed my life in those years. The sense of being popular, from which I would now like to escape to the extremities of the earth, was sweet and pleasant at the age of twenty-one. "Journalist" was an important title in the Russian provinces in those days. It was pleasant to enter the city theater, one of the most beautiful in the country, for free, with the usher dressed in the solemn attire of the time of Marie Antoinette, bowing and accompanying you to a seat in the fifth row, which was adorned with a bronze plaque engraved "Mr. Altalena." Heifetz, the editor, knew how to assemble young talent. Under his wing "Karmen," who wrote stories from the life of the *bossiaki* (tramps) in the Odessa harbor and from the lives in the pauper districts, began his literary career.[80] So too did Kornei Chukovsky, who is now one of the foremost writers of Red Russia's literature. When we came into a café, the neighboring patrons looked up and whispered into one another's ear. Perhaps it was better that we did not hear what they whispered, but we believed these were compliments; and Karmen used to twirl the extremities of his blond moustache, Chukovsky spilled his glass on the floor out of bashful confusion, while I put forward my lower lip to express indifference, although I knew that there was no need for that since my creator had already put it forward more than enough.

In that fall of 1901, my first play, *Blood,* was produced in the city theater.[81] Who will believe that in my youth I wrote a pacifist play against war in general and against England in particular? I had written it while still in Rome. The subject, connected with the Boer War, I had taken, to tell the truth, from the manuscript of one of my friends ("Goffredo" in my story "Diana"), but I changed the plot, introduced new characters, etc.: three acts and in verse. The best stars of our city company, headed by Anna Paskhalova, played in it, but the theater was empty—perhaps three hundred persons, maybe fewer, and half of them were my acquaintances and friends. They of course cheered and even summoned me to appear before the curtain at the end of the performance. I came out to take my bow dressed in a long, black redingote that I had ordered expressly for that day and stumbled over the cord of the curtain. I certainly would have fallen on my face if Mrs. Paskhalova had not caught my hand. I did not sleep the whole night. I got up at dawn and rushed to buy the newspapers, all the newspapers, even the *Police Gazette,* and I greedily swallowed the reviews. The critics proved considerate, even the reviewer of the *Police Gazette,* and did not spoil my joy, but my play appeared in the Odessa theater only twice. True, a year later they produced my second play, also in verse, but one act only, and Paskhalova acted in it as well (we became friends after she saved me from humiliation in front of the curtain); however this time the critics showed no compassion, and every one of them, as if by a common agreement beforehand, launched at me with the same jokes about the name I had given the play: *Ladno* (which means something like "all right," but not quite).[82] They wrote, "Ne ladno, ne skladno" ("Not all right and not well done").

Although I do not remember—and thank God—what I wrote day after day during those two years, I am certain that there was no fixed political tendency. I did not neglect or forget the theories of Labriola and Ferri, but I did not use them or was not interested in them. Perhaps the only idea I did stress in newspaper columns as well as in my speeches at the literary club (in spite of the offense I had not stopped going there) was the idea of individualism, "Pan Basileia," that I already mentioned earlier. If my creator had bestowed on me sufficient wisdom and knowledge to formulate an original philosophical doctrine, I would have founded and constructed this doctrine: In the beginning God created the individual, and every individual is a king equal to everybody else. Everybody else is likewise a king, and it is better that the individual sin against the community than society sin against the individual. It is for the good of individuals that society was constituted, not the other way around. In the end, in the future, the vision of the Messiah's time is the paradise of the individual, the reign of splendid anarchy, the intricate play of individual forces without rules or limits. "Society" has no other function than to give comfort to those who stumble and help them get up, and enable them to reenter the competition. If my poems "Noala" and "Schafloch," beautifully translated by Mr. Reichman, should appear, the reader might be surprised at their contents, by the denial of any obligation on the part of the individual toward the nation and society—I must confess that this is my creed to this very day.[83]

People may point out to me the contradiction between this concept and the essence and contents of my national propaganda. One of my friends who read this manuscript already reminded me that he also heard from me another refrain: "In the beginning God created the nation"—there is no contradiction. The second formula I used against those who assert, "In the beginning 'humanity' was created." It is my unshakable belief that between these two the nation comes first, just as the individual has priority over the nation. And the individual also should subordinate his whole life to the service of the nation. I do not see any contradiction if that is his desire and free will and not obligation. In my small play *Ladno*, produced at the Odessa theater in 1901, I devoted a long monologue to this idea. Briefly, its contents: A person is born free—free of obligations toward Heaven and Earth; do not make sacrifices—the blessings of achievement do not spring from sacrifice. Thou shall build an altar to Will; that is your leader, go wherever it will lead you—whether its road be up the mountain or down to Hell; majesty or crime, frivolity or servitude—or even the yoke of service to the people—this yoke too you should accept not as a slave submitting to an order, but as a free man fulfilling his sovereign.—Who knows, although I have grown old and do not expect changes in my life, still it is possible that before I finish this story I shall have the privilege to inscribe in it a chapter that will impress and embody my fundamental belief.

Most of the readers of *Novosti* enjoyed reading my articles, but not one of them gave them serious attention, and I was aware of that. The only one of all my articles of that period that deserves to be saved from oblivion is the one in which I openly, in black and white, called myself and all the rest of my fellow journalists "jesters."[84] I devoted one of my articles to one of the writers of a rival newspaper—a decent, quiet, "neutral" man, neither clever nor stupid, anonymous in the full sense of the expression—of whom I had made a kind of dummy, and who I used to ridicule at every opportunity and even without one, just for the fun of it. That time I addressed myself directly to him, and I said: "Of course I have persecuted you without any reason or necessity, and I shall continue, because we are jesters for the reading public. We preach, and they yawn; we write with the bile of our heart's blood, and they say, Well written; give me another glass of compote." What is there for a buffoon to do in the circus but to slap the cheek of his fellow buffoon?[85]

My Zionism was also considered something frivolous. True, I did not join any group, nor did I even know who the Zionists were in the city, but several times I devoted one or two fragments in a feuilleton to the subject. In a big and decent monthly published in St. Petersburg, an article by a certain Bickerman appeared, couched in the style that was then called scientific, in which he demolished Zionism, demonstrating that Jews were a happy people, satisfied with their fate.[86] I wrote a lengthy answer, using arguments that would satisfy me even now. The next day I met one of my acquaintances, Ravnitzky, also a "lover of Zion," no doubt, and he said to me, "What is this new plaything you are toying with?"[87]

I lived in my mother's house along with my sister. Great changes had occurred during my stay in Italy. My sister had married a doctor from Alexandrovsk, on the Dnieper, my father's river. I too went to that town for the wedding. About half the inhabitants there still remembered "Yona"; they received my mother as a sort of king's widow, and at the receptions, around the table on the terrace, they told me legends about Father's deeds, the Dnieper's days of past glory, and Ukraine's grain trade. About a year and a half later, my brother-in-law died while I was in Rome, leaving two women widowed and a four-month-old baby (who is today an engineer at the electrical company in Haifa). My sister overcame her grief and opened a girls' school, and began to expand it gradually until it became a *gymnasium*. In their home there was always a room that was mine, and every time I returned to Odessa, they had only to put blankets on my bed.

In the beginning of 1902, in the middle of the night, my sister woke me and whispered, "Police." An officer wearing the blue uniform of the gendarmerie groped for an hour among my books and papers, found some "forbidden" pamphlet and a bundle of my articles published in an Italian newspaper in Milan, and invited me to follow him: "I received orders to conduct you to prison." I kissed my mother and sister—they did not cry nor complain; Mother only told me quietly, "God bless you"—and we drove away. The "fort" [the prison] stands outside Odessa, on the other side of Plague Hill and the Christian and Hebrew cemeteries. On the way I had a polite conversation with the police inspector, who told me, "I read your articles; they are excellent."

The Odessa prison is a magnificent building. I can compare it with others, but, God, it has not shamed my patriotic pride. It was constructed in the form of a cross, with cement and steel all the way through. At that time it had no electricity, and in my cell I found a tiny kerosene lamp. I lay down and fell into a heavy sleep. In the morning shouting from all sides woke me; I mean really that the shouts came from all sides, but what woke me was one steady refrain, constantly repeated. "New neighbor—number 52—come to the window—don't be afraid—we are all friends here, we are all political prisoners. New neighbor, number 52." I did not understand at once who the shouter was addressing, but finally I remembered that on the door of my cell I had seen the number 52. The window was high, but with a chair I climbed onto its large sill and introduced myself—through the bars—to my neighbors. They gave me the nickname "Lavrov," after one of the first founders of the Russian socialist movement. True, the former inhabitant of my room had been given the name "Zhelyabov," and he was now in Siberia, and according to tradition I ought to have inherited his name, but I renounced this dangerous honor, since the real Zhelyabov had been one of the murderers of Tsar Alexander II.[88]

I learned the nicknames of my neighbors: "Ghed," "Mirabeau," "Garibaldi," "Labori" (in honor of the defender of Dreyfus).[89] My upper neighbor was called "Salamander," my neighbor below, "Duck," and the chap on the top floor was the "Supreme Being." After two days I knew the stories of most of them and their social functions here in prison. About half of them had been arrested a month earlier in connection with the unfurling of a red flag in Deribas Street.[90] "Garibaldi," a carpenter from the suburb of Moldavanka, carried the red flag and was "given the works" thoroughly in the police station.[91]

He laughed when he described it. Several were from among the veterans of the movement, especially "Mirabeau," the king of the group, the permanent chairman who always presided over the "meetings." He was the supreme judge in all the quarrels and the spiritual leader who decided on every controversial point of Marxist doctrine; his real name was Abraham Ginzburg, an engineer from Lithuania. About two years ago, I read his name in the newspapers of Red Russia—he had been sentenced to a severe punishment for the crime of "sabotage" at one of the trials characteristic of the Soviet regime.[92] Woe to the proletarian state if such are its saboteurs. He was a decent man in the full sense of the word, a learned Marxist, a revolutionary *sans peur* and *sans reproche,* a born leader. I never saw his face, but day in and day out, seven weeks in a row, I heard his voice conducting, through the bars on his window, the government of our republic, with his quiet and polite orders, tactfully and at the same time firmly.

I said he presided over all our "meetings," but truly we did not enjoy freedom of speech even at the literary club. Every evening, when the clamor from the wing occupied by the simpleminded folk—who fell asleep at sunset, the thieves on the other side of the main building of the forest—died down, we arranged lectures followed by debates. "Mirabeau" lectured on the great revolution in France; another veteran nicknamed "Zayda" (grandfather in Yiddish) narrated the story of the Bund; and I too was invited to lecture on my professional subjects—the Decadents, Italian revival (in honor of the aforementioned "Garibaldi"), and of course individualism.[93] But after this lecture they did not invite me to speak anymore. For the workers who were in the group, the prison was a school for revolution. Demonstrations were also staged. On the first of May, those who had money bought a special brand of tobacco in the prison canteen; the tobacco was bitter, but it was sold in packages with red paper. Pieces of this paper were distributed among all the inhabitants of the "political" wing, and in the evening we pasted the paper on the glass of our lamps, and put them in the windows, and the people in the train on their way to the fountain or Arcadia saw the red illumination in the distance and cheered.[94] Or perhaps they did not cheer, and maybe they didn't even see, as on the first of May people do not go to their summer dachas. However, between reality and the legend, it is better to believe the legend.

I was called for an inquiry. In the prison office I found the prison director and the assistant deputy state prosecutor, whom I had seen many times at the literary club. I asked, "The 'forbidden' book you found at my home is a memorandum of the minister Witte, *Zemstvo and Autocracy;* what is the offense?"[95]

I was told that the book had been printed in Geneva, and this was very bad; that it has a preface written by Plekhanov, some four pages, and that this is still worse. Besides, at my place there also had been found Italian articles, under my name.

"Is it forbidden to write newspaper articles in Milan?"

"It is allowed; one is also allowed to write in them whatever you please, except false testimony that harms the state. That is why we submitted your articles to the official translator, and he will ascertain whether you have committed the offense of harming our state."

I spent seven weeks in this prison, one of the most pleasant and the most cherished of all my memories. I liked my neighbors, although I never saw their faces. I became skilled in the art of "telephone": a rope with a weight at its end that you could swing outside the bars and then let go at a certain moment, so that it could move toward the neighbor on the right side or the left or above, so he should catch it. This way it was possible to transmit a book, a note, or a piece of red paper. In the thieves' wing this contraption was called the *lecha dodi*, as the Hebrew national influence was strongly felt in this particular milieu and was its lingua franca.[96] I also liked the thieves, especially the young men who used to bring me the soup and meat: "Here is the champagne!" I even liked the director of the prison, the gendarmes, and the wardens. They treated us politely and with respect—perhaps owing to an order from their superiors, perhaps also because of the intricate situation prevailing in the country: who knows but that tomorrow they may be thrown into jail while that very "Mirabeau" may don the blue uniform?

Several months after I was set free, this idyll came to an end. One night the wardens attacked my friends and pounded them with their fists and bludgeons. The warden of the "fort" was discharged from his office without a pension. He met me once in the street and asked whether I could find him another job.

I was set free because the official interpreter could find no offense or harm. But the criminal offense of the pamphlet by Witte continued to cast a shadow on my reputation, and I was ordered not to move from Odessa before the judgment. I did not move, except once: in October of that year, my turn to be inducted for military service came up, in Nikopol, my father's native town. I arrived there at night, and early in the morning, policemen had already arrived to search the valise of the revolutionary from Odessa. In the draft board I was lucky to receive a very high number, and I returned home happy and fully confident that I would never have to wear a Russian soldier's overcoat.

Kishinev

The beginning of my Zionist activity is connected with two things: the Italian opera and the idea of self-defense.

We always had Italian opera at the Odessa City Theatre during the winter. That winter Armanda degli Abbati was singing.[97] She was a friend of my friend Lebedintsev, and he used to come to the theater every evening. Once, during the intermission, I met him in the lobby in the company of an elegant gentleman with a black moustache and Western manners, whom I had already seen several times before; he was always seated in the second row. Lebedintsev introduced us to one another: the gentleman was the special correspondent for a Milanese review of music and opera.[98]

Afterward I met him at the house of Miss degli Abbati. We spoke French, and when we left together, I continued the conversation in the same language.

"We can speak Russian, too," he told me. "I too am from Odessa, like you, although born in Lithuania."

I knew already that he was a Jew—"Signor Zal'tsman."[99] It was clear who and what he was. Now he suggested that I call him Solomon Davidovich; he revealed that his position as correspondent with the Italian magazine was only a hobby, and that his main occupation was commerce, as was every Jew's. He also told me that he was a Zionist.

We met many more times at the theater; he showed me his article in that Italian review, but we did not speak of anything else.

In the meantime Pesach was drawing closer, Passover of 1903. From several acquaintances I heard strange words of concern. In the city, the whole vicinity, and in the entire territory, there was a danger of pogroms, a thing the likes of which had not happened for twenty years or more. Some argued that the rumors were twaddle and nonsense; the police wouldn't allow it. Others whispered that in fact the police were going to organize the outbreaks; while a third group advocated that a delegation of the community's notables go to the city governor—these were strange propositions to which we were not accustomed.

I sat at my table and wrote ten letters to ten Jewish community leaders, most of whom I did not know, proposing that we organize self-defense.

They did not answer. A week later one of my old friends came to see me; he was a student who had contacts and connections in all kinds of movements, and he told me: "Mr. So-and-So showed me your letter, strictly confidentially of course. Why did you write? First of all, those to whom you wrote will not dare act, and secondly, and this is the most important point, there already is a self-defense group. Come and see for yourself."

We went to Moldavanka, and there, in a large and empty room resembling a commercial office, I found several young men. One of them was Israel Trivus, who became my friend from that day and later was also a colleague in the Revisionist movement (the "Tsohar").[100] I have forgotten the names of the others, and it is a pity; as far as I know, that was the first attempt to create organized self-defense in Russia even before the Kishinev pogrom.[101] We did good work and gathered money—up to five hundred rubles, if my memory does not fail me, a mighty amount in our opinion; Rouchwerger, the owner of a gun store, gave us some twenty pistols as a gift, and the remainder he sold us at cut rate and mostly on credit, without much hope of being paid. The arsenal was in the same office: pistols, metal rods, kitchen knives, butcher knives. Day and night two guys sat on guard in the office. Young men came in, one after the other, each holding a note signed by one of the "committee" members, and received the weapons they were entitled to. In the second room behind the office, we had a hectograph on which we printed proclamations in Russian and Yiddish. Their contents were very simple—two paragraphs from the penal code providing explicitly that he who kills in self-defense is free from punishment, as well as some brief encouragements to the Jewish youth, exhorting them not to let themselves be slaughtered like cattle.

At first I used to wonder at the patience of the police. It was impossible that their attentions were not aroused by our activities. After a short investigation, an explanation of this mystery was revealed to me when the owner of the office was introduced, and I was told in whispers and behind his back about his peculiar role. He was a quiet and polite young man with a beard soft as silk, and he himself was involved in diverse activities that were typical of the type we called a "silk young man."[102] His name was already famous in leftist circles and infamously—Henrik Shaevich.[103] But I had not yet even heard his name, nor was I aware of the whole matter in connection with him. Now I was told that Shaevich was the emissary on a special mission of the famed chief of the gendarmes Zubatov, the inventor of a new policy toward the worker's movement.[104] According to law and tradition, strikes of workers were considered a political crime in Russia. Zubatov said, "Why? In this way you will only make the workers enemies of the government. Let us permit strikes and not obstruct the organization of labor under the sole condition that they don't interfere in political matters." The authorities accepted his advice. He chose emissaries—for the most part simple people who believed candidly that this scheme would alleviate the situation of the workers in the future—and they had already begun their propaganda in Petersburg, Moscow, Vilna, Minsk, Sormovo, and in the Don mining district. The most important of these was Gapon, the priest who created a large movement in St. Petersburg.[105] As for Henrik Shaevich, he was sent to Odessa. I do not think that organizing Jewish self-defense was included among the tasks he was assigned by Zubatov, and there is no doubt that Shaevich risked his official position. But the local authorities were afraid to touch Zubatov's agent. Perhaps they did write reports to Petersburg and received no answer. I do not care whether Shaevich was an honest man gone astray or a spy and traitor by profession. From the day he gave us shelter to arm Jews, he redeemed all his crimes in my eyes.

Pesach came and then the Christian Pascha, too, and then the pogrom, however not in Odessa, but in Kishinev.

It is a strange thing: I do not remember the impression this event made on me, the turning point in our whole life as a nation. In general it made no impression. I was already a Zionist before it happened; I had also thought about it before. Neither was the Jewish cowardice revealed in Kishinev a discovery for me, no more than for any Jew or Christian. I always had the feeling that there is nothing to learn from pogroms; they hold no surprise.[106] I had always known that such would be the case, and it was. The editorial offices of *Novosti* were inundated with contributions for the victims of the Kishinev pogrom; I was sent to distribute money and clothes in the city of ruin. I visited the places of the slaughter; I spoke with eyewitnesses. At the hospital I saw a Jew, an artisan I think, who years ago had his left eye accidentally pierced; from that time on he lived in one of the suburbs of a Christian neighborhood, working his craft, talking and interacting with his neighbors, until the day those neighbors came and pierced his right eye.[107]

For the first time I came to know the representatives of Russian Zionism. Cohen-Bernstein was a native of Kishinev; Ussishkin hailed from Yekaterinoslav; Vladimir Tiomkin from Elisavetgrad; and Sapir from Odessa.[108] I also saw Bialik there, and I was told who he was—to my great confusion I hadn't heard of him earlier.

After I returned to Odessa, Signor Zal'tsman came to me and said, "I came to see you on behalf of the Zionist group 'Erets-Yisrael.' We decided to propose that you go to the Zionist Congress as a delegate from our group."

"But I am completely ignorant of everything in the movement."

"You will learn."

I agreed. They invited me to a meeting of the group. It was composed of "*ba'alei-batim*," middle-aged or even older men—I didn't see one young face at the meeting except that of Zal'tsman himself—and they asked me to expound my program.[109] With His all-forgiving mercy, the Lord has let me forget all the twaddle I poured forth on that occasion: the members of the gathering were also apparently full of mercy and understanding and did not expel me. On the contrary, they asked me questions, and one of them I still remember: "What was my attitude to the 'El-Arish' scheme—would I vote for it or against it if it comes up before the congress?"[110] Zal'tsman had managed to explain to me a couple of days before the meeting that we were offered the opportunity to colonize the area, situated in Egypt on the border of Palestine, and that a delegation had been sent there by the Zionists to explore the district. I remember my reply, too, which I found on the spot and without any mental efforts:

"My vote will depend on the attitude of the majority in congress. If I see that there is no danger of a split in the Zionist Organization, I shall support the plan; but if I see that the movement will divide on this question—it is a sign that Zionism is only for Zion, and then I shall raise my hand against El-Arish."

I was elected, and I went to Basel to the Sixth Congress; and that is the beginning of a new chapter in my life.

The Congress

A very amusing comedy could be written about my adventures at the congress. First of all, I was not entitled to participate in it, as I was almost a year and a half too young with respect to the legal age for a delegate, and I do not remember who the friendly false witnesses were who attested to my being twenty-four years old; my face was that of a boy, and the official in charge of the delegates' cards did not want to accept me until I brought the witnesses. After that I loitered by myself in the corridors of the casino; I did not know anybody except those bigwigs I had seen in Kishinev, but they were members of the executive committee and were busy with secret meetings inside.[111] I was introduced to a thin and tall young man—with a black triangular beard and a shining bald head—called Dr. Weizmann, and I was told that he was the leader of the opposition: I felt immediately that my place was also in the opposition, although I did not know yet why.[112] So when I saw that young man sitting with a group of his friends around a table in a café, engaged in a conversation full of intensity, I came toward them and asked, "I hope I am not intruding?" Weizmann answered: "You are"—and I went away.

I tried to ascend the podium of the congress and to speak precisely on a burning question: some months before that, Herzl had gone to Russia and talked with the minister of the interior, Plehve; the same Plehve whom we considered the instigator of the Kishinev pogrom.[113] A passionate discussion broke out among the Zionist circles in Russia—whether it is admissible or forbidden to conduct negotiations with a monster such as him. True, both sides had agreed not to touch on this dangerous subject from the tribune of the congress, and I also knew it. Nevertheless, I decided that the interdiction did not apply to me because my experience—the experience of a journalist in Russia, skilled in the art of writing on a risky question without irritating the censor—would help me on this occasion, too, to steer clear of the reefs.

My turn came when the time allotted to the speakers had already been limited to fifteen minutes, but I was not allowed even that quarter of an hour for my eloquence. I began to demonstrate that the two issues of ethics and tactics ought not to be confused. The delegates in the corner of the opposition sensed immediately what was in the mind of that young man, unknown to everybody, with a black head of hair, speaking a polished Russian as if he were reciting a poem at a *gymnasium* examination, and began to stir and to shout: "Enough! No more!" Panic broke out in the hall. Herzl himself, who was busy in the adjoining room, heard the noise, came out hurriedly to the tribune, and asked of one of the delegates, "What is it, what does he say?" It so happened that delegate was the same Dr. Weizmann, and he replied briefly and emphatically: "Quatsch" ("Nonsense"). At that, Herzl came toward me from behind the podium and said: "Ihre Zeit ist um" ("Your time is up"), and these were the first words and the last I ever had the privilege to hear from him.[114] Dr. Friedman, one of the close associates of the leader, emphasized these words with the outrageous bluntness of his native Prussian: "Gehen Sie herunter, sonst werden Sie heruntergeschleppt" ("Come down or else you will be hauled down").[115] I came down without finishing the defense unwanted by the man in whose defense I had taken the floor.[116]

I realized that my task in that congress was to keep silent and to observe, and that is what I did.[117] I found a lot of things to observe there.[118] The Sixth Congress, the last in Herzl's life, was perhaps the first congress of adult Zionism. The name of that examination of maturity is known as Uganda.[119] I was one of the minority that voted against Uganda and, together with the rest of the "Nein-sagers," walked out of the hall.[120] I wondered myself at the motive hidden deep within my soul that prompted me to vote against, in spite of what I had told my electors. I had no romantic love for Eretz Yisrael then—I am not sure that I have it now—nor could I have known whether there was a danger of a split in the movement. I did not know my people, I saw my delegates for the first time, and I did not yet have time to approach any of them; and the great majority of them, among these many who, like myself, came from Russia, raised their hand to vote "for."[121] Nobody tried to persuade me to vote as I did. Herzl made a colossal impression on me—this word is no exaggeration, no other description would fit: colossal—I am not one of those who will easily bow to a personality. In general I do not remember, out of all the experiences I have had in my life, one man who made any impression on me whatsoever either before Herzl or after him. I felt that truly there stands before me a man of destiny, a prophet and leader by the grace of God, deserving to be followed even through error and confusion. And even today it seems to me that I hear his voice ringing in my ears, as he swore to all of us, "*Im eshkahech Yerushalayim*...."[122] I believe his oath; everyone believed. Yet still I voted against him, but I do not know why: "just so"—that same "because" that is stronger than a thousand reasons.

It is a strange thing: I felt that, after that vote, the congress reached such a height that the level at which it began simply could not be compared to it. In spite of the split, the tears, and the indignation, some deeper inner cohesion between the "Neinsager" and the "Jasager" came about. Perhaps they learned to have more respect for one another or for the movement than they had before; and it seems to me the movement as a whole also attained greater elevation on that day, when the delegates of the people mourned their first political victory. I am sure that Chamberlain, the author of the Uganda proposal, and Balfour and many more statesmen in England and in other countries, only on that day realized what Zionism meant, and that the same is true also of many veterans of the movement.[123]

From Basel I went to Rome; now I observed her with new eyes. I looked for and found Jews among my friends whom I had left two years earlier. Several times I visited the historical ghetto, not for the sake of the Palazzo Cenci as before but to acquaint myself with the Jewish people who, despite civil equality and the absence of anti-Semitism, for the most part had not left the Hebrew quarter mentioned in one of Cicero's speeches and in the *Satires* of Juvenal.[124] I came into especially close contact with the used clothing sellers—as in Italy this trade was also concentrated in the hands of "members of the tribe." They had an official association with the beautiful name "Negozianti de generi usati"—and they invited me to the celebration in honor of their yearly meeting. In the editorial offices of the *Tribuna*, which played the same role in those days in Italy as that of the *Times*, I spoke with the famous publicist Primo Levi, who wrote editorials with the byline "Italico."[125] All of them—students, dealers, and journalists—were classical examples of perfect assimilation, the peak of assimilation, such as had not been reached even in Germany, France, and England. Nevertheless, after my first conversations, I also heard from them the word "goy," and in their hearts, too, I found some germ of care or fear, some inner unrest, as if they sensed dangers in the air that I did not feel either before or then, dangers that perhaps really did not exist. However, what matters are not facts but the feelings.[126]

I learned a great deal during this trip, in Basel as well as in Rome. First of all, I learned that I knew nothing about the theory of my new field. I returned to Odessa, found Ravnitzky, who taught me Hebrew when I was a boy, and asked him to continue to teach me. With his help I came to read the writings of Ahad Ha'am and Bialik.[127] Now if I am not mistaken, even the readers of the *Novosti* began to realize the seriousness of my Zionist thought: that same Zal'tsman printed a selection of my articles under the general title *To the Enemies of Zion*, and had it distributed as far as Vilna and St. Petersburg and Saratov on the Volga River.[128] The public accepted me.

St. Petersburg

What my plans were at that time, at the end of the year 1903, I do not remember. Perhaps, as youth is wont to, I dreamt about conquering the two worlds on whose thresholds I stood: laurels as a Russian writer and the captainship of the Zionist vessel; or maybe I didn't have any definite plan. I doubt very much in general whether I received from the gods the talent or even the desire to make my way in life. It was destiny that decided—fate manifested as a *goy*, tall and corpulent, the police commissar of the Central District of Odessa, whose name was Panassiuk.

I had a permanent seat in one of the first rows not only in the city theater but also in the others as well. That evening—it must have been a short while before the Christian New Year—Panassiuk did not recognize me as I rose from my chair during intermission at the "Russian Theatre": he stopped me in the passage and asked me in his famous voice, the voice of a buffalo: "How did you steal a place in the front rows?" My face was that of a boy, and I was dressed as a dandy. According to the yardstick of the police, my place was apparently among the students in the upper balcony and not here among the best company in the city. I took offense and told him what I thought. A fair-sized crowd gathered around us. General Bezsonov, the chief of the blue-clad gendarmes, whom I had met once while I was in prison, also became interested in the disturbance. He came over and spoke, and I also told him what was on my mind. Two days later I received an invitation to appear before Count Shuvalov, the city's governor.[129]

I donned formal dress (my Shabbat suit) that was worn in those days—that same black redingote that I had ordered to commemorate the presentation of my first play, and a stiff collar that bruised my ears—and went in a sledge to the governor's palace. Before leaving, I put my passport in one of my pockets, and in the other pocket all the cash I had at home, some thirty rubles. When I arrived before the palace, I told the driver, "Wait." The interview was at eleven, and at noon the direct train northward was leaving. I also packed my valise and gave it to one of my friends, who was instructed to bring it to the station in time for the train.

My conversation with the governor was very brief. "It is his habit to roar," said Shuvalov, pointing at Panassiuk, who stood at attention in front of us. "When he speaks to me, he roars, too. I shall let you know today what your punishment will be. Good day."

I went out, leaped into my sledge, and hurried to the railway station. I bought a ticket for St. Petersburg. My friend with the valise was late, so I left on the two-day journey without soap and brush. It is easy to imagine the impression made on the passengers by the young man dressed in a redingote on the third-class bench.

In St. Petersburg I knew only two people: one was distant relative my own age who was a student of dentistry; the other I had never seen, but about a month before he had written me a letter, informing me that he was going to start a Zionist monthly review in Russian, and he invited me to send an article. His name was Nikolai Sorin.[130] From a station en route, I sent a cable to my cousin. He met me at the railway station in St. Petersburg, brought me to his room, let me wash and shave, and gave me a shirt and drawers—everything except a place to sleep because, although I possessed a passport, the identification "Jewish" was in it, and people like me were not entitled to reside in the capital.[131] My cousin's house superintendent (*dvornik*) was a police agent, as were all the *dvorniks* in Holy Russia, and very strict in the performance of his duties. I slept the whole day through, and that night we spent at the theater. My poor faithful cousin did not want to leave me; after that we went to a noisy restaurant, and after it closed, to "the Isles," that point of land jutting into the Gulf of Finland called "Strelka" (little arrow). The pleasure and the drunken sledge cost us all the cash we possessed.

In the morning I went to see Sorin. He was a young lawyer who spoke Russian with the accent of a St. Petersburg native. His wife, a beautiful blonde, was born in Kovno and raised in Paris. They received me as if I had always been their bosom friend. Sorin enlisted the services of a Jew expert in such matters to resolve the problem of my residency by having me stay in a remote hotel where the police were bribed to refrain from inspecting the passports of the Jews dwelling under its protection. Almost from that very first day, we began to prepare the material for our review's first issue.[132] The name of the monthly was *Evreiskaia Zhizn'* (*Jewish Life*). For this title and the permit [to publish the paper], Sorin had paid seven thousand rubles, which he procured through an interest-free loan to be repaid as money came in from subscribers. This monthly, which later became a weekly, and then was closed several times by the authorities, changed its name several times. It moved from St. Petersburg to Moscow, and from there to Berlin, and finally to Paris. It is actually today's *Rassvet*, and Sorin is still the most active editor.¹³³

Another gentleman, also a journalist, wrote me from St. Petersburg before I left Odessa: Alexei Suvorin, son of the famous editor of *Novoe Vremya*, the citadel of Russian anti-Semitism.¹³⁴ Alexei Suvorin turned away from his father and founded a radical daily called *Rus'*, and he tried to rally young and promising journalists around it. I was also invited to contribute to his paper from a distance or at its place of publication, as I chose.¹³⁵ I came to his office and introduced myself: "Altalena. I came at your invitation, sir." He assigned me a salary that I did not expect, of four hundred rubles per month for two articles a week; he did not print even half of them, but the salary he paid with punctual regularity. Thus my subsistence was settled in this new chapter of my life, and I plunged wholeheartedly, free of care, into the activities of the Zionist kitchen with which I am occupied to this day and apparently will be until the end of my life. Is it for my good or ruin? Does it benefit Zionism? I do not have the slightest regret.

I used to spend my days at the end of the month, before the paper appeared, as well as my nights, in Sorin's apartment, which served as the office for our editorial board. This was the first attempt, in Russian, to create an official periodical of the Zionist movement: subscribers responded from every corner of Russia; the spirit in the editorial offices was high, especially as all its members, with the exception of the chief editor, M. M. Margolin, were as young as I was, or even younger.¹³⁶ Margolin was about forty and was known in Russian Zionist circles for his book *Basic Currents in Jewish History*, a short but valuable volume from which I learned a great deal, and which would be worth translating and distributing even now. He was a scholarly man, the general editor of two big encyclopedias, the Russian and the Hebrew, that were published by Efron.¹³⁷ During World War I, I came to know his younger brother, Eliezer, who immigrated to Palestine while still in his early youth. He was Colonel Margolin, commander of one of the battalions of the Jewish Legion.¹³⁸

The other mainstays of our monthly were Shlomo Gepstein, Alexander Goldstein, Arye Babkov (he also taught me Hebrew), Arnold Seideman, Max Soloveichik, and an engineer named Moshe Zeitlin, who left a well-paid job in Baku and moved with his family to St. Petersburg to join our group.¹³⁹ From among the notables of the generation we had Dr. J. Brutzkus, a physician, economist, and journalist who enjoyed the public's respect on our editorial board.¹⁴⁰ I stress the word "respect," as such an attitude toward Zionists on the part of the intelligentsia was rare in St. Petersburg in those days. The well-known adage, "X has two sons: one is clever, the other a Zionist," was widely used. Among its purposes, our journal fulfilled this one as well: it destroyed tradition. This was especially true from the second year of its existence, when we supplemented it with a weekly, and Avram Idel'son came from Moscow to edit it—and thus our group found its spiritual leader.[141] I am sure that it would not be an exaggeration if I say that the word "talent" is inadequate to describe Idel'son. That man stood on the threshold of genius. "An acid, all-corroding brain," Grusenberg once said to me, speaking of Idel'son, and he was right.[142] But that was merely one facet of a multifaceted crystal. His acid consumed only the shells; he knew how to inject vivifying fluids into the kernels. He was prevented in the end from summing up his ideas in the form of a finished treatise because of the curse of his destiny, the fate of a pauper—like that of most members of our circle—or perhaps also because of a self-negligence originating in the source of that same acid. I heard the wistful phrase from him: "Would the Lord have it that I be imprisoned for a couple of years, then I might perhaps be able to write my works." But to us youngsters his company as it was seemed like a university.

Israel Rosov and his family were outside the writers' group but nonetheless mainstays of "the Company"—that was what they used to call us in St. Petersburg, using the Polish word "Halastra."[143] There were then several homes like his, here and there, in the remote corners of the Russian *galut*, which, without any prior arrangement or premeditation, served as centers of the Zionist movement.[144] If the story of those homes was written, it would constitute a complete history of Zionism during the period: the homes of Isaac Goldberg in Vilna, Betsal'el Yaffe in Grodno, Hillel Zlatopolsky in Kiev, and Ahad Ha'am in Odessa. There was also the house of Israel Rosov in St. Petersburg.[145]

Wanderer

My connection with the Halastra lasted almost seven years.¹⁴⁶ I did not spend all of that time in St. Petersburg; mine was a nomad's life. In Vilna a hotel owner once told me: "This is the fifty-fifth time that you have come to our place, sir!"

A new Jewish world was revealed to me in Vilna, a world that I knew until then only from my contacts with the "externs" as well as through brief contact with prison inmates.¹⁴⁷ Lita [Lithuania], too, was like a university for a man like me, who until then had never breathed the air of the Hebrew cultural tradition and did not even suspect that there was such an air in God's world.¹⁴⁸ True, in my time the "Jerusalem of Lithuania" was less flavorful than the original idea, but what was left of it made an overpowering impression on me. I saw a Jewish autonomous (in the literal meaning of the word) universe, moving according to its inner law, as if it had no other connection to Russia than barely a political one, but certainly not a moral one. Every street corner was a miniature Wall Street, with its dozens of firms. Yiddish was a powerful conveyor of thought and culture, and it was not the jargon it was considered in Odessa and St. Petersburg. Hebrew, too, was a language spoken by the daughters of Isaac Goldberg. The poems of Bialik, Tchernichovsky, Cohen, and Shneur directly influenced the young generation—while I, a lover of poetry in four foreign languages, had already become accustomed to the thought that the art of verse had degenerated into a plaything for loafers, apparently to flatter the aesthetic sense of an elite but unable to move the multitudes.¹⁴⁹

As I was saying, the center for Vilna's Zionists was the home of Isaac Goldberg. And not only of Vilna—countless were the general meetings from the various districts of the Pale that were convened in that house. The plan claiming national rights for Russian Jewry, known as the Helsingfors Program, was formulated explicitly in Landvarovo, near Vilna, at the Goldberg family dacha and not in Helsingfors.¹⁵⁰ As for myself, most of the Zionists I knew—those of my generation as well as those belonging to the generation preceding mine—I met in that house. I received half of my Zionist education there.

It is not worthwhile to record the details of my wanderings between 1904 and 1908. First of all, I do not remember them, and secondly, at that time there were many who, like me, were "residents" of the railways of Lithuania, Volhynia, Podolia, and Kiev. I took part in the meetings of the Tsiony Tsion in Kiev, which set the stage for the failure of the Uganda proposal at the Seventh Congress.[151] Rosov and I toured the Lower Volga, downstream all the way from Nizhny [Novgorod] to Astrakhan, and from there to Baku. I spent several months in Odessa; apparently that political "crime" that had made me a fugitive had been forgotten.

I should mention two short visits to jail: one in Kherson, after an unauthorized Zionist meeting, and the second in Odessa, at the end of 1904—that period of "meetings" famous in the history of the first Russian Revolution.[152] A meeting was also organized in Odessa, and I gave a speech. I remember that I concluded it with that word, a favorite of mine—"Basta!"—on that occasion against the tsarist regime. Once every two years I went to the Zionist congresses, but I played no special part, and there is nothing to speak about.

In the meantime, I continued my work in the Russian press, but without real success. Alexei Suvorin, the editor of *Rus,* used to bury most of my articles in his table drawer: "they were not in conformity with the paper's policy." I thought that perhaps his political attitude is really not mine; maybe he is not sufficiently radical. After all, Suvorin was brought up under the influence of his anti-Semitic and conservative father. I went to see him and said, "Aleksei Alekseevich, I have decided to leave you. I have joined the editorial board of another paper that has just been established in St. Petersburg, *Nasha Zhizn'.*"[153]

Two months earlier I had received a letter of invitation from the editor-in-chief, one of the liberal professors. But he also acted like Suvorin: he paid my salary but buried most of my articles—"not consistent with the political attitude." In that case it was already impossible to be mistaken about the tendency, or to suspect his radicalism. The writers worshipped radicalism with a reverence that reminds one of rabbis supervising the *kashrut* of fowl. After my imprisonment in Odessa (for the "basta" speech), I wrote that "the whole town laughed at the stupidity of the police." My article got buried "because it is necessary to protest in such a case."[154] Finally I burst out: "Why did you invite me?" Mrs. Katherine Kusskova, one of the mainstays of the editorial board, answered candidly, "Mr. J., you have an excellent style, and we thought that you would consent to express in that style the ideas we would submit to you."[155]

I leapt into a cab, went straight to *Rus'*, and asked for Suvorin. "Will you take me back? At least you do not think of me as a gramophone." "With pleasure," he replied. Whatever his politics may have been, he had a character and knew how to respect the character of other people. He did not prevent me from writing, "We Jews . . ." This was something unprecedented and a violation of all the traditional principles of Russian liberalism.[156]

By the way: I do not know who spread the rumor that in my time I was considered one of the top-ranking journalists in Russia. That is an exaggeration—one of those legends. In Odessa and the southern districts, I was popular mostly among Jews, but I did not "conquer" St. Petersburg. If I am not mistaken, my newsletters from London during the war years, published in the Moscow daily *Russkie Vedomosti*, made a greater impression.[157] But I was unable to enjoy that reputation because I did not return to Russia, and that newspaper was destroyed, and the public that read it is no longer alive.[158]

Through the Storms of the Russian "Spring"

In the meantime Plehve had been killed, and the workers in St. Petersburg, whom the priest Gapon had promised Zubatov would disengage from politics, organized a procession to the Palace of the Emperor, on January 9, to demand a constitution. The soldiers—their own brethren—killed scores of them. It was already clear to everybody that this victory spelled the decisive defeat of the regime.

My activity in those years followed three basic lines: polemics against the assimilationists, and even more against the Bund, and propaganda in favor of self-defense and national rights for Russian Jewry. I no longer found pure assimilation in St. Petersburg. Those who denied Zionism and who gathered around Vinaver and Sliozberg and their organ, the weekly *Voskhod*, knew already that Russia was not France or Germany, and that there was no place in Russia for "Katsaps of the Mosaic faith."[159] The government itself issued the results of the population census of 1897, and people saw with their own eyes that there were more than a hundred nations, and that even the mightiest of them all—the Russian—did not constitute a majority.[160] In fact the Jewish nation stood fourth on the list. Thus the assimilated also became aware that there was a "Jewish nationality" in Russia, but they did not yet know what we were to demand as a nationality; and they were content with the old slogan—"equality of civil rights"—the Bund's platform.[161] Of course, things were more complex and intricate.

The recognition of a separate nationality had already crystallized. The slogan of "cultural autonomy" was based, on the one hand, on the writings of the Austrian Rudolf Springer, and on the other hand, on the theories of Dubnov.[162] The reader must bear in mind that in those days the influence of the Bund was decisive in all the people's actions, and no "progressive" bourgeois in St. Petersburg would make a speech or write an article without showering compliments on the powerful proletarian movement. In the shade of that Bundist oak, furtively, were emerging the first buds of leftist Zionism. We in the Halastra resisted thinking about class, and we defended Zionism against attacks by the Bund. It is not really important what I wrote and said publicly, but one year after my arrival in the north, I was already despised in the circles of *Voskhod*—we called them National-Assimilators—and even more in the Bund group, whose historical function I formulated as a sort of bridge for our working masses to cross from pure Marxism to Zionism.[163] Regarding self-defense, I worked as an organizer. After the Odessa experience Zionism was not very active, although I took part in a conference in Odessa, if I am not mistaken. I heard that my proclamations and pamphlets, distributed undercover, did help the movement in terms of morale, especially Bialik's "Tale of the Pogrom," in my translation and with my introduction.[164]

That summer of 1905 I visited Warsaw—for the first time, I think. Ever since my childhood I had liked Poland—which is not astonishing, of course: that attitude reflected a kind of general tradition among the progressives in Russia and worldwide. I had studied Mickiewicz's poetry by heart.[165] A pianist from Warsaw once came to Odessa, and the article I devoted to his performance was translated in a Polish newspaper representative of the extreme national movement. I had already made speeches and lectured in many cities and towns in the north, the south, and the east, but it had never occurred to me to make a speech in a Polish town. I did not know Yiddish yet, and to make a public speech in the language of the "Moskal" was considered an insult to Polish pride.[166] I came to Warsaw only to consult with the Zionist youth, centering around our Zionist weekly, *Głos Żydowski,* and to arrange along with them a time and place for a conference devoted to the formulation of the national autonomy in the *galut*.[167]

We considered the Zionist youth in Warsaw the very elite of the new Zionist generation; and we were right. A particular depth and refinement, a sort of echo of the *neshama ha-yetera*, were perceptible in their whole being, in their approach to the problems of national existence, and in the modes of reaction to every decisive event.[168] Perhaps this was due to their proximity to the West; perhaps to the atmosphere of the country, saturated with Polish tragedy and romanticism. Also individually—such spiritual individuals as Jan Kirschrot and Noah Davidson were rare in our world then as well as now.[169]

The news of the pogrom in Bialystok reached us there, in Warsaw.[170] It was the first serious pogrom outside Ukraine, and in a town in which half of the populace was made up of factory workers. Along with young Hartglass, we leaped on the train, and we went to the city of slaughter.[171] Till my last day I shall not forget that trip. The car was full of Jews, but by the time we reached Grodno, Jews disappeared, one after another, and the few Poles refrained from looking at us and spoke among themselves in whispers. A lady nevertheless tried to sympathize with Hartglass—he was a good-looking young man—and insisted that he should leave the train. He declined her advice with refined Warsaw politeness, explaining to me in a low voice the psychological secret of her compassion as follows: Of course she does not care whether they murder one more, but she told me she was going to Grodno, and that is farther than Bialystok, which means that if he was murdered, he would be murdered in her presence, and that would be unpleasant. Perhaps he was right; as I remember, she got up suddenly, gathered her belongings, and went into another car.

As we neared the Bialystok station, we came to the window: The place before the station was crowded by a mob that stood in tight rows, behind the fence alongside the rails, and looked at the train. When they saw us, they began to point at us, get excited, and shout. At the same time, even before the train came to a stop, an old porter came into the car and said:

"For God's sake, if there are Jews in here, do not get off, go on."

We asked, "Is it not over?"

"What do you mean 'over'? It's in full blaze ..."

Of course we obeyed. Our train stood some ten minutes in the station; I do not remember my thoughts, but I do remember well that I was ashamed to meet Hartglass's eyes, and so probably was he.

We went to Grodno; and there, I do not know why, we decided to visit the famous Polish author Eliza Orzeszkowa, a friend of the Jews, and in general a noble personality of that humanistic generation that became extinct with the twilight of the nineteenth century.[172] In her salon, on the walls, she had a Polish flag with the white eagle in its center. We were welcomed by a white-haired lady, generous and noble, her manners full of that ancient *courtoisie* that also died away with that generation. She read my name on one of the two cards we gave her, and she said to me in Polish: "I saw your article in the last issue of the *Głos Żydówski*. Are you opposed to self-government for Poland?" I replied:

> That depends on one thing, Madam. I am prepared to support with all my heart the revival of Poland "from one sea to another"—a state that would include within its borders the majority of the Jewish population of Russia and Austria, if Polish public opinion would agree to give us equality of rights, both civil and national. However the tendency prevailing today among the public of Warsaw is entirely different. Mr. Dmowski proclaims openly that his group would use autonomy in the first place to ruin Jews.[173] Would you say, Madam, that we ought to support his coming to power under these circumstances?

She did not answer me directly. In general, she did not argue with us; that would not be consistent with the tradition of hospitality of such a noble soul as she was. However, later on, in the course of the spontaneous flow of our conversation, she commented with quiet sadness: "All my life I tried to promote mutual understanding and neighborly peace between your people and mine. Apparently I worked in vain."

The Helsingfors Program, its history and principles:[174] Few are those who would be interested today, but in our generation's Zionist evolution there was a psychological and philosophical crisis. We began by negating the *galut:* that is, the idea that there is no purpose in reforming the Diaspora, there is no other cure for *galut* than exodus. However, life led us to the necessity of improving the *galut*, improving it systematically and extensively, and not merely gaining civil equality but also national rights. Regarding this demand we are obliged—precisely we Zionists—to go twice as far as any other Jewish party, since our national appetite is stronger than theirs.

Our opponents ridiculed us, saying that we fell into contradiction and apostasy toward the principles of Zionism, because if national revival is possible in the diaspora, what need for Zion? And therefore we had to find a logical justification for building national palaces in the *galut*, with the intention of abandoning them without regret on the day of their completion. A number of philosophical theories were born with this justification in view. One of those left-wing parties I mentioned—Takiya or SERP, a small but select group of the young Zionist intellectuals—proposed a certain theory according to which Zionism is not an interruption or leap in our national history but only the uppermost or final point on the staircase leading to the revival: Zionism will be fulfilled by the concentration of forces and by winning positions, by means of building up a Hebrew nation in the *galut*, a Hebrew nation free and respected by other peoples, while still scattered among those nations, and only then will it erect a longed-for national perfection and not the *"Judennot."*[175] It will be a special country, somewhat like a millionaire who already possesses a hundred houses in all the capitals and who now builds himself a villa on an island in the midst of the ocean.

Ber Borochov, the spiritual leader of Poale-Tsion, who also stood on the threshold of genius, formulated another theory: normalization of the *galut*. *Galut* is leprosy and plague, and all attempts to reform the *galut* are nothing but delusion and deceit. But even leprosy, like every disease, comes in two forms, the normal and the acute, poisonous form. *Galut* with the absence of rights, *galut* with pogroms—this is the poisonous *galut*. The normal *galut* is the Western variety: *galut* full and fat, a *galut* with honors but nevertheless *galut*, against which a people conscious of its worth will also rebel in the end. And our mission in Russia consisted merely in normalizing the *galut*, realizing fully that this is not a solution to the problem. It is a situation similar to that of a traveler hastening to his goal: the road is long and hard, he is thirsty, and his face is covered with dust; and lo and behold, he finds a spring, drinks from it and washes, and continues on his way.

I must admit that I, too, immodestly, came out to compete with those eminent men and evolved a third theory. What is the meaning of national autonomy in the *galut*? It is the sole means of organizing only a part of the people in the form of a private group, such as the Zionist organization. And what will the people do once it is organized? They will do that same thing Herzl, of blessed memory, had in mind: they will implement *shivat Zion* [return to Zion]. National rights in the *galut* are simply the organization of the Exodus.

At first we tried to disseminate in the general Jewish milieu the idea of a fight for the national rights of Russian Jews. From the beginning of 1905, we started to organize nonpartisan circles in St. Petersburg: We arranged meetings of doctors, and lawyers, and others of merchants, artisans, and so on, and to all of them we introduced the slogan of "complete" civil and national rights—this substitution of the word "complete" was considered a vary daring innovation.[176] In the end we called a meeting of the delegates who had been elected from each of the circles, and a plan was adopted, the details of which I do not remember. The center of this whole movement was our paper's editorial offices. We printed invitations on our broken printing press, and despite the fact that we were only Zionists, and for the most part youngsters without stable social standing, many of the most prominent members of the community responded to our appeal. Naturally, the Vinaver-Sliozberg group did not join us. They convened a special conference in Kovno and established a group there.[177] Finally, both these organizations merged under the lengthy name of Union for the Attainment of Full Rights for the Jewish People in Russia, and I was elected to the central committee. Those of my generation still remember, no doubt, the waves of laughter that greeted the name everywhere—the use of "attain" instead of "fight for." We received the nickname *Die Dergreicher* ("the Attainers").[178]

That summer I went to the Seventh [Zionist] Congress, the first without Herzl, and after it was over, I went hiking in the Swiss mountains with a small group of friends—young girls and boys together. Oh, how I would enjoy it, and how the reader would have an incomparably better time, if, instead of the autobiography of a public man, I could tell him the story of that excursion, which brought us as far as Venice—without as much as a penny in all our pockets! Here, in this story of mine, it will be sufficient if I connect that story with the general trend by mentioning two facts: the first—on the shores of Lake Lugano, I bought an Italian newspaper in which I read about the humiliating end of the Russo-Japanese War, the recognition of Japan's victory, and about the new victory of the liberation movement in Russia; and the second fact—that in the middle of October, while I was in Montpellier in Southern France, word reached me that a constitution and State Duma had been granted, and the next day a wave of pogroms occurred, which was the price we paid for that day of joy for the whole of Russia.[179]

I returned to St. Petersburg. Zionists organized a public meeting in a hall called Solianyi Gorodok ("Salt City"), and I was among the orators.[180] For the first and last time, I saw a meeting devoted to Jewish protests to which non-Jews came, and there were many of them. Only two days before, a proclamation signed by the two labor parties, the SD and the SR, had appeared. The contents of the proclamation included a vigorous denouncement of the government, which had deceived the people and promised liberation but instead had acted in such and such way. I do not remember anymore what crimes were mentioned in that protest, but the murder of Jews in a hundred cities of slaughter (or were there more than a hundred?) was not mentioned altogether. When my turn to speak came, I told them: "People have tried to comfort us that there were no workers among those who murdered, that the Russian proletariat stands guard for the equality and fraternity of all races. Perhaps. Perhaps it was not the proletariat who carried out a pogrom against us. The proletariat did worse; they forgot us. That is the real pogrom!"—I should praise the *goyim:* not only did they come to listen, but they listened in silence and bent their heads.[181]

Soon after, the electoral strife began: the revolutionary parties boycotted the elections, because the right of general suffrage had not been granted, but there was plenty of noise even without them.[182] Jewish candidates were presented for election in the Pale of Settlement as well as outside it. We in the Halastra sat in the office of our paper for a whole night and deliberated. We demanded from all the candidates a promise to join a Jewish faction following their election. Vinaver and his group opposed our demand with extreme force, but even Vinaver himself was compelled to sign the pledge that he would submit and join the "Union of Attainers," whose conference was to be convened after the elections, when the faction would be formed. Twelve Jews were elected, five of them Zionists, and the conference took place in St. Petersburg.[183] Although I was not among those elected, nor was I even a candidate (I had not yet reached the legally required age of 25), my fellow Zionists honored me with the task of speaking about the need for the separate faction.[184]

Ostrogorsky was appointed the principal speaker on behalf of the Vinaver group.[185] He was a delegate from Kovno, an expert on politics and well known even abroad; he was the author of a classical treatise on political parties in North America. Never, either before that day or after it, did I experience such fear while preparing for a public debate: What should I say?—how could I oppose an expert and a specialist with scientific arguments? Ostrogorsky spoke after me; I listened—and I marveled in unmitigated bewilderment. Is that the speech of a scholar, an authority among authorities in the mysteries of grand politics, on which the fate of six million people depended? Not even in the days of my early youth, when I wrote frivolous feuilletons for *Novosti*, did such airy twaddle pour from my pen. On that occasion I learned for the first time what subsequent experience has confirmed: that there exists as yet no "science" of Jewish politics, that there is no precedent to suit our position and needs. My generation is one of beginners, and we must create the science of politics in Israel from A to Z; the same applies also to Zionism, especially to Zionism.

By a majority of delegates, the conference decided in favor of our demand, but in spite of their obligation to join the faction, our opponents did not comply.[186] Our delegates broke into two groups—six against six. (Frenkel, a non-Zionist, joined the five Zionists.)[187] Finally, arbiters intervened and produced a compromise, the details of which I have already forgotten. As for myself, I left the committee of the "Attainers," and on the night following the end of the conference, the Halastra gathered in the editorial office to draw its conclusions.[188] We decided that, in the future fight for rights in the *galut*, the Zionists would act independently, under a Zionist flag.

The speech of the late Dr. Daniil Pasmanik remains in my memories from that conference of the *Die Dergreicher* ("Attainers").[189] He was one of the most elegant and profound orators I ever had the privilege to hear in my entire life. In general, I always believed he possessed a talent out of the ordinary as a speaker. He stuttered slightly, but he even knew how to exploit that defect to intensify the impression. He knew how to emphasize the speed of his speech in such a way that the silences would fall just before the central and decisive word, thus intensifying the effect. This is what he said at the closing session:

> We have arrived at a compromise, and this too is good for the time being, since we are still weak. However this peace is but a preface to war. One after the other, eminent orators rose here to praise peace: they

reminded me of the sweet sounds of the Italian music of Donizetti and Bellini, a caress to the ear.[190] But that music has outlived its time. The new generation likes Wagner, music founded on dissonance. These vessels are coarse; it does not matter if they break: the gap is patched up, and the crack—forgotten. But there is also the antique Greek urn, the delicate and refined creation of an artist, and should a break occur, you will find it beyond repair. And we Hebrews, we are a precious vessel, costly and beautiful, and that crack has no remedy.

In those days Pasmanik was a member of the central committee of Russian Zionists (together with Isaac Goldberg and his late brother, Boris; Leib Jaffe; and Dr. Joseph Lurie, the editor of the official weekly in Yiddish), which then had its seat in Vilna.[191] The destiny of that man is a mystery to me without any visible cause; a cleft existed between the real personality and the impression he created. Even today I am told that he was a hypocrite who put a hat on his head when he took the floor at a Mizrachi gathering.[192] But I happened to be an eye-witness to this at the Sixth Congress, and I remember what Pasmanik said then: "If you demand of me that I should express in this way my feeling of respect toward your meeting—I shall put on my hat; but if you see in it a respect for religion, it is better that I withdraw." The meeting answered him unanimously, "No, no, we do not demand that." Then he covered his head, not as a "hypocrite" but as a polite person, and I would have acted the same way.[193]

The fable about his tendency to change his views frivolously as well as to win the applause of the crowd is also a lie. On the contrary, in my memory Pasmanik remains a fighter against the current tide. Even in Helsingfors he was one of those few who expressed grave doubts regarding the value of the new line. He particularly opposed the belief in "minorities"—the dream that something like an alliance would form among us and the Ukrainians, Latvians, Tatars, and the rest of them against the dominant people.[194] He argued that they all hate Jews, the majority people as well as the minorities, but that the best of them all were especially the Russians. It is well known that he persisted in this belief until his death, and for its sake, he fled the Zionist camp and died in cold and bitter solitude.[195]

Regarding the flaw of superficiality, perhaps it is true; yet it was not his fault but rather a cause of suffering. All his life he read and studied a great deal. I do not know a scholar like him in that Zionist generation, with the exceptions of Ber Borochov and Avram Idel'son. But the talent for expressing knowledge in terms understandable to the masses is the rarest of all gifts. Only a few can do this in such a way that audiences can understand him and at the same time not make his science sound cheap and shallow. He did not succeed, and in general I would not consider him a great talent. But without a doubt he enriched the doctrine of Zionism with many ideas that took root, and he was among the first who taught us to study the economic and social physiognomy of the *galut*.

Helsingfors

In the summer of 1906, we gathered at the conference that I mentioned earlier, at the summer dacha of Isaac Goldberg, in Landvarovo, near Vilna. We called it the Commission of Zionist Journalists. We were joined by the "gang" from St. Petersburg, the group from *Głos Żydówski* in Warsaw, and the editors of *Evreiskaia Mysl'*, which had been founded some time earlier in Odessa.[196] Over the course of three days and three nights, among the trees of the old estate of the Polish count Tyshkevich, on the shores of a beautiful lake on which we rowed during the breaks, we established what was later called the Helsingfors Program.[197] On the third day we learned the shocking news that the tsar had dispersed the First Duma, and that the elections to a new Duma were to begin within several months.[198]

In October I turned twenty-five. In Volhynia, in a forlorn town in the vicinity of Rovno (but which bore a proud name—Alexandria!), I bought a one-story house with three windows, and therefore acquired the right to elect and be elected.[199] I toured the provincial towns, sometimes by train but mostly by sledge. By that time the situation had become more complicated than in the first elections, as the leftist parties had shifted their position and even the Bund participated and proposed candidates. One night in November I assembled the delegates of the Zionist clubs of Miropol, also a small town, and they ratified the plan that had been formulated in Landvarovo, electing me as their candidate under the Zionist flag. And early in the morning I went north to Helsingfors, to the sixth Conference of Russian Zionists.[200]

I reached Helsingfors, but not without some mishaps. I stopped in St. Petersburg on the way, for a final consultation in the editorial office of *Evreiskaia Zhizn'*. In the middle of the meeting, Archipov, Idel'son's faithful servant, who was devoted to him as only a *muzhik* from Yaroslav might be and in due time even acquired the accent of his master—speaking Russian with a Jewish accent!—came in and whispered, "Police!" I do not know why the police arrived suddenly; they did not bother the others, but since I did not have the right of residence in St. Petersburg, I was arrested.[201] I sat in the police station until midnight, and had already resigned myself to missing the conference. Finally, I was rescued by Sliozberg, the lawyer.[202] He came to the police station and attested that I was no revolutionary. "All right, sir," said the police officer, "we shall release you, but we will put the red stamp on your passport." The red stamp meant that this Jew had been expelled from St. Petersburg and must leave the capital within twenty-four hours.

"From which railway station shall I send you off, sir?" asked the policeman. "From Nikolaevskii to the Pale of Settlement?" "To the Finland Station," I answered, and my heart dropped in fear he would refuse, as I had no right to reside in Finland either. He looked at me, looked at the passport, pondered, hesitated—finally, he yawned and said: "All right, go to Finland." I traveled to the station accompanied by a policeman, a splendid fellow who on the way told me about the distress of the peasants: no land, all of it in the hands of the aristocrats! I gave him a silver ruble, and he stood at attention until the train moved off; he took leave of me by giving me a military salute, his hand on the visor of his cap.

The Helsingfors Conference was the peak Zionist experience of my youth, and I am sure that many of those who took part in it would say the same thing, even those who belong to the generation preceding mine: because youth was not only inside us—it was in the air; the youth of the entire country, the youth of the whole of Europe. Such periods in the history of the world do not occur often—periods when many peoples quiver with hopeful expectancy, like a young boy waiting for his girl. Such was the case for Europe before the year 1848, as it was also at the beginning of the twentieth century, that deceitful century that frustrated so many of our hopes. To say that we were naive then, without experience, that we believed in easy and cheap progress—like an instantaneous leap from darkness to light—would be incorrect. We had already witnessed murder on the cusp of the holiday, and especially then, precisely that winter, we already knew that all the reactionary elements were shaping their ranks into a huge and mighty, powerful army. But in spite of all these facts, that faith, the charm of the nineteenth century, had not died in our hearts. We were certain in the belief in abstract principles, in the sacred slogans—freedom, fraternity, justice—and in spite of everything, we were certain that the day of their triumph had come and would overcome all obstacles. I, who had just escaped arrest—even I saw no contradiction between that humiliating experience and the bold demands that I would advocate the next day in my speech at the conference: that there is no dominant nation in Russia, that all her nationalities are nothing but "minorities"—Russians, as well as Poles, Tatars, and ourselves, all have equal status, with all deserving self-government.

I will not compare the Helsingfors Conference to a World Zionist Congress: with the exception of the Sixth Congress (my first), I did not like them; I always used to "wander" like a stranger, and now it is real mortal torture for me to think that I may be compelled to participate once more. But the conferences of Ha-Tsohar and Betar—those I like very much.[203] I have no memory dearer than that of the conference in Helsingfors. The reason lies perhaps in the fact that Revisionism and Betar are mingled with bitterness, because the struggle we now lead is directed also against our Zionist brethren, and every new initiative put forth at our gatherings is a severe condemnation of what is dear to them. Earlier, in Helsingfors, we stood shoulder to shoulder, hand in hand; all the branches of the Zionist movement in Russia—the center of world Zionism—and everything we proclaimed, we proclaimed in the name of all. We believed that we were creating a new Zionism, a synthesis of Hibbat Zion in the past and the political dream of Herzl (as the slogans of "practical work" and the "conquest of positions in Eretz Israel" were proclaimed at Helsingfors).[204] We envisioned a synthesis of the citadels built for our people in the *galut* and the great citadel, which we would gain for ourselves west and east of the Jordan.[205]

Yitzhak Gruenbaum headed the delegation from Poland. (We called them the "Koło" [Circle] and considered them to be the conference's heart and soul: there were among them Noah Davidson and Jan Kirschrot, two excellent men—of the type not easy to find in our midst nowadays.)[206] Gruenbaum summed up our aspirations in these words: "We came here to raise the Zionist idea from a catastrophic conception to evolution, and to base our national revival on world progress." I am afraid that the young reader will not understand this terminology. I should explain, but it is not worthwhile; those days are gone, and they will not return. There is no longer any value or reality to those problems, but at the time we understood and believed. Even now I am one of a very small number who believe in the Helsingfors Program and claim that, in spite of everything, the morning will come, and the tempests of chaos will calm. In the countries that sent delegates to the capital of Finland thirty years ago, order shall be established forever, and it will be that same order about which we dreamt in Helsingfors.

My conscience compels me to make a bold and impudent confession here: in my heart's inner depths, I feel I am the author of the Helsingfors Program. Of course I am aware that the individual who directed our thinking was not me, but Idel'son; and I also know that all the details of the program—all of them bar none—were worked out and took shape in many conversations during the conference, including those with the members of the Warsaw group and the Odessa group with whom we had permanent contact (Israel Trivus, Nahum Sirkin, Shalom Schwartz, and Hayim Grinberg).[207] Nevertheless, if I did not curb my enthusiasm, I would not hold back, and would fill this page with evidence proving that precisely me, and nobody else, had the privilege of formulating the final text. However, it is best that I hold back, since those others—and there are perhaps two or even four of them—also feel the same certainty deep in their hearts, and maybe even carry the same page of evidence and the same right. The art of politics obeys the same laws as that of an architect. That reminds me of a university building I saw some time ago in one of the cities in the United States—a tower fifty stories high, beautiful as a dream, as a wave in the middle of the ocean, rising *de profundis* up to the sky's edge. But in the whole of the city I could not find anyone who could remember the name of its builder. Even the waiter in the restaurant, a fellow who knows everything (it was he who advised me to go and see the new university)—he did not know the name of the architect. In his profound wisdom he told me, and I quote: "This is not important, sir. The architect made the design, others came and improved it; then the contractors arrived and harmed what they could, and then the fools from the municipal council came and destroyed whatever there was to destroy. But the result of it all—there it is, and that is what really matters. Who built it? America did."

Elections, Marriage, Vienna

I hurried back to Volhynia from Helsingfors. The National Assimilationist Party had declared war on us. It was forbidden, they argued, to stress the Zionist program or raise the Zionist flag in the Russian Duma lest even our progressive-minded allies abandon us. They would say, "If you are Zionists, why do you demand citizens' rights in Russia?" I hurried to St. Petersburg and mobilized my good friend S. Poliakov-Litovtsev. (He was a veteran Zionist, and the only one of all the journalists I have ever known, from that time and up to now, who possessed the art of the interview, rendering the interlocutor's words in a way that was true to their spirit and content.)[208] He visited the leaders of the Liberation parties—Milyukov, Kovalevsky, Kerensky, and many others; all of them swore to him that they would faithfully defend the rights of Jews, regardless of who was elected from the Pale of Settlement—Zionists, assimilationists, or rabbis. I published these interviews in *Rus'*, and hurried to Rovno, etc., etc.[209]

In the end I was not elected to the Duma. The Jewish voters (the elections were on two ballots) chose as candidates the Jew Ratner and the Ukrainian Maxim Slavinsky—the same Slavinsky who afterward, fifteen years later, was appointed minister in the Petliura government, and with whom I signed the agreement for which I was cursed in every corner of the Jewish world, and which I am willing to sign again.[210] But these two were not elected either. In Volhynia, the Black Hundreds won, as well as in the other western districts, so that the Jewish Pale of Settlement contributed to a mighty contingent of inveterate Jew-haters to the Second Duma.[211] Of all the Jewish candidates, only three were elected. This Duma, too, did not last long: it was also dispersed, and at the end of that year, I appeared again before the electors—this time in Odessa, my native town—but again I failed to get elected.

However for me the fall of October 1907 was memorable for an entirely different reason. A couple days before election day, I called a cab and went to the synagogue, accompanied by my mother and sister. On the threshold of the synagogue, I met Anya, also accompanied by her mother and sisters and her brother; Anya, that same girl whom I had called "Mademoiselle" when she was ten years old, thus winning her heart, as narrated earlier in the memories of my boyhood. The assistant, the rabbi, a *minyan*, and a *huppa* awaited us in the synagogue.[212] I said to Anya: "*Harei at mekudeshet*" ("Thou art consecrated"), and in my heart I swore, "*Hareini mekudesh*"; and from the synagogue I hurried to an electoral meeting.[213]

I must mention here that, strictly speaking, from the point of view of Hebrew law, there was no need for a wedding. I remember an evening at Anya's home seven years before: we were among friends, her brother Eli Galperin was with us, and three other students—Elie Epstein, Alexander Poliakov, and Moshe Ginsberg—all those friends about whom I would have so much to say if I had the privilege of describing that other, "second half," of my life, which I decided to keep off the record.[214] I had received my salary at *Novosti* that day, and I still had in my pocket a gold coin. I gave it to Anya, saying in front of everybody: "*Harei at mekudeshet li*, by this money, *kedat Moshe ve Yisrael*."—The old Mr. Ginsberg, the father of my friend Moshe, a pious Jew and one of the Orthodox elite of Israel, shook his head and said to Anya—and he meant it seriously—that she would have to ask me for a divorce if she intended to choose a more "solid" partner.[215]

I spent the day after the election by the telephone in Ussishkin's office. We received news on the number of votes counted every hour. Already by noon it was clear that I had not been elected. I do not remember if I was upset; I remember that I thought about something else in those hours. From the days of my youth until now, I have been inclined to have periods of meditation—what they call in foreign parlance "introspection." For two or three years, I habitually carry on the routine of my life without complaining—I even enjoy it for the most part—and then all of a sudden the great inner secret becomes revealed to me: namely that I am tired of everything and that this is not my path. On this occasion, and actually already some time earlier, such a revolt had begun inside me. I saw no definite thread whatever in my life, no "seam line" of my own personal desire and will. I was like a log cast around by waves, a shipwreck. I had been driven to and fro at the hazard of external circumstances, led and not leading, dissolved in the midst of the Zionist crowd, just as I had been drowned in the ranks of the professional humorists, hired earlier in the days of the light feuilletons to amuse the lazy readers. Before that, in Rome, I had been assimilated among the Italian youths who drank wine from the vineyards of Frascati and Grot in the company of a young seamstress. And I, where am I? What has become of me? I give but do not receive. I am preaching to the public—me, an ignoramus—teachings that I do not know. Ever since I left the university, I did not learn a thing but just taught others. Every journalist knows this hunger of the brain that he empties every day, pouring its contents onto the readers. He has no time to replenish the empty vessel . . . "Basta!" Enough of that!

My wife was packing her things to travel to France, where she studied agronomy in Nancy. I told her, "I shall accompany you as far as Berlin; we will separate there, and I will go to Vienna. I want to study." I spent about a year in Vienna. I did not meet anyone, nor did I go to Zionist meetings, except for once or twice. I devoured books. In those days Austria was a real school for studying "the problem of nationalities."[216] I would spend the whole day at the university library or at the library of the Reichstag. I learned to read Czech and Croatian (I've since forgotten, of course); I studied the history of the Ruthenians and the Slovaks, and even the story of the forty thousand Romanians in the canton of Grisons in Switzerland, the customs of the Armenian church (there is a Michitar cloister in Vienna that also has a library), and the life of gypsies in Hungary and Romania. I made notes from every book and pamphlet; I wrote them down in Hebrew in order to train myself in our language, which I also did not know sufficiently well. By the way, I became accustomed to writing Hebrew in Latin letters, a style of writing that is easier for me than the Assyrian square script.[217]

Constantinople

In the meantime revolution broke out in Turkey, and one of the newspapers in St. Petersburg proposed that I go to Constantinople.[218] The Young Turks craved publicity: countless ministers received me and proclaimed unanimously that their country from then on and eternally would be a paradise, and that there is no difference between a Turk, Greek, or an Armenian—all are "Ottomans," one nation with one language. "What language, *effendi*—Turkish?" "There is no Turkish language, sir—Ottoman!" I was told the same story in Salonica, where I met Djavid Bey, a Muslim of Jewish descent who belonged to the sect of Shabbetai Tzvi; and also Enver Pasha, a young and refined officer with a handsome face like that of a *friseur* for ladies' coiffure.[219] I heard the same opinion from all of them regarding Jewish immigration as well: "Why not? We shall be very glad if they would scatter over all the provinces of the country, and particularly in Macedonia, especially if they commit to speaking 'Ottoman.'"

I found Zionists in Constantinople as well as in Salonica. A branch of the Zionist bank in London had been established in Constantinople already before the revolution. It was a real bank, although it had a neutral name, and Victor Jacobson was appointed as its director.[220] I made speeches in Italian on the revival of Israel and Zion, and the next day I read in the Spanish paper *El Tiempo*: Señor J. made a speech full of the purest Ottoman patriotism ("vibrante de patriotism Ottoman"). When I reached Salonica, especially after a conversation with Enver and Djavid, my patience gave out; I was invited to give a lecture at the students' club of the Alliance—the citadel of the assimilationists who until yesterday considered themselves French and did not know what to do, with whom to assimilate, now.[221] I told them not to hurry. I told them about the Austrian example: the Germans didn't succeed in "Germanizing" the Slavs in spite of the overwhelming superiority of their high culture and wealth. I hinted that in Turkey the cultural and economic advantages lay not with the dominant race but precisely with the Greeks, Armenians, and Arabs. I left the "new" Turkey absolutely convinced of two things: first, that this new regime is blind and mad, and that it is bound to accelerate the dissolution of the empire of the Padishahs; and second, that this dissolution will bring nothing but benefits to all the peoples of Turkey, beginning with the Turks themselves, and perhaps even to us.[222]

From Salonica I sailed to Eretz Yisrael. As this is a book that will appear in Tel Aviv, there is no need for me to describe the Hebrew *Yishuv* as it was in 1908. I will mention only some details that may have been forgotten, and some of which will perhaps surprise you, owing to the tremendous difference between the past and the present. In Jaffa I stayed at the house of Meir Dizengoff, my friend from Odessa.[223] Every morning his wife had to go to the pump, turn the handle with her delicate hands, and with a cheerful smile on her refined face—while her husband took me for a walk in the sands north of Jaffa, saying to me: "We bought this land here, and if the Lord is with us, we will build a Jewish city, and in its center we will erect a building for the school; I mean if we can find somebody to provide the money." In the settlements I found small groups of workers; they received me like brothers and asked me to tell them about what was going on in the world. When I told them, in my poor Hebrew, what was happening in Turkey, they answered me the same way everywhere: "So what? This does not matter; the important thing is this—why is there no immigration from Russia?" I went to the Galilee, from one settlement to another; I saw groups of workers looking for work who accompanied me. Most of them had rifles slung over their shoulders, and belts of cartridges. On the road we frequently met a Jewish guard (*shomer*) on horseback, also holding a rifle in his hand. "What if you should bump into a Turkish gendarme?"—"He will say, 'Shalom, hawaya.'"[224] In Meska, below Mount Tabor, I visited a teacher—a burly fellow, tall and square-shouldered—and he told me the following story: "The day before yesterday I rode over to Sejera. On the way I met an Arab who was also on horseback. He stopped his mare and asked me to light a cigarette from the one I was smoking. This is the usual trick of bandits in our region. If he suddenly wanted to grab me, that would be the end. I took out my revolver, put my cigarette into the barrel, and stretched it out to him: 'Go ahead, light it!'" He told me that only a week ago "the war" in their neighborhood had come to an end. The belligerents, two Bedouin tribes, had fought the last couple months, and there were casualties. In Tiberia I tried to speak Hebrew to the son of the hotelkeeper, a boy of fourteen, a student at the Ashkenazi yeshiva, but he replied in Yiddish. "Don't you know *leshon ha-kodesh?*"[225] He bent his head and explained: "My rabbi says: 'Who speaks Hebrew? Non-believers speak Hebrew.'" And from the top of Mount Tabor, I saw the Jezreel Valley, at that time a desert.

On my return from Palestine, I stopped in Odessa to speak with Ussishkin, and then in Vilna, the seat of the central committee of Russian Zionists. We decided to collect money and to propose to David Wolfsohn, the president of the World Zionist Organization, that it establish a newspaper in Constantinople.[226]

In the spring of 1909, I found myself again in St. Petersburg. I was still full of a desire for learning; it did not matter what [I would study] as long as I could immerse myself in a printed page not written by me. Arnold Seideman, one of my fellow members on the editorial board of *Rassvet* (I do not remember what the name of our paper was at that time: from now on I will call it *Rassvet*), gave me good advice: "If that is what you want, why don't you get a university degree?" I was twenty-seven, an age somewhat old for diplomas. Nevertheless I agreed, and it is difficult to imagine the pleasure that I found in the forgotten ABCs, the Latin grammar, and even Russian grammar. (Consider that Edgar Allan Poe's "The Raven" in my translation had been printed in an anthology several years before this.)[227] In Russian history I found the patriotic version of Ilovaysky; in math the theorem that we in the Odessa *gymnasium* used to call "Pythagoras's trousers."[228] The only examination that I almost failed was Russian composition. I received a mark I was not proud of, and one of the other students, a reporter for a popular newspaper, insisted on propagating this sensation in his paper, and it was very hard indeed to persuade him to give it up. But I did receive a diploma.

After that I was called again to Constantinople. I found Wolfsohn there, and we consulted together to work out a program. I was to remain in the Turkish capital to supervise, along with Jacobson, not one paper but a whole Zionist press that consisted of (a) a French daily of a general character called *Le Jeune Turc;* (b) a Zionist weekly, also in French, called *L'Aurore* (*The Dawn*); (c) *El Judio*, a weekly in Judeo-Spanish. Some time later we also added (d) *Ha-Mevasser*, a Hebrew weekly. I doubt whether the sum we raised in Russia for this purpose amounted to twenty thousand francs, although the value of the franc was very high in those days, especially in Turkey.

Of course I could not possibly edit so many newspapers. My role was similar to that of the person they call "politcom" in the land of the Soviets.[229] The editor of the daily was an ethnic Turk, Djelal Nuri-Bey, the son of a high official—a governor of a province in Asia or something similar. He himself was a young man who had studied in Belgium.[230] The Spanish weekly was edited by David Elkanav, or more exactly—why would he need to "edit" it when he himself had literally written every line in the paper? And he also licked the stamps, kept the books, and collected the subscriptions as well as the advertisements. He was a diligent, enthusiastic young man, a faithful Zionist, and in general a splendid fellow. As for Lucien Sciutto, the editor of the French *Rassvet* (*L'Aurore*), he was a journalist by God's own grace; he successfully combined realism, good intuition, adaptability, and a rich and succulent style.

Hochberg was appointed to deal with the financial details of this complex business.[231] He belonged to the generation between Hibbat Zion and political Zionism, and had spent some twenty years in Palestine and Syria. He knew the East and its ways, as well as the men of the preceding regime. I soon realized, too, that this was no less important than knowing the leaders of the new regime. We also had a legal and political advisor, Isaac Nofech, who had come to Constantinople several years earlier to study Turkish law.[232]

In Jewish circles, our work was a success. If reincarnation does exist, and if I were reborn again, and were I to be granted from above permission to choose for myself a nation and race, I would say: "All right, let it be Israel, but please Sephardi." I fell in love with the Sephardim, perhaps precisely due to those qualities that are ridiculed by their Ashkenazi brothers: their superficiality, which I prefer a thousand times to our cheap deep-mindedness; their inertia, which holds for me a greater appeal than our tendency to pursue every passing fancy; their generations of intellectual passivity, which have preserved their spiritual purity. And regarding cultural vigor, I doubt that a liter of French and Italian education or a ton of Russian mysticism really brings a man closer to the threshold of Western civilization (in my view there exists no other—civilization and Occident are the same thing). In Salonica, Alexandria, and Cairo, you will find a Jewish intelligentsia of the same level as in Warsaw and Riga; and in Italy they surpass that of Paris or Vienna. I am prepared to admit they have one great defect as far as Zionist activity is concerned (although the national idea is more widespread among them, relatively speaking, than it is among us): they have no appetite for conquest in their hearts, no ambition. But these too will awaken in due course.

Our propaganda succeeded in both the Ashkenazi and Sephardic communities. But I did not succeed with Nazim Bey, the general secretary of the Young Turk Party, the author and true initiator of the revolution, and perhaps also the one who played a decisive role in accelerating the downfall of the Ottoman state.[233] I found him to be modest and as poor as a monk of the Middle Ages, with a cold and quiet fanaticism like that of Torquemada.[234] He was as blind and deaf toward reality as a wooden log. Again that same refrain: there are no Greeks, no Armenians; we are Ottomans, and will welcome Jewish immigration to Macedonia. All of them—ministers, members of parliament, and journalists—sang the same song. As a general rule I do not regularly overestimate the first refusal uttered by those in power; if it comes to that, even the second refusal or the third for that matter. They will change their minds; let us wait and press on. But here I felt at once that no experience or pressure would help. The refusal is an organic necessity, general assimilation is the central condition for the existence of the nonsense that is their state, and there is no hope for Zionism but for the nonsense to self-destruct.

I hated Constantinople and my useless work. In the winter I went to Hamburg to the Ninth Congress. I enjoyed the intermission, the beauty of Europe that made me forget for a while the hateful East—yet I had nothing to do but vote at the congress once again, which I did for the most part with the rest of the delegates from Russia. I returned to Constantinople, my heart again full of that disquiet, reluctance, and revolt against myself, similar to those feelings that had driven me to Vienna. Jacobson was ill even before we left for Hamburg, and he stayed in Europe for treatment after the congress. And in Constantinople Hochberg showed me the accounts: very little of the money collected in Russia remained in our cash register. I wrote to Cologne, Wolfsohn's home, to Odessa, Vilna; all of them asked my advice: What to do? Nevertheless, we carried on with unrelenting energy.

In the summer of 1910, a very serious conflict broke out between me and Wolfsohn. In those days the Zionist leadership consisted of a trio: Wolfsohn as president, assisted by Jacobus Kahn in The Hague and Bodenheimer in Cologne.[235] About a year earlier, Jacobus Kahn went to Palestine and wrote a book on his travel impressions, printing it beautifully in three editions—Dutch, German, and French. I received the book in Constantinople—and was appalled.[236] With candid outspokenness Jacobus Kahn demanded political autonomy and a Hebrew government for Palestine, as well as a Jewish army to preserve order, and all these—immediately. He was a Revisionist *avant la lettre*. Such is the irony of fate, and even more than irony, a comedy, that precisely I, and nobody else, was appalled by these ideas. However, believe me when I say that what appalled me were not the ideas but rather the chaos of our executive.

Here in Constantinople barely a year earlier, we had articulated our program with the president and Jacobson. Our demands were immigration and language; these and nothing else—immigration and language. Dangerous issues like autonomy would not even be hinted at. "Autonomy" was the most abhorrent word to the ears of the Young Turks, the ultimate anathema and the highest summit of aversion; we could not deviate even by a thin hair from this course, neither to the right nor to the left, or we would be expelled from Turkey and our publications closed. And now the vice president of that same organization comes out and proclaims that the representatives of the Zionist Organization in

Constantinople are nothing but deceivers. I hold political Zionism dear—from my boyhood I knew no other Zionism than this one—but logic is even dearer to me. Not only was I appalled, I also felt angry, and I wrote a detailed letter to Wolfsohn, requesting emphatically that he stop the distribution of the book.

However, about two days after I sent the letter, we learned that Jacobus Kahn had sent his book as a gift to a number of prominent Turks, members of parliament and editors of patriotic newspapers. A couple days later, one of these papers announced that it would soon start the publication of "this interesting book, a detailed official statement of the demands of the Zionists"—extract by extract, day after day, in a clear and exact translation.

Panic broke out in our Zionist community. We gathered for a discussion: about twenty of us, all the best Zionists of the capital, the editors of all our papers (except of course Djelal Nuri-Bey), journalists, the heads of organizations, the leaders of the Maccabi, teachers, and so on, including the rabbi of the Ashkenazi community, Dr. Marcus, a veteran Zionist.[237] We decided unanimously to dispatch an urgent cable to Wolfsohn to prevent the utter destruction of our work. We demanded the resignation of Jacobus Kahn and public repudiation of his book by the executive. And I signed it.

It is not worth recounting in detail the exchange of telegrams and letters that followed this ultimatum, nor do I recall the details. It is sufficient to mention that angry words and admonitions were uttered on both sides, and of course Jacobus Kahn did not resign, but instead I did, although not immediately. At any rate I had spoken with Wolfsohn before our conflict and already had decided to go to Russia to replenish my bank account. So I went, and I received no money, because the Zionists in Russia also despaired of the prospects for propaganda in Turkey—"talking to the trees and the stones," was how S. Rosenbaum described the situation.[238] He was a member of the large action committee and of the central council in Vilna. It was then that I resigned. But I must mention that before I left Constantinople, Hochberg—the Hochberg who "knew the East and its ways"—visited the editor who intended to publish that book in the columns of his newspaper, and the translation did not appear.

I have affection and respect for Jacobus Kahn, and if he needs comfort, here it goes. In fact, none of this really mattered, even had his work been printed in Turkish and posted on the walls of the mosque of Hagia Sophia—it would not have been harmful. It is impossible to harm when there is nothing to achieve. As for me, I am forever grateful to him for having helped me free myself from a useless predicament; although I very much regretted parting from my Zionist friends in Constantinople.

Crossroads

From the middle of the summer of 1910 until the world war broke out, I stayed in Russia. Deep in my heart I doubt whether I was right in giving this chapter the title "Crossroads." From the perspective of its contents, that period of my life in Russia deserves a more distinguished name. Precisely during this period I achieved a certain fame, of which one shouldn't be ashamed, as a writer as well as a public figure (a lone one in most cases). Nevertheless, every single day that same discontent which had made me flee to Vienna continued to grow in my heart, and I felt that this time even Vienna would not save me, that I would not be satisfied with only studies. My whole being yearned for something that was yet embryonic, and despite the fact that there was nothing to be ashamed of, I do not like the memory of these four years, and I will skim over them.[239]

We settled down in Odessa and stayed there for about two years; and it was there, in December 1910, that my son, Eri-Theodore, was born.[240] In 1912 I went to Yaroslavl, a city north of Moscow and home of an ancient law school. I passed the exam and received a university diploma, which meant the right of residence outside the Pale; even more precisely—the right to live in St. Petersburg without paying tips to the porters and police officers as before.[241]

After my return from Constantinople, I finished my translation of Bialik's poems. We were then neighbors in a resort area near Odessa, and he helped me with the translation, explaining passages in the original which I had failed to understand. We became quite close in those weeks. I do not know whether his character changed later, as we almost never saw each other after that, but that summer I enjoyed his great modesty very much. I showed him my Hebrew translation of Edgar Allan Poe's "The Raven": he suggested several corrections and finally said: "But the euphony makes up for everything." Apparently there were a great many things to "make up" for. I sent my translations of Bialik's poems to different publishers in St. Petersburg: they didn't want them—except one offered me 400 rubles for the copyright *in perpetuum*, without regard for whether one or many editions would be published. He explained in his letter that he doubted whether we would find buyers for such a book. At that time Zal'tsman, having arrived from St. Petersburg (he had been invited there much earlier to take charge of the administration of *Rassvet*), read the letter, and said to me, "I will publish it." That is what he did, publishing seven printings, about thirty-five thousand copies. Some say that more people read Bialik in Russian than in the Hebrew original. If that is true, it is to Bialik's credit, not mine. Practically none of my own books warranted a second printing.

I again began to write articles once a week for *Novosti*, mostly on Jewish subjects. Many quarrels broke out between me and the other members of the editorial board due to "chauvinism," but Heifetz, the editor of the paper, remained steadfast and defended me. Most of the articles translated in *Feuilletons* appeared in *Novosti* between 1910 and 1912. I consider this period the high point in my career as a journalist.

During that same period, our attacks on the Society for the Promotion of Culture, the citadel of Russification in Odessa, intensified.[242] This struggle had been started by Ahad Ha'am a number of years earlier, but in the interim he had moved to England, and "the land grew quiet."[243] We renewed the struggle again, but there is nothing to relate about that either: meetings, addresses, articles, elections, defeats; and every defeat, like a mighty stride, brought us closer to victory. But victory came after I had left Odessa. I will mention only one incident, an anecdotal one, because I learned from it that, in the heat of debate, your opponent does not hear your voice, nor does he read what you write; he listens only to his own voice and understands only what is agreeable to him. Our slogan in that struggle was "two-fifths"—that is, two-fifths of time in a Jewish school should be devoted to Hebrew studies. I wrote an article with that same name: "Two-fifths!"[244] The next day the leader of the assimilationists answered me in his paper, quoted my article, quoted my name in full—and concluded: "This is how Zionists demand that more than half the time should be devoted to the study of the Hebrew language and history."

In 1911 a controversy between me and the Warsaw press emerged. Endecja circles even now have not forgiven me, and neither have I them, but free Poland is now the slogan of Piłsudski, not of the ND, and I hope and pray that the government of this noble nation never again falls into the hands of men such as those who then, in the time of Dmowski, betrayed the tradition of nobility.[245] And this is enough—I shall not write any more about it.

However the main part of my Zionist activity in those years consisted of promoting the Hebrew language: Hebrew as the language in which all subjects were to be taught in the schools of the *galut*. The young reader will not believe me if I tell him that I was compelled to fight for this idea not against the assimilationists, God forbid, but against Zionists like myself. But it is the truth. This demand was considered foolish twaddle. In fifty cities and towns, I made the same speech: "The language of Hebrew culture." I learned it by heart, every word of it, and although I do not value nor like myself as an orator, this speech is the only one of which I will be proud to my final day. In every one of the cities, Zionists listened to this address of mine and applauded but afterward came to me to speak in the tone of a serious person talking to a mischievous and naughty child.

In 1911 the Tenth Zionist Congress was convened. I refused to be elected, nor did I go to Basel, for the first time since I joined the movement. I do not remember the reasons now. I remember the most important one was the sum total: a feeling of estrangement. For a long time, many years in fact, my relations with *Rassvet* and the central committee of Russian Zionists had become distant. I was angry with them because they had no ideological position, because they did not know how or want to lead the movement. Actually they made fun of these very words—"position," "to lead"—in a friendly way, of course, but friendliness does not exclude irony.[246] With regard to the Western Zionists, I had no relations with them at all. Go to Basel? I did not go, in spite of insistence from all sides; it was typical of the heartfelt relationship that at that time still united all of us that the Conference of Russian Zionists sent me a cable saying: "Your spirit is with us." It is a pity that two years later I did go to the congress in Vienna, the last before the war. If I had not, they might perhaps have also sent me a friendly telegram from Vienna instead of severing the last thread that still connected me with that naive Zionism.

In 1912 the Third Duma came to an end, and the Zionists in Odessa again asked me to run for election. I pleaded for mercy; I wrote to the central committee (which had in the meantime been transferred from Vilna to St. Petersburg) that there was no sense in it; what use would one Jewish deputy, or two, or even three be in facing a mob of wild beasts such as the one we saw in the preceding Duma and which we would probably also see in the new Duma?[247] But the central committee decided otherwise, and I submitted. A month later those same Zionists decided to remove my candidacy and replace it with Sliozberg's, because they found that, in the first round of ballots on which he was registered, the chances of a Jew being elected were higher than with my candidacy in the second round. I did not agree with them, but I submitted. In both races anti-Semites were elected. After that I moved to St. Petersburg, and there I remained until the war.

In the summer of 1913, I went to the Vienna Congress, the eleventh, and there, at the Conference of Russian Zionists, I submitted the following resolution: "Hebrew should be the exclusive language of teaching in every national school in the country." Approximately one month before the conference, a bill of law had been submitted and approved by the government and passed to the Council of State (i.e., the upper chamber of the legislative body, whose lower chamber was the Duma): the essence of the bill was that the founders of a private school are entitled to choose the language of instruction. It is hard to believe and impossible to explain, but I was received with anger and mockery at the Zionist convention. Perhaps the reason is me and that strange ability of mine, which I already mentioned before, to irritate people. They were angry not only because of the proposal—they did not believe the facts I told them, even though the new law had been published in all the newspapers; they thought it was fiction. Of course they could not reject such a motion at a Zionist meeting; so they adopted it amid laughter and exclamations: "This is a law that will be realized only when the Messiah comes." And I left the meeting feeling like a stepchild who departs from the house he had always called his home. Suddenly now he was called a stranger.

There was a prophet in Israel who, when a son was born to him, gave the child the name "*Loammi*" ("My people for him"). I am not exaggerating: if a son were born to me in those days, I would have called him "*Ivriani*" ("I am a Hebrew").[248] But again I felt that estrangement in my innermost self, and this time with a violence as though a hurricane had broken out in my soul, a revolt against my life, all my past and present. For the first time I realized clearly that there are wild creatures for whom there is no home or refuge even among their own brothers. Such a creature must build himself either a sukkah, tent, booth, or something less than that, a shed—but entirely his own—or else he will be doomed to wander in the spiritual diaspora like a solitary vagrant. Zionism? The name of my air is Zionism—there is nothing else for me to breathe; but that Zionism is not mine either.

If I were asked at that time to define succinctly what "my" Zionism was, it would perhaps have been difficult to say; but it is silly twaddle to pretend that the absence of a formulation means the absence of a clear notion. Russian Zionism's fundamental flaw in those days was very clear to me. I was not interested in Western European Zionism, nor was it worthwhile—it did not produce practical results. True, the Second Aliyah to Eretz Yisrael had already begun—the immigration of workers with the goal of seizing labor in the settlements; I had also seen them in Palestine. However, I returned from Constantinople certain that the *sine qua non* of a serious undertaking was the expulsion of the Turks. Nevertheless, whether it was too much or little, there in Palestine they were trying to build something. But here in Russia it was as if we had no other care than to elaborate theories and programs, to make a *Stellungnahme* ("formulate a position") with regard to every important problem and nothing more.

Struve, the editor of the well-known monthly *Russkaia Mysl'*, asked me to write an article about the Jewish national movement.[249] I remember that I stressed this strange disease—an excess of philosophizing and an absence of action. An important book appeared then, edited by the late Kastelianski—a review of the political movements among the various nations of Russia—and I pointed out in my article a typical characteristic: the chapter on the Estonian movement quotes the number of schools they established, while the chapter on Jews written by Dubnov describes the eight programs of eight parties.[250] Perhaps I am really light-minded, but a program makes no sense to me unless it is translated into achievements. I do not care whether it is successful or not; it is nonetheless a step forward. I remember that a conference of the friends of our language had been organized in Kiev, on the invitation of Hillel Zlatopolsky, who had already begun propagandizing for the spread of spoken Hebrew. I could not attend it, but I sent a written proposal: "Do not adopt any decisions except this one: Establish schools!" Ussishkin, to whom I entrusted my letter, told me afterward that he intentionally did not read that sentence. "This is not practical." In local politics I proposed an alliance among the minorities, asking for negotiations with the Ukrainians and the Lithuanians. I myself also took a number of steps: I had many friends in Ukrainian circles because I supported their movement in my articles in *Novosti*, but the other Zionists looked at these initiatives with indifference and undisguised mockery. In the arena of general Zionist politics, I also felt for a long time that we should return to Herzl's tradition. I began to write a German article, "Back to the Charter," and started to write a Hebrew article with the title "We Sit and Will Not Lift a Hand." I did not finish either of them because of my deep feeling that nobody would care.

At that same Vienna Congress, Weizmann's proposal to create a Hebrew University was adopted, and I agreed to be elected to the committee appointed for this purpose. But it soon became obvious that Dr. Weizmann wanted only "research institutes" in which scientists would work and strive to win the Nobel Prize, not a school in which students would study. I wrote a letter of protest to the central committee of the Zionist Organization in Berlin, and I still remember one of the passages in it: "I also realize that at this point we are unable to create a good university; it does not matter—let us begin with a bad one, since you will see that it will have national and educational value equal to a dozen excellent institutes of research." In the meantime I went to Belgium to investigate the budget question at two private universities, Louvain and Brussels. I also went to Padua, where a famous university also operated with a limited budget. On my way back I stopped in Berlin for a meeting of our committee, demanded a repeal of the program for research institutes, and called for the adoption of the principle of a school focused on students. Only one member of the committee supported my demand: Avram Idel'son. The majority ratified Weizmann's plan. And once more, instead of a decisive and revolutionary achievement, we got a toy.

This was the beginning of the summer of 1914, a fortnight before the shot in Sarajevo. A strange memory: In that same city of Louvain, I became interested in the problem of anatomy, as I knew that in Belgium, too, it was difficult to get corpses for dissection, and in our Palestine this question was even more complicated. Arthur Van Gehuchten, the famous neurologist, who was in charge of the Institute of Anatomy, almost wept before me as he was telling me about the obstacles standing in his way.[251] "No corpses! The public, the municipality, and the churches—all of them—object to giving up the dead for dissection. If I were to describe to you the devices, the stealing, to which I am compelled so that we might continue to have a future generation of doctors who know their business, why, sir, you would think that I am telling you stories from the Middle Ages." This was the same Louvain which, two months later, was flooded with the blood of German slaughter.

Here ends the first part of the story of my life, because the thread became interrupted on its own; it was a period that had no continuation. If I wanted to live, I had to be reborn anew. But I was thirty-four, long past my youth and half into middle age, and I had wasted both. I do not know what I would have done if the whole world had not turned upside down and thrown me into unforeseen paths. Perhaps I would have gone to Eretz Yisrael, perhaps to Rome; maybe I would have created a political party, but that summer the world war broke out.[252]

When the Volcano Erupted

The critic of *Kiryat Sefer* indicated some errors in the first part of my story; some of them bad ones—for instance, the Helsingfors Conference I called "the Sixth Conference of Russian Zionists," whereas it was the third, and who if not I, one of its initiators, should know and remember? Or when I described my involuntary visit to the governor of Odessa, Neidgardt, calling him Shuvalov; for me also this is a strange mistake—I mocked that Neidgardt in various articles many times.[253] On the other hand, it seems strange to me how I could have confused (when I spoke about the anti-Semitic speech that constituted my first step in Zionism, in Bern, 1898) Nachman Syrkin with Nahum Sirkin: it was not Nahum but Nachman who participated in that meeting, and I doubt whether I met him even once after that; while Nahum Sirkin was my friend, whose memory still lives in my heart today.[254]

I will commit errors such as these, probably as numerous and even worse, in this second part. I am writing it aboard a ship (the first part was also written on a ship). I shall continue it or finish it in South Africa, the destination of my journey. But even if I were writing in the city where I live and in my very apartment—a wanderer has no archives, and even what is stowed away in files or valises, most of it is difficult to find, and I have no time to look.

I do not remember whether I "believed in the war" then, during the summer of 1914. True, about two and a half years prior to that, on January 1, 1912, I published an article in an Odessa newspaper in which I predicted the event in its full scope—half of it right, half not. The name of the article is "Horoscope"; it was printed in one of the volumes of my Russian writings.[255] I doubt, however, that I realized that summer, despite the murder of the Austrian crown prince and all its consequences, that the day had arrived. It seems to me that I recall my feelings toward the war: from the first moment, with all my soul, I hoped and prayed for Russia's defeat. If the fate of the war had depended on me in those weeks, I would have decided it this way: a quick peace in the West without any victors or defeated—but first of all the defeat of Russia. I doubt I need to swear here that it was not because I hated my homeland that I wished the destruction of her army: I thought that if Russia would be beaten on the battlefield, she would gain inner freedom. But if she were to win, the regime of slavery would win.

Ten years earlier, during the war with Japan, that opinion was shared by the whole of the intelligentsia, even within Christian progressive circles. But now I found myself isolated even among Jews: nearly all of them were "on Russia's side." Perhaps they were more farsighted than I and could appraise the difference between the results of the Japanese conquest in Eastern Siberia and those of a German invasion here, on the threshold of two major cities on the Ukrainian map, or perhaps it was the traditional charm of the name "England." I knew Zionists like me, young men from the *Rassvet* group (that paper bore another name in those days, but it has already been agreed between the readers and me that I would designate it here under its last name, which is dear to me)—young men who went to a mass demonstration on the square in front of the Winter Palace and bent their knees, along with the thousands around them, when Tsar Nicholas appeared on the balcony. That evening, when we assembled to have dinner at the home of Israel Rosov, one of them told us: "It was not only by compulsion that I knelt—it seemed to me at that moment as if nine generations stood before me on the balcony of the palace, the whole golden chain, with Peter the Great in the middle." If my memory does not deceive me, I attacked him angrily. He also answered sharply, and everyone present took part in that discussion—so that in a short time we were all clamoring and shouting around the table "for" and "against"—even in front of the Christian servant girls, who could feel the agitation. I mention them because I heard that now, in the new Russia, nobody would dare to say even one word "against," even to one's own sons.

One more incident, also typical of the description of the regime of slavery for whose destruction I prayed: At the house of some friends, I met the editor of a popular newspaper, *The Stock Market News,* a politically moderate paper but very extreme with regard to patriotism. He listened to my "against," and invited me to state my heretical views in an article. I wrote it cautiously, but I was quite explicit: All hopes for the reform of the regime were hopeless if "we" won, and all those who want victory must be aware that they are sacrificing their progressive dream. And the article was printed, and the editorial did not receive even a rebuke from the censor.

Not only was this matter of the "pro" and "con" clear to me from the beginning of the war, but so too were several other important aspects as well. For instance: it was "clear" to me that the dispute would not last more than six months; it was also "clear" to me that I, thirty-four years old, with spectacles for nearsightedness, would be free and would stay free from military service under all circumstances, whatever might happen. Only one thing was not clear, not clear at all: How would I feed my family?

My steady participation in the Russian press had ceased some two years earlier, as I had refrained from interesting myself in almost any of the things that interest the editor and reader. *Rassvet* was not a source of income. There was a newspaper in Yiddish, *Der Fraynd,* in St. Petersburg, but it did not even occur to me that a fellow like me could produce articles in the language we then called "jargon," and in which I did not know how to express even simple terms (so it seemed to me).[256] For about two years I was living mostly by giving lectures: a solid and a wide field of activity in a country with a Jewish population of six million. Lectures all year round; but this income source was destroyed in the world catastrophe, or so it seemed to me. What to do?

It was sheer accident and nothing else that made me think of a journey to the West. The late Isaac Goldberg, my close friend, happened to be in St. Petersburg at the time, and he came to see me. During our conversation he told me that he needed a man to go to Holland for his business. I asked him, "Would you send me?" and he agreed.

The next day I hastened to the station and took a train to Moscow. The newspaper *Russkie Vedomosti* was something like the great-great-grandfather of the entire Russian press, the temple of the progressive liberal tradition, a supreme court of good and evil. Nowadays there are no longer any papers like it in the whole world; only the *Manchester Guardian* in England, before the war, had a moral prestige similar to this. Why I went there, I do not know. I knew next to no one in the editorial office, but I was well aware that they were all very scrupulous with regard to progressive purity, whereas the status of a Zionist as a progressive was still dubious in those days. However I received quite a cordial welcome, and they also accepted my proposal to be the newspaper's special correspondent "on the Western Front and around it."

I asked, "For how long is the agreement?"

"Until you come back."

This way of doing business was called the "broadness of the Russian soul," a quality which even in business is frequently more advantageous than any minute calculation. My salary was also measured according to that same "broadness." I hope, and what I heard also from competent persons, that they did not regret the arrangement. As to me, I certainly did not; it is not an exaggeration if I say that my whole fight for a Jewish legion, or almost—about three years in a row—I fought at the expense of the Moscow newspaper.

What exactly was the business assignment I received from Goldberg? I don't remember. Did I accomplish it properly? Of that I am also not sure; but I am certain that he also, up there in the midst of heavenly repose, does not repent having given me the impulse to travel.

My son was then three and a half years old. From his first day, I spoke to him exclusively in Hebrew—but in my wanderings, I did not often have opportunities to talk to him in general; he learned to understand me but used to answer me in Russian, with the accent of his nurse, a native of the Kaluga region.[257] When I came into his room to say goodbye, he said to me: "S Bogom!"[258] His mother told me, as she always did before that, as well as after: "Everything will be all right; do not worry about us, and take care of yourself." My mother, sister, and nephew lived in Odessa. I went away without taking leave of them. One year later I visited them for three days, and after that we did not meet again until we met in Palestine after the war.

It was only a month after the war started that I began my journey. I traveled through Finland, and I stopped in Helsingfors to exchange my Russian banknotes for gold coins; the gold I put in a leather wallet, the opening of which I sewed with a strong thread, and I hung it around my neck under my shirt. We all had a naive notion at that time about the dangers of traveling in countries that were not involved in the war. Of course I soon found out that the most suitable place to keep money even during a world war is the pocket of your trousers, and only a fool would carry gold coins instead of paper or checks.

There was a customs house on the Swedish frontier, and in it were Russian gendarmes of course. (In those days Finland was still a part of the Russian Empire.) It was not until that moment, when I stood before the blue-clad officer for the verification of my passport, that I realized that I had made a dangerous and foolish mistake. Before leaving Moscow I had taken letters from Efim Tchlenov, a member of the Zionist world executive, to his colleagues in Berlin, Dr. Hantke and others.[259] Naturally these letters dealt with Zionist matters, but then I thought to myself that, if I were king, I would not permit correspondence with the subjects of an enemy country. It is typical that we did not pay attention to the danger even for a second—neither I nor Tchlenov, cautious pedantic as he was. It was typical of that atmosphere of paradoxical freedom in that country of obscurity, which I already mentioned before, and it is a wonder that the paradox did not stop even during the war. The officer returned my passport and did not search my pockets, nor did he ask any questions. It is hard to believe nowadays.

Who among the wise men knows the name Haparanda? It is a small town, forgotten and forlorn, on the frontier between Finland and Sweden, and I am not sure that we would find it marked by a circle and a name even on the maps of these countries. Nevertheless it has already twice been the destiny of Haparanda to play a decisive role in world politics. The first time she played such a part was in the Crimean campaign, in the middle of the nineteenth century, when the British navy blockaded Russia's shores on the Baltic Sea. The entire trade between Germany and Russia was forced then to change its course, and turned to Haparanda. The woman orderly in the municipal bath told me: "We have here fifteen families—millionaires who got rich in those days—and their children's children would not leave the town because they knew fully well that our turn would come again." Now it was the Germans who made the blockade, and the goods this time were English. I do not know whether "bath woman" needs any explanation. In Scandinavia, even in men's baths the person in charge is a woman, and if you feel shy and disgusted, you would be considered crazy. Her age? I did not dare look closely at her shape and face, so I just asked in a voice full of pious reverence, "Do you still remember the Crimean War, madam?" For such a provocation I was immediately punished with a friendly slap: "Even my grandmother had not married yet, you fresh young man," she answered merrily.

Lust for a Fight?

In the beginning of September, I crossed the frontier; in the middle of December, I arrived in Egypt; for ten weeks I visited Sweden, Norway, England, Holland, Belgium, France, Spain, Portugal, Morocco, Algeria, Tunisia, Sardinia, and Italy. I could fill a whole book with my impressions of the journey—about the world that had already been struck with madness but had not yet realized that it was poison—but since a whole book would be impossible, let me try to focus on the most important things.

And the most important was the madness. I found the first symptoms the day after passing through Haparanda, in Stockholm. I did not expect such a surprise. I must confess that until then we in general did not suspect that there was also a political mood in Sweden, a longing for imperial statecraft, an appetite for greatness, and so on. True, at the beginning of the century, for some twenty years in a row, the literary and theatrical worlds had satisfied us with Scandinavian productions, and we received this spiritual outflow as some balm coming from beyond the Sambatyon, from some legendary paradise outside reality.[260] We had the impression that Christiania (nowadays it is called Oslo), Stockholm, and Copenhagen existed to supply us with books and theater, and that is all. The possibility did not occur to us that these capitals had other concerns as well. In the Russian press we used to read long articles praising Knut Hamsun and Selma Lagerlöf, but in the foreign news section, their native countries were practically never mentioned, as if nothing that deserved the designation "event" had happened or would ever happen there.[261]

But even before I had time to meet with anyone in Stockholm, I saw a book in a store window with a color picture on its jacket of six U-boats: a sea fight, two warships spitting fire and smoke at each other, one of them flying the Russian flag and the other the Swedish flag. I came inside and bought the book; it was cheap, a book for the masses. The author had left off his name, but the foreword said he was an officer in the navy. I looked through the book: its contents

Cover of *Betar*, the journal of the Betar Organization in Eretz Yisrael, issue 7 (1933). Courtesy of Brian Horowitz.

described a war between Russia and Sweden in the near future; after many ups and downs, Sweden wins.

I went to the editorial office of the most important newspaper and asked to speak with the chief editor. I think I already mentioned in the first part of these memoires that a serious journalist who looks for a profound, serious, and exact understanding of what is going on should not speak with government officials: they know little, because their palace is surrounded with a rampart and a moat with no bridge, and what they know they cannot reveal. A journalist should talk with a fellow journalist: he knows, and he is glad to tell. I showed the book to my colleague and asked:

"What is it? An accident or symptom?"

He told me secrets about which I had not the slightest hint or ever heard of. He spoke about the occult designs of Russian politics of which we—neither my humble self nor colleagues in the major newspapers—were not aware in St. Petersburg, whereas here in Scandinavia (so he told me), it is public and known in all its details to every man, woman, and child. Russia desires an ice-free winter port. Since England will never let her conquer Istanbul in the south, the Russians have long set their eyes on the western shore of Scandinavia. The Norwegian port of Bergen—that is their aim. The gulfstream passes there, no ice, and the rest is clear without explanation. Russia is waiting only for a favorable moment to attack her northern neighbors. The plan is not connected to the war; it is a historical goal, from time immemorial; and here in Sweden people know it, prepare themselves, and spin their dreams.

I tried to persuade him that this whole matter was actually a lie, that in Petersburg there was no official or advisor in the foreign ministry, or even a writer in the cheapest newspaper, who dreamed about such things. And the proof is that, ten years earlier, the same irritated Russia went to seek an ice-free port in the Far East, and not here in the north, and so on. I tried in vain. He did not believe me. All of Scandinavia would not believe, because it is clear that Bergen is close, that Sweden and Norway are weak, and ... In short, his arguments reminded me of the famous Jewish accusation: "Are these not silver spoons? Don't you have two hands? Are you not a thief by birth and vocation? It's clear."

The editor advised me to pay a visit to Sven Hedin, the famous explorer.[262] The greatest explorer of our generation received me in his office, and on the walls, on the tables, in every free space, there were, close together, pictures of kings, princes, earls, dignitaries, generals, and diplomats, each one inscribed and signed. He told me: "Here is the picture of His Majesty Nicholas II, which he gave me as a present only five years ago. I was his guest at the Winter Palace. And here are also the presents from his uncles, cousins, and his ministers.[263] And now they are all against me, all of them call me a traitor because I dared tell the truth to my people. . . . You ask what 'truth,' sir? The danger that threatens Bergen!"

I did not argue with him of course; after all, it was not my affair. But a strange impression remained in my mind after these conversations: as if fear was not the most important thing but some other psychological phenomenon—let me call it an itch for a fight. Afterward, already on the Transjordan front, Colonel Patterson (he was Irish-born) told me the story of a countryman of his, a wanderer who came to a foreign city and saw a riot in the marketplace; about a dozen hard young men battering each other with lethal blows.[264] He stopped to look, and his face expressed envy, nostalgia, and longing; and finally he turned to one of the onlookers and asked politely: "Pardon me, sir: is this a private fight, or may a stranger also take part?" Sweden was a peaceful country, and so was Norway; however both of them had a romantic past, and apparently, to countries such as these, the thunder of the cannon in the distance and the polishing of swords echo a hidden and exciting appeal.

Later I talked with journalists also in Christiania; I found that they also felt the obvious and well-known dangers awaiting Bergen, although they discussed them more quietly and with less concern than their colleagues in Stockholm. I asked them, "Why the difference?" They replied: "The population of Sweden is six million; ours is only two. Of course, even Sweden is too small to meddle in the war between the titans, but in Stockholm they may at least dream. As for us here, we cannot afford to dream."

Several weeks later, I found myself at the other end of the European diagonal, in Lisbon. I also encountered a similar mood there. True, Portugal was not officially a neutral country: already more than three hundred years earlier, she had concluded an old treaty with England and now had sent several detachments to France. But they took part in the war only from behind the front, in auxiliary unarmed services: nor did England and France ask more than that of them—thanks for that, and it is enough. Nevertheless in Lisbon I felt at once that, for them, it was not enough. Again that same mysterious, magnetic force raging in the distance: of course Portugal, too, has a small population, like that of Sweden, but during the last four years they have been involved in making revolutions and counter revolutions—and now I found in their newspapers most encouraging mathematical calculations, offering bright hopes: revolution #1 was made by 532 men, and they were successful; revolution #2 two was made by seventy-seven men, and they also were successful; the third revolution . . . Who said that in an external foreign war there was no place for such a miniature-scale method? And minds were already busy trying to invent motives, causes, and aims that would justify the theory of active dynamism. Somebody pointed out that the Germans were a threat to Angola, and that consequently Portugal must arm itself against Germany earnestly and not only superficially, as is the case now. Another hints that England herself, in spite of the old alliance with Portugal, made a secret agreement with that same Germany, providing for a partition of that same Angola—and consequently . . .

"It does not matter, sir!" the journalist who had given me most of this information told me calmly:

> Our government will not follow these dreamers, and even if it attempted to, we dreamers would ourselves overthrow it. Nostalgia for heroic deeds is only natural for the descendants of Vasco da Gama.[265] Even in our daily life you will find naive expressions of this megalomania: Everybody has three or four names, in addition to the family name, which is already doubled (father and mother); the street numbers indicate the number of windows and not of the houses; and the basic monetary unit is the "Mille-reis." That is why when you receive a bill from the laundress, sir, please do not be surprised: "Maria-Emilia-Catarina Magaliance-Di-Fonseca, 472–474–476, so and so street, sum due 4,850 reis . . ."

Two weeks later I found that same longing for action also in Italy. Here it was not restrained by a natural inferiority complex and feeling of weakness due to one's small population. I arrived there from Tunis, on a steamer that had a tonnage of 250 tons or less; on the way we passed an Italian cruiser, and he began to "converse" with us from a distance in semaphore, and one of the ship officers with whom I had become friendly translated for me. "Are there foreigners aboard?"—"One. A Russian."—"His profession?"—"Journalist."—"His name?" (Here I saw my names "written" in a combination of all the seven rays of the rainbow; really delightful.) Italy was still neutral in those days.

I went ashore in Cagliari, the southernmost port of Sardinia, and spent about half of the night talking with a friend from my youth in Rome, Emanuel Silla. In Rome I had known him as a poet; here he was a professor of economics at the university. He explained to me the mood that I would find the next day in Rome. For us strangers the situation in Italy was very obscure. For several decades she had been considered a sworn ally of Germany and Austria, however she abstained from taking their side in this conflict. Newspapers in Vienna and

Berlin concealed their anger. To the contrary, they complimented Italy for fear that she would join the enemy camp. I already knew (I do not remember if it was from rumors or whether it had already been announced officially) that Franz Joseph intended to offer the Italians a large bribe.[266] The province of Trento would be given to Italy, an Italian university would be established in Trieste, and so on. All these concessions would be promised the Italians not for the sake of their help, God forbid, but only to keep them from "going to the other side." All this I knew, but I did not know the Italian public's opinion.

"And I am sure," Silla said to me, "that we shall fight, and entirely on the side of France and England. Tomorrow you will be in Rome, and you will see that this is the general opinion."

I asked:

What for? What will you gain? Trento is already in your hands. If you are looking for profit, you will also get Trieste without firing a shot. What more could you want? On the other hand, the day before yesterday I spoke with the editor of the Italian newspaper in Tunis, and in his cautious words I heard the ancient dream that you also know— "Tunisia, an Italian colony." That means that the situation is one of profit and loss on both accounts: so where do you get your confidence that public opinion is already crystallized and convinced?

To this he answered: "Where my confidence comes from, I don't know, but I am sure. What shall we gain? Perhaps Dalmatia or Albania, or nothing. But . . ."

My friend was right; in Rome, too, all my acquaintances displayed the same confidence, and he was also right in his prophecy. Even now political leaders in Italy continue to debate the question of whether that step was worthwhile for them. It is a moot question from the viewpoint of utility and profit. But I am certain that, when the final decision came, it was neither utility nor profit that mattered most.

Two years later it was again not profit that proved decisive in America's decision. I had not yet visited the United States, but I was sure that, from the very beginning of the European conflict, the remote echo of the same mighty, gigantic, global factor was felt there, too. Patterson explained to me his nostalgia for his poor Ireland. I am certain that, already during the first months of the war, on that very same day when President Wilson exclaimed, "There are nations whose pride does not allow them to fight!"—he already knew and already wanted to fight.[267]

The magnetic power of war was one of the fundamental and dominant forces of the world. If I were allowed the time and had the talent to write a story of the history of the mysteries within the heart of the individual and society, I would speak a lot about the depth, the meaning, and the scope of this factor, and I would also analyze its moral nature: was it for good or evil that the Creator planted it in our soul? However, I am writing the story of my life, part of what I saw; and in those pregnant months, when the world was at a crossroads in its fate, I saw this in the north, west, and south. If someone were to say—perhaps—that in my soul "this" [feeling] and not calculation prevailed, I would not agree, but I would not argue or feel ashamed.

Around the Front

However, I should also report my personal and professional memories as a journalist wandering around the front.

From London I sailed to Holland—not much to tell—and from there I went to Belgium. There I came face to face with the reality of war: half of the city of Malines, famous for its lacework industry, was already destroyed, and in the other half I saw a row of paupers waiting their turn before the municipal kitchen, with tin plates in their hands. I heard that among them were some who only yesterday were considered wealthy. In Ostend I was awakened at night by two explosions—the Germans passed in the sky and dropped bombs.

From Belgium I went to France, and by strange and complicated routes, changing trains at least a dozen times, I finally reached Paris. I had never been to Paris, although I had already visited other cities in France. It is not worth describing what I found in the capital of lights and gaiety: no gaiety, no lights, and also no capital, as the authorities had already been transferred to Bordeaux, and its inhabitants had vanished, dissolved, or simply hid inside their homes. It was not as though they felt fear, but as though they were ashamed. If my memory can be relied upon, maybe only by this word could I sum up the entire impression of my first contact with this multinational city, stricken with disaster, really suffering, as was London or St. Petersburg: "People were ashamed." It was a sort of depressing feeling, a general humiliation. Every woman was ashamed that her husband and sons, and not she herself, risked death; the clerk at the window in the bank, the grocer in the store, the typesetter in the printer's shop hastened to explain to a stranger (who did not even ask them) that this one limps, that one is fifty years old, although his face may mislead, and this man is a very important specialist irreplaceable in his profession; even the soldiers you met in the train—they also tried to justify the fact that they had not yet been killed. I went to the theater: the same impression, as if all of us we were committing a great and ugly betrayal, the actors as well as the spectators, by gathering at such a time to amuse ourselves; in everything you could sense a subtle poison that pervaded every atom of air, from which there was no escape.

My professional pride prompts me to mention here the incident that, in the book of my life, was considered the height of my cleverness as "our special correspondent on the western front," even though I am afraid my story will not cause any thrills nowadays. The incident was on the occasion of my trip to Reims, the capital of Champagne and the center of production for the famous wine. About two weeks before my arrival in Paris, the entire civilized world was shocked to learn that the Germans had shelled Reims and damaged its antique cathedral. This news made a very strong impression. Now it is already difficult to understand why—to me as well—but then it still was clear to all of us that, although it is permitted to shoot at human beings, one nevertheless is forbidden to bomb a historic building, especially if it possesses artistic value. The articles I read on my way to Paris expressed extreme anger, but the main thing that struck me was that no journalist, neither French nor foreign, had yet succeeded in visiting Reims, and there was no hope of the interdiction being lifted soon. I decided to have a try; I did, and was successful. In Paris I tried to get a permit for this trip for about a week, from I do not remember how many authorities, and every one of them refused. So I went without a permit; even the word "trip" should be taken loosely. I went by train as far as Epernay; from there I continued on foot through hills and woods and military posts. I do not know why I was not arrested; apparently I have been favored by luck sometimes, though not often.

Finally, I reached Reims and saw the damaged cathedral. I spent the night in the hotel in which all the army chiefs stayed; I talked with them, and they showed me the local "money" printed by the municipality of Reims, and I showed them the city "money" of Epernay and Aix. During the night the Germans bombarded the city again, and once again in the morning. One of the bombs fell in front of the barber's in which I'd had a shave. I sent my newspaper a cable of nine hundred words—a cable the kind of which there was not in the *Temps* of Paris, the London *Times*, or the *New York Times;* or at least I hope there was not. After all, it is possible to send a long cable even without visiting Reims . . .

There was another incident—also an adventure of "our special correspondent" around the battlefronts—that I did not report in my newspaper but which is worth describing here. Once I traveled outside Paris with another journalist;

I do not remember what destination we were trying to reach, but we stopped at Senlis. By chance, the assistant to the prosecutor of the district court was staying in the same hotel, in the room adjoining ours, because his private home had been destroyed by German bombs. From behind the thin wall, he heard our conversation—we spoke in Russian—and it seemed to him that the language was German; one word he heard exactly, and he even understood what it meant: the word was *durchaus*, which means, as is known, in translation "to cross the lines." (I swear that he said this.) A military investigation commission was summoned immediately—the commanding officer, along with two officers and the assistant to the prosecutor. We explained to them the meaning of *durchaus*, and clarified which language I used to converse with my friend. "But nevertheless," roared the commander, "you admit that you understand German!" "Yes," I answered, "and I also understand Italian, and Hebrew, too . . ."

"Hebrew? This is very bad, this is very suspicious: the Jews have no country . . ."

Here his officers and the assistant prosecutor intervened—the inspection of our papers had already convinced them that we were "all right," and they wanted to quiet their chief. But I did not relent: I demanded that he should retract the accusation. He swore, shouted, thundered, and wanted to arrest me—"You will sleep on hay tonight, sir!" He already ordered "four soldiers, bayonets on the rifles!"—until one of his officers gathered courage and pulled him outside, while another took me to another room. When I returned to Paris, I sent a complaint to Bordeaux, to the war minister, Millerand, and received from him the following answer: "It appears from our enquiry that the officer did not act in that case with the necessary tact, and he was reprimanded accordingly."[268]

However, as a rule and speaking generally, the work of a military correspondent is a tedious one nowadays. Fifty years ago, perhaps, he was really allowed to write. If he was not afraid, he could enjoy battle scenes from a mountain perch a hundred paces away, and there below, a messenger was waiting to take his manuscript to the telegraph; now the commander himself does not see or know anything. What to do about it? It was impossible, simply out of sympathy for the poor reader, to avoid rhetorical embellishments. I want to confess one more thing: Among my "correspondences" that made an impression, there was a conversation called "The Hun." (That is how the German race was referred to in those years, in honor of Attila and his ancient tradition.) It dealt with a German scholar, who was wounded and captured, with whom I talked onboard a prisoners' train; what about? Of all things, about Provençal poetry, and about the poet, Mistral, the author of *Mirèio*.²⁶⁹ That also, to my regret, never happened. The origin of that "correspondence" is a literary sin committed by me. During the Parisian tedium, I translated the "Song of Magali" from the poem, and I was pleased with the translation, and it was a pity to bury it.²⁷⁰ That is why I tried to create for it something like a setting with a military background, of course—and . . .

The Jewish Accent

In these chapters devoted to my impressions from the journey that brought me from Moscow to Bordeaux, I did not mention any Zionist matters. Nor is there anything to mention. True, I cabled from Stockholm to the Zionist central committee in Berlin, and from there a messenger came to meet me, and, if I am not mistaken, it was Julius Berger.[271] He told me that there was nothing to report. I also heard the same from Dr. Weizmann, who traveled from Manchester while I was in London: no news. And we remembered with a tolerant smile the disagreement we had had half a year earlier, among the members of the Committee for a Hebrew University, over the urgent and heated issue regarding whether the university would be devoted to studies or to scientific research. I did not find Nordau and Marmorek in Paris, as Hungarian and Austrian subjects had been forced to leave France; nor do I remember whether I tried to get in touch with other Zionists, or what we talked about if we did get in touch: there was simply nothing to talk about.[272] The world was busy with matters utterly unconnected with the Zionist vision; a Jewish accent was conspicuously absent from the entire situation.

This situation changed all of a sudden, in a single night. I was then in Bordeaux—I had come to see what a government-in-exile does—and there it was that the news reached me that Turkey had joined Germany and Austria, and would fight against England, France, and Russia.

I do not know, nor am I interested in knowing, whether I should be proud or ashamed of what I am going to confess: In one night I changed my previous opinion and embraced the new goal, going from A to Z. I stifled in my soul all my objections and grievances regarding the Russian regime; I "buried" all my calculations about the prospects for equal rights in the event of victory and in the event of defeat, etc. . . . I eliminated everything except what mattered most: Our fate depends on the liberation of Eretz Yisrael from Turkish rule, and we must participate as a Hebrew military unit in this liberation.

NOTES

A Note on the Text

1. *Sippur yamai* (*Story of My Life*) appeared first in Hebrew in 1936 and was published again in 1946–47. *Story of the Jewish Legion* (*Slovo o polku*) appeared in Russian in 1928 and in English in 1945; it appeared in Hebrew in a single volume, with *Story of My Life*, in 1946–47. Each version is somewhat different, especially with regard to where *Story of My Life* ends and *Story of the Jewish Legion* begins.
2. Vladimir Jabotinsky, *Sippur yamai*, in *Golah ve-hitbolelut* (*Exile and Assimilation* [Tel Aviv: Sh. Zal'tsman, 1936]), 15. Three volumes of Jabotinsky's collected works were published between 1936 and 1946: *Golah ve-hitbolelut* (1936); *Be-sha'ah harat olam* (*Historical Hours* [Jerusalem: T. Kuf, 1943]); and *Ha-medini'ut ha'tsionit* (*Zionist Politics* [Tel Aviv: Eri Jabotinsky, 1946]).
3. Jabotinsky, *Sippur yamai*, in *Golah ve-hitbolelut*, 15.
4. V. Jabotinsky, *Tirgumim* (Berlin: Ha'Sefer, 1923).
5. This paragraph is based on research by Zoya Kopelman, "Zhabotinskii i ivrit," in *Zhabotinskii i Rossiia: Sbornik trudov Mezhdunarodnoi konferentsii (Russian Jabotinsky: Jabotinsky and Russia), posveshchennoi 130-letiiu V. E. Zhabotinskogo (Evreiskii Universitet v Ierusalime, iiul' 2010)*, ed. E. Tolstaia and L. Katsis (Stanford Department of Slavic Languages and Literatures, 2013), 23–24.
6. Jabotinsky, *Golah ve-hitbolelut*, 16.

Introduction

1. *The Story of My Life* (*Sippur yamai*) was published in Hebrew in 1936. It can also be found in V. Jabotinsky's *Avtobiografia* (Jerusalem: Eri Jabotinsky, 1946–47), 9–187. The work originally appeared in fragments in various newspaper articles. For a bibliography of Jabotinsky's works, see Mina Grauer, ed., *Kitvei Ze'ev Jabotinsky 1897–1940: Bibliografia* (Tel Aviv: Jabotinsky Institute, 2007).
2. Among recent works on Jabotinsky, we want to mention particularly the new *Completed Works of Vladimir Jabotinsky*, which is being published in Russian, five volumes of which have already appeared (*Polnoe sobranie sochinenii v deviati tomakh* [Minsk: Met, 2007–]); Dan Miron's book, *Ha'gavish ha'memaked: Prakim al Ze'ev Jabotinsky, ha'misaper ve ha'mishorer* (Jerusalem: Mosad Bialik, 2011); and Arye Naor, "Mavo," in *Leumiot liberalit* by Ze'ev Jabotinsky (Tel Aviv: Machon Jabotinsky be'Yisra'el, 2013),

11–56; Svetlana Natkovich, *Bin inyanei zoher: yatsirto shel Vladimir (Ze'ev) Jabotinsky ve ha'kesher ha'haverti* (Jerusalem: Magnes, 2015).
3. Dalia Ofer, *Escaping the Holocaust: Illegal Immigration to the Land of Israel, 1939–1944* (New York: Oxford University Press, 1990), 11–13.
4. See Zev Golan, *Stern: The Man and His Gang—The Story of the "Fighters for the Freedom of Israel"* (Tel Aviv: Yair, 2011), 63–65; also Joseph Heller, *The Stern Gang: Ideology, Politics and Terror, 1940–1949* (New York: Routledge, 1995).
5. See Nachum Orland, *Der Faschismus in zionistischer Sicht* (Frankfurt am Main: Peter Lang, 1986), 14–15; also Eran Kaplan, *The Jewish Radical Right: Revisionist Zionism and Its Ideological Legacy* (Madison: University of Wisconsin Press, 2005).
6. I. Benari, *Herut, Gahal, Likud: An Analytical Survey and Review of the Evolution of Israel's Main Political Opposition Bloc* (London: Information Department of the Herut Movement of Great Britain, 1974).
7. Although admittedly not everything his followers attributed to him actually conformed to his politics. In particular, Menachem Begin reinterpreted Jabotinsky for his own needs. See Yachias Weiss, *Bin Zeev Jabotinsky le'Menachem Begin: Kovets ma'amarim al ha'tenua ha'revizionistit* (Jerusalem: Magnes, 2012).
8. Colin Shindler, *The Land Beyond Promise: Israel, Likud and the Zionist Dream* (London: St. Martin's Press, 1995), 17.
9. The first printing was in Russian, V. Jabotinsky, *Slovo o polku: Istoriia evreiskogo legiona po vospominaniiam ego initsiatora* (Paris: Imprimerie d'art Voltaire, 1928). The English version was titled *Story of the Jewish Legion*, trans. Samuel Katz (New York: Bernard Ackerman, 1945).
10. See, for example, his articles, "Nabroski bez zaglaviia," in *Rus'*, from January 22, 1908, and February 4, 1908.
11. For example, "Fun tog-buch," which appeared in *Haynt*, April 20 (1932), and in *Der Morgen Journal*, May 1 (1932). Some of the autobiographical articles were translated into Hebrew and published in Jabotinsky's collected works (*Ktavim*) in the volume *Zichronot ben-dori* (*Reminiscences of My Generation* [Tel Aviv: Eri Jabotinsky, 1958]), 25–80. It is important to realize, however, that the translations into Hebrew ("*Odesa sheli*," "*Gimnaziya*," "*Be'shem ha'eile shtot—Ladrover*," "*Bern 1898*," and "*Be'nashaf 'razvet' [meayin reportazh]*") do not include all the articles that appeared in *Der Morgen Journal* between 1932 and 1934.
12. It is important to note that Jabotinsky continued to use the rubric "From My Diary" in his newspaper writing in Yiddish. After 1934, however, he invested these articles with discussions of current events rather than autobiography.
13. This last paragraph is based on Michael Stanislawski, *Zionism and the Fin de Siècle: Cosmopolitanism and Nationalism from Nordau to Jabotinsky* (Berkeley: University of California Press, 2001), 118–19.
14. We found two drafts of *Sippur yamai* in Hebrew that have Jabotinsky's own corrections and thus reflect his work on the manuscript.
15. Michael Stanislawski, *Autobiographical Jews: Essays in Jewish Self-Fashioning* (Seattle: University of Washington Press, 2004), 3.

16. Hillel Halkin, in contrast, approaches Jabotinsky's memoir writing as fact. He writes, "For the most part, I believe, his memoirs are a sincere if artful attempt to describe times and episodes in his life as he recalled them, and I have treated them as essentially reliable accounts despite whatever inaccuracies in them are attributable either to the vagaries of memory or to literary and personal considerations." H. Halkin, *Jabotinsky, A Life* (New Haven, CT: Yale University Press, 2014), 61.
17. See Jabotinsky letter to David Wolfsohn, February 15, 1910, located in the Jabotinsky archive.
18. Jan Zoupla, "Vladimir Jabotinsky and the Split within the Revisionist Union: From the Boulogne Agreement to the Katowice Putsch, 1931–33," *Journal of Israeli History: Politics, Society, Culture* 24, no. 1 (2005): 52–53.
19. Shabbtai Tevet, *Retsach Arlosorov* (Jerusalem: Schocken, 1982).
20. V. Jabotinsky, *Inyan Stavsky* (Tel Aviv: Ts. Feinberg, 1934), Tevet, 265–66.
21. Armanda degli Abbati (1879–1946) was an Italian opera singer who performed in Russia. Jabotinsky mentioned her performances in his articles "S beregov Tibra," *Odesskie Novosti*, March 25, 1901; and "Vskol'z'. Radi Boga," *Odesskie Novosti*, December 8, 1901.
22. Vladimir Jabotinsky, "O zheleznoi stene," *Rassvet* 19, nos. 42–43 (November 4, 1923): 2–4.
23. One scholar believes that he is at heart a liberal. See Raphaella Bilski Ben-Hur, *Every Individual, a King: The Social and Political Thought of Ze'ev Vladimir Jabotinsky* (Washington, DC: Bnai Brith Books, 1993). Another example of how Jabotinsky wanted to appear to be a liberal in *Story of My Life* is the formulation of his supposed credo: "In the beginning God created the individual, and every individual is a king equal to everybody else. Everybody else is likewise a king, and it is better that the individual sin against the community than society sin against the individual. It is for the good of individuals that society was constituted, not the contrary." Acknowledging that such a statement seems to contradict the notion of the primacy of the nation, he continues: "People may point out to me the contradiction between this concept and the essence and contents of my national propaganda. One of my friends who read this manuscript already reminded me that he also heard from me another refrain: 'In the beginning God created the nation.'—there is no contradiction. The second formula I used against those who assert, 'In the beginning "humanity" was created.' It is my unshakable belief that between these two the nation comes first, just as the individual has priority over the nation."
24. Yitzhak Conforti, "Between Ethnic and Civic: The Realistic Utopia of Zionism," *Israeli Affairs* 17, no 4 (2011): 569
25. Yosef Gorny, *Zionism and the Arabs, 1882–1948* (Oxford: Clarendon Press, 1887), 176–77.
26. See Arye Naor, "Jabotinsky's New Jew: Concept and Models," *Journal of Israeli History* 30, no 2 (2011): 141–59.
27. Gorny, *Zionism and the Arabs*, 162.
28. Svetlana Natkovich, *Bin inyanei zoher: yatsirto shel Vladimir (Ze'ev) Jabotinsky ve ha'kesher ha'haverti* (Jerusalem: Magnes, 2015), 201–9.
29. Betarist: a member of the Revisionist Zionist youth organization, Betar.
30. The Hebrew word here is *kushi*, which means Ethiopian; it is likely an allusion to the great Russian poet Alexander Pushkin, who was descended from an Ethiopian prince.

Of course *kushi* is used pejoratively in Israel, and Jabotinsky appears to be portraying himself in an unflattering and jocular light.

31. From the Old Testament; Japheth, along with Shem, was one of Noah's sons.
32. Jabotinsky, *Die idee des Betar: Ein Umriss Betarischer Weltanschauung* (Lyck: A. Kaulbar, 1935), 18.
33. Jabotinsky's followers collected his essays that reflect his views of women. See Ze'ev Jabotinsky, *Shelk i stal': Zhenskaia tema v zhizni i tvorchestve Zeeva Zhabotinskogo*, ed. J. Nedava (Jerusalem: Gesharim, 1993).
34. The "May Laws" decrees of May 3, 1882, imposed a series of liabilities on Jews in Russia, including a restriction on living in the countryside. Pogroms took place in Russia in 1881–82, 1903–6, and 1914–21. The term "blood-libel trials" refers to the trials of Jews who were accused of killing non-Jews to use their blood for Passover matzah. The most famous of these was the Mendel Beilis trial of 1911–13. The "Black Hundreds," a vigilante group that received support from the tsar, was responsible for several assassinations of Jewish political figures.
35. "Bilu," an acronym used to refer to the first immigrants to Palestine after 1881, derives from Isaiah 2:5: "*Beit Ya'akov lekhu ve-nelkha*," or " Let the House of Jacob go!" "Hibbat Zion" refers to the proto-Zionist organization in Odessa that supported immigration to Palestine in the decade and a half before the First Zionist Congress.
36. See the first volume of Shmarya Levin's memoirs, *Childhood in Exile*, trans. Maurice Samuel (New York: Harcourt, Brace, 1929).
37. Jabotinsky is described in Chukovsky's memoirs, but his name is not given. See Kornei Chukovsky, "Kak ia stal pisatelem," in *Zhizn' i tvorchestvo Korneiia Chukovskogo: Sbornik* (Moscow: Detskaia Literatura, 1978), 144.
38. See Jarrod Tanny, *City of Rogues and Schnorrers: Russia's Jews and the Myth of Old Odessa* (Bloomington: University of Indiana Press, 2011); Rebecca Jane Stanton, *Isaac Babel and the Self-Invention of Odessan Modernism* (Evanston, IL: Northwestern University Press, 2012); Charles King, *Odessa: Genius and Death in a City of Dreams* (New York: Norton, 2011).
39. Jabotinsky published the poem in his translation, along with an introduction, in *Evreiskaia Zhizn'*, November 11, 1904, 160–62. The poem was published many times thereafter, including in a collection of Bialik's poems in Russian translation: Kh. N. Bialik, *Pesni i poemy: Avtorizovannyi perevod s evreiskogo i vvedenie Vl. Zhabotinsky* (St. Petersburg: S. D. Zal'tsman, 1911).
40. Sh. Zal'tsman, *Min he'avar: Zichronot ureshumot* (Tel Aviv: Zal'tsman, 1943), 254.
41. Avram Idel'son should not be confused with the prominent musicologist Abraham Zevi Idelsohn. See Brian Horowitz, "What Is 'Russian' in Russian Zionism? Synthetic Zionism and the Fate of Avram Idel'son," in *Russian Idea, Jewish Presence: Essays on Russian-Jewish Intellectual Life* (Boston: Academic Studies Press, 2013), 54–71.
42. Joseph Klausner, "Real'nye zadachi russkgo evreistva," *Evreiskaia Zhizn'* 3 (1906): 125.
43. V. Jabotinsky, "U kolybeli Gel'singforskoi programmy," in *Sbornik pamiati A. D. Idel'sona*, ed. Iu. D. Brutskus, et al. (Berlin: Lutse & Bogt, 1925), 90.
44. Taro Tsurumi, "An Imagined Context of a Nation: The Russian Zionist Version of the Austro-Marxist Theory of Nationality," in *Bounded Mind and Soul: Russia*

and Israel, 1880–2010, ed. Brian Horowitz and Shai Ginsburg (Bloomington, IN: Slavica, 2013), 86–87; also Dimitry Shumsky, *Ben Prag li-Yerushalayim: Tsiyonut Prag ve-ra'ayon ha-medinah ha-du-le'umit be-Erets-Yisra'el* (Jerusalem: Merkaz Zalman Shazar, 2009).

45. V. Jabotinsky, *The War and the Jew* (New York: Dial Press, 1942), 212–13.
46. Gorny, *Zionism and the Arabs*, 163–64.
47. Yehuda Slutzky, *Ha'itonut ha'yihudit-rusit be'mea ha'esrim (1900–1918)* (Tel Aviv: Ha'aguda le'haker toldot ha'yihudim, 1978), 205–6.
48. Simon Rabinovitch, *Jewish Rights, National Rites: Nationalism and Autonomy in Late Imperial and Revolutionary Russia* (Palo Alto, CA: Stanford University Press, 2014), 79–119.
49. Shlomo Haramati, "*Ze'ev J'abotinsky—yozam beyt ha'sefer ha'ivri-leumi be'tfusot*," in *Ish ba-sa'ar: Masot u-mekharim 'al Ze'ev Z'abotinski*, ed. Avi Bareli and Pinhas Ginossar (Be'er-Sheva: Universitat Ben-Guryon ba-Negev, 2004), 299–324.
50. Pyotr Struve, "Velikaia Rossiia: Iz razmyshlenii o probleme russkogo mogushchestva" and "Otryvki o gosudarstve," in *Patriotica: Politika, kul'tura, religiia, sotsializm* (St. Petersburg: Zhukovsky, 1911).
51. Chaim Weizmann, *Trial and Error: The Autobiography of Chaim Weizmann* (Philadelphia: Jewish Publication Society of America, 1949); Shmarya Levin, *Forward from Exile: The Autobiography of Shmarya Levin*, trans. Maurice Samuel (Philadelphia: Jewish Publication Society of America, 1967); David Ben-Gurion, *Memoirs* (New York: World Publication Society, 1970).
52. World literature also offers models for a mythologized autobiography. Charles Dickens's *David Copperfield* (1850), Jean Jacques Rousseau's *Confessions* (1782), and Johann Wolfgang von Goethe's *Wilhelm Meister's Apprenticeship* (1795–96) form a genre with certain literary characteristics, such as a first-person narrator who resembles but also differs from the protagonist; the use of two time frames (the present and recollections of the past); and the depiction of a hero who ages during the narrative and learns through experience the purpose of his or her life. We also know of other texts that were important to Jabotinsky which knit together personal narrative and philosophical import, such as Giuseppe Garibaldi's *Autobiography* (1861), as well as fiction that joins historical meditations with a story of personal experience, such as Ivan Goncharov's *The Precipice* (1869).
53. Vladimir Korolenko, *Istoriia moego sovremennika*, 5 vols. (Moscow-Berlin: Vozrozhdenie, 1922). Vladimir Korolenko (1853–1921) was a Russian writer and humanitarian. Jabotinsky corresponded with Korolenko regarding his own development as a fiction writer. Jabotinsky's letters to Korolenko (1898–99) were published in *Vestnik Evreiskogo Universiteta v Moskve* 1 (1992): 203–5. Michael Stanislawski examines Jabotinsky's attempt to abandon provincial journalism and become a more significant Russian writer. See Stanislawski, *Zionism and the Fin de Siècle*, 116–18. The episode is also mentioned in I. Gal'perin's article, "V. E. Zhabotinskii (biograficheskii ocherk)," in *Evreiskii mir: Sbornik 2* (New York: Union of Russian Jews, 1944), 209. See also Vladimir Korolenko, *Izbrannye pis'ma v trekh tomakh*, vol. 3, ed. N. V. Korolenko and A. L. Krivinska (Moscow: Mir, 1932–36).

NOTES TO INTRODUCTION

54. In the late 1890s Jabotinsky asked Korolenko to help him find a publisher for his poetry..
55. Korolenko, *Istoriia moego sovremennika*, 6.
56. Ibid., 6–7.
57. Vladimir Jabotinsky, *Story of the Jewish Legion*, 181–82.
58. Ibid., 60.
59. Whitehall is home to the chief headquarters of the British army, located in central London.
60. Jabotinsky, *Story of the Jewish Legion*, 37. General Anatoly Stoessel led Russian forces at the siege of Port Arthur in 1904.
61. Ibid., 39.
62. Ibid., 159.
63. Yael Zerubavel, *Recovered Roots: Collective Memory and the Making of Israeli National Tradition* (Chicago: University of Chicago Press, 1997), 152.
64. Vladimir Jabotinsky, "Za militarizm," *Betar* (Sofia), November 1, 1934, 225–28.
65. David Niv, *A Short History of the Irgun Zevai Leumi*, trans. D. Shefer (Jerusalem: World Zionist Organization, 1980), 18.
66. Jabotinsky, *Story of the Jewish Legion*, 31.
67. V. Jabotinsky, "Yener Maks Nordau (tsu tseyn zaynten yartseyt)," *Der Moment*, February 3, 1933, 4.
68. Laurence Weinbaum, *A Marriage of Convenience: The New Zionist Organization and the Polish Government, 1936–1939* (Boulder, CO: East European Monographs, 1993), 9.
69. Ibid., 210–11.
70. Michael Stanislawski writes, "It does not take much detective work to establish that this self-portrayal is not only entirely retroactive and polemically charged, but almost totally invented out of whole cloth. Jabotinsky's autobiographical writings are chock-full of factual errors—incorrect dates, years, names, and the like, on matters both trivial and substantive" (*Zionism and the Fin de Siècle*, 119).
71. "*Im eshkahech Yerushalayim*": the line in Hebrew from Psalm 137:5, "If I forget you Jerusalem." The psalm continues, "May my right hand forget its cunning." Herzl made this the cornerstone of his speech at the Sixth Zionist Congress in order to undercut those who accused him of indifference to Palestine for promoting East Africa as a possible place of settlement.
72. Vladimir Jabotinsky, "Sidia na polu . . ." *Evreiskaia Zhizn'* 14 (April 10, 1905): 17.
73. Vladimir Jabotinsky, "Hespêd," *Evreiskaia Zhizn'* 14 (April 10, 1905): 8–10.
74. V. Jabotinsky, *Was wollen die Zionisten-Revisionisten* (Paris: Polyglotte, 1926), 16.
75. Ibid.
76. Ibid., 3.
77. Kh. N. Bialik, *Pesni i poemy: Avtorizovannyi perevod s evreiskogo i vvedenie Vl. Zhabotinsky*, 6th ed. (St. Petersburg: S. D. Zal'tsman, 1922), 43; the first edition came out in 1911.
78. Ibid., 43–44.
79. Dan Miron, *Ilan metsak ba-gai: Ze'ev Z'abotinski ve shirato* (Tel Aviv: Ha-Misdar'a sh. Ze'ev Z'abotinski, 2005).
80. Yehuda Friedlander, "*Ha'erot le'yitsarto ha'sifrutit shel Ze'ev Z'abotinsky*," in *Ish ba-sa'ar: Masot u-mekharim 'al Ze'ev Z'abotinski*, 283–98; see also Barry Scherr, "An

Odessa Odyssey: Vladimir Jabotinsky's *The Five*," *Slavic Review* 70 (2011): 94–115; Marat Grinberg, "Was Jabotinsky the Zionist Nabokov?" *Tablet Magazine,* August 4, 2014, tabletmag.com/jewish-arts-and-culture/books/180735/jabotinsky-the-zionist, accessed August 4, 2014.

81. See Simon Karlinsky and Alfred Appel, *The Bitter Air of Exile: Russian Writers in the West, 1922–1972* (Berkeley: University of California Press, 1977).
82. "Edmée," in *Razskazy* (Paris: Tip. d'Art Voltaire, 1931), 103–14; "Diana," 11–56.
83. V. Jabotinsky, *Samson Nazorei* (Berlin: Slovo, 1927). See Mikhail Veiskopf, "Mezhdu Bibliei i avangardom: fabula Zhabotinskogo," *Nezavisimyi Filologicheskii Zhurnal* 80 (2006), magazines.russ.ru/nlo/2006/80/va9.html, accessed December 14, 2014.
84. V. Jabotinsky, "Evreiskaia kramola," in *Fel'etony* (St. Petersburg: Aktsionnoe obshchestvo v SPb, 1913), 39.
85. V. Jabotinsky, *Samson Nazorei* (Tel Aviv: Biblioteka aliyah, 1990), 307–8.
86. Zoya Kopelman depicts Jabotinsky's commitment to Hebrew culture in a number of interesting contexts. See Z. Kopelman, "Zhabotinskii i ivrit," 207–36.
87. First edition: Vladimir Jabotinsky, *Piatero* (Paris: Ars, 1936).
88. Ze'ev Jabotinsky, *Igorot*, vol. 1 (May 1898–July 1914), ed. Daniel Carpi (Jerusalem: Jabotinsky Institute in Israel/Hassifriya Haziyonit, 1992), 17–30.
89. The next section is based on my essay, "Hail to Assimilation: Vladimir 'Ze'ev' Jabotinsky's Ambivalence about Fin-de-Siècle Odessa," which appeared in *Empire Jews: Jewish Nationalism and Acculturation in 19th- and Early 20th-Century Russia* (Bloomington, IN: Slavica, 2009), 87–89.
90. Alice Stone Nakhimovsky, *Russian-Jewish Literature and Identity: Jabotinsky, Babel, Grossman, Galich, Roziner, Markish* (Baltimore, MD: Johns Hopkins University Press, 1992), 63.
91. Ibid.
92. Vladimir Jabotinsky, *Piatero* (Jerusalem: Biblioteka Aliyah, 1990), 229.
93. Ibid., 229.

Story of My Life

1. Chava (Eva) Jabotinskaia (née Zak), Jabotinsky's mother (1840–1926), blended a traditional upbringing with secular education that was typical for Jewish girls in mid-nineteenth-century Russia. See Eliyana R. Adler's *In Her Hands: The Education of Jewish Girls in Tsarist Russia* (Detroit, MI: Wayne State University Press, 2011). Interestingly, although Jabotinsky tells us that his mother taught him prayers such as "*Mode ani,*" he did not remember them later. Something is not right here; Jabotinsky is likely playing a game, pretending to forget and remember. Michael Stanislawski grapples with this issue: "Given his later ideological turn, it is not surprising that he could never really sort out the subtleties and complex contradictions of Jewish acculturation and embourgeoisement in late nineteenth-century Russia. [...] Thus, to cite just one example, Jabotinsky later seemed truly baffled that, on the one hand, as a child, teenager, and young adult, he had virtually no interest in anything Jewish, never read a book on a Jewish topic, never studied any ancient Jewish lore; and yet, on the other hand, in school the Jewish children sat together and played together, barely associating with the

non-Jewish children." Michael Stanislawski, *Zionism and the Fin de Siècle: Cosmopolitanism and Nationalism from Nordau to Jabotinsky* (Berkeley: University of California Press, 2002), 123.
2. The Maggid of Dubno, or Jacob ben Wolf Kranz of Dubno (1740?–1804), was a Jewish preacher and storyteller. One story about Kranz describes how he went to Berlin and met with Moses Mendelsohn, who called the preacher the Jewish Aesop for his sharp wit and love of folktales. By claiming that the Dubno Maggid was the only religious figure in his biography, Jabotinsky contradicts his mother, who claims that their family was Hasidic. The Dubno Maggid subscribed to Lithuanian Orthodoxy.
3. Berdichev is a city in the Zhitomir district of Ukraine. In the sixteenth to eighteenth centuries, Berdichev was part of the Bratslav province in the Polish Commonwealth. In 1793 it became part of Russia. The first evidence of Jewish life in Berdichev is found in 1721. In the last quarter of the eighteenth century, Berdichev was one of the centers of Hasidism. In the first quarter of the nineteenth century, it became known as one of the centers of Jewish publishing in Russia. In the first half of the nineteenth century, Berdichev became a center for wholesale trading, especially of agricultural products. Much of the trade was in the hands of Jewish middlemen. In the second half of the century, the trade fell and moved to other areas, such as Odessa.
4. *Maskil* refers to a secularized Jew in Eastern Europe in the nineteenth century. The term *apikores* refers to a Jewish heretic, often used to describe a so-called enlightened Jew. "Modernized *heder*" refers to elementary schools with trained teachers and advanced methods of teaching Hebrew. Zionists were sometimes the initiators of such schools.
5. Friedrich Schiller (1759–1805), German poet and writer. Johann Heinrich Daniel Zschokke (1771–1848) was a Swiss poet who wrote in German. He worked as a translator, Evangelist theologian, teacher, and government official.
6. *Hasidim* (from the Hebrew for "pious ones") are followers of a Jewish sect founded by the Baal Shem Tov in the middle of the eighteenth century. The movement gained many adherents, especially in Ukraine, Romania, and Eastern Hungary. *Mitnagdim* (from the Hebrew for "opponents") are the Orthodox Jews who opposed Hasidism.
7. Tamara Jabotinskaia-Kopp was Vladimir's sister. She was a teacher and established her own school in Odessa.
8. Abraham Zak, Jabotinsky's uncle on his mother's side, was a wealthy Jewish lawyer in Odessa.
9. *Ezrat-nashim* (in Hebrew, literally, "women's help") refers to the women's section in a Jewish Orthodox synagogue.
10. From the Old Testament; Japheth, along with Shem, was one of Noah's sons.
11. Alexandrovsk is located in the district of Zaporizhia, on the west bank of the Dnieper River, in Ukraine. It was one of the largest administrative, industrial, and cultural centers of southern Ukraine. It was named, prior to 1921, for the Alexandrovsk fortress, which was built in 1770.
12. ROPIT is an acronym of Russkoe obshchestvo parakhodstva i torgovli; the shipping company, founded in 1856, was nationalized in 1918.
13. Nikopol is located in the district on the right (eastern) bank of the Dnieper River.

14. *Ha-Melits* was a Hebrew-language Jewish weekly that started publishing in 1860.
15. Nicholai Chikhachev (1830–1917) was an admiral in the Russian navy who held several government positions. He was the director of ROPIT from 1862 to 1876.
16. The German emperor known as Wilhelm I, William Frederick Louis (1797–1888), ruled as the king of Prussia from 1861 to 1888.
17. Yakov Petrovich Polonsky (1819–98) was a Russian poet and writer. After receiving his university diploma, Polonsky moved to Odessa. In 1851 Polonsky moved to St. Petersburg. His impressions about Odessa form the basis of his novel *The Cheap City* (*Deshevyi gorod*, 1879).
18. The well-known English writer Rudyard Kipling (1865–1936) was widely read in Russia before the October Revolution. The actual text from the first quotation is: "If you can meet with Triumph and Disaster; / And treat those two impostors just the same" (from the poem "If—" in the chapter "Brother Square-Toes," published in the book *Rewards and Fairies* [1910]). According to Kipling expert Thomas C. Pinney, the second quotation is a "misattribution." The original Kipling text could not be located.
19. October 18, 1880, was the thirteenth of Cheshvan, 5641. The weekly portion of the Torah read that week was "Vayerah," which Jabotinsky imprecisely transliterates as "Va yar" (וירא).
20. The writer, journalist, editor, publisher, and famous Hebrew scholar Yehoshua Ravnitzky (1859–1944) was a member of Hovevei Zion and one of the founders of Bnei Moshe. In 1889 he was appointed editor of the Yiddish periodical *Der Yid*.
21. Yehuda Leib Gordon (1830–1892), the famous Hebrew poet and proponent of Haskalah.
22. "*Mode ani*" is a Jewish morning prayer; the "*Shema*" prayer (Deuteronomy 6:4) is traditionally recited twice a day.
23. Thou/you (Rus. Ты / Вы) refers to the distinction some languages make in addressing someone politely versus informally.
24. Pan Basileia derives from the Greek: *Pan* = all, *Basileia* = king. Thus "Everyone is a king."
25. "Squirrel" ("Belka") and "Love Affair" ("Diana") were two stories that appeared in his collection *Razkazy* (Paris: Tip. D'Art Voltaire, 1931). "Diana" first appeared in *Novoe Slovo* (St. Petersburg), vol. 5 (May 1910): 24–40.
26. Jabotinsky notes the year 1888: the decree that created quotas for Jews at Russian institutions of education was instituted in 1887. The phrase "candidates of the Mosaic religion" refers ironically to those Jews who dreamed of getting into a Russian high school or university under the anti-Jewish quotas. Sometimes Jews became baptized as a way to gain entrance to Russian educational institutions, which thereby led to the candidate's alienation from the Jewish people. Here Jabotinsky mocks the expression that Jews of Poland often used: "Poles of the Mosaic law." Denial of Jewish identity is one of the central themes of Jabotinsky's journalism.
27. *Bezvremennye* refers to the period of the late 1880s and 1890s in Russia, which was characterized by political stagnation. In Russian history it is associated with the reign of Alexander III and depicted as following the civic and patriotic period that was

connected with the abolition of serfdom. In literature it is associated with the late work of Leo Tolstoy, the most accomplished works of Anton Chekhov (and his death in 1904), and the birth of Russian Symbolism and Russian religious philosophy. In terms of state policy toward Jews, this period is characterized by the May Laws, a series of decrees affecting primarily Jews in the countryside, and the imposition of quotas that limit the numbers of Jews in Russian schools and universities—10 percent in the Pale of Settlement, 5 percent outside the Pale, and 3 percent in Moscow and St. Petersburg.

28. Vsevolod Lebedintsev (1881–1908) was a close friend of Jabotinsky and a "revolutionary." He was executed by tsarist authorities.
29. Alexander Pushkin (1799–1837), Russia's national poet; Mikhail Lermontov (1814–41), after Pushkin, the greatest poet of the Golden Age of Russian poetry.
30. Nineteenth-century writers: Thomas Mayne Reid (1818–83), Bret Harte (1836–1902), Walter Scott (1771–1832), Alexandre Dumas, père (1802–70).
31. Friedrich Spielhagen (1829–1911), German novelist.
32. Ivan Goncharov (1812–91), Russian novelist; *The Precipice* (*Obryv*, 1869).
33. Edmond Rostand (1868–1918) authored *Cyrano* (1897); Esaias Tegnér (1782–1846), the Swedish epic "Frithjof's Saga" (1825); Adam Mickiewicz (1798–1855), the Polish epic poem *Konrad Wallenrod* (1828); and Edgar Allan Poe (1809–49), the American narrative poem "The Raven" (1845).
34. City Park was originally called Alexandrov Park in honor of Emperor Alexander I. It was founded in 1840.
35. The game is played with six or more players (the more the better). The players agree on the boundaries of the game and divide into two groups. Lots are used to decide who will play a Cossack and who will be a robber. Sometimes leaders, known as "atamans," are selected. The robbers gather and guess the password. When they get the signal, the robbers run and hide. The playfield is demarcated by arrows drawn on the asphalt and other surfaces, such as walls or fences, which help the Cossacks find the robbers. Often at first the group of robbers runs together, but a little later they separate to confuse their rivals. The faster the robbers run, and the more confusing their arrows, the greater their chances of hiding successfully. After some time (15–20 minutes), the Cossacks begin looking for the robbers. When they capture a robber, they bring him to the prison, from which he cannot run away.
36. Anya (Jeanne, Johanna) Galperin, Jabotinsky's wife. A great deal about her can be found in Eri Jabotinsky's memoirs. He describes his father's farewell in Eri Jabotinsky, *Avi, Zeev Jabotinsky* (Jerusalem: Steimatsky, 1980), 24–28.
37. Vladimir Lenin (the pseudonym of Vladimir Ilyich Ulyanov, 1870–1924), was the leader of the Russian Socialist Democratic Labor Party (the Bolshevik faction) as of 1903. After the October Revolution of 1917, he became the chairman of the Council of People's Commissars, the leader of Soviet Russia, and later the leader of the Soviet Union. "Lenin" was only one of Ulyanov's many pseudonyms, although it became his official name.
38. *Voskhod* was a Russian-language Jewish newspaper that appeared from 1879 to 1910.

39. Jabotinsky's translation of "The Raven" was published numerous times under the pseudonym Altalena, even in the Soviet Union, without anyone realizing the identity of the translator. The journal *Northern Messenger* (*Severnyi Vestnik*) began to appear in 1885 under the editorship of Anna Evreinova. After the closure, in 1884, of *Otechestvennye Zapiski* (*Notes of the Fatherland*), *Northern Messenger* became the journal connected with the populists (*Narodniki*) associated with N. K. Mikhailovskii. Gleb Uspenskii, Vladimir Korolenko, and Anton Chekhov published in this journal as well.
40. "A Remark on Pedagogy" appeared as "Iz detskogo mira. Pedagogicheskaia zametka," *Iuzhnoe Obozrenie* (Odessa), September 11, 1897, 2.
41. Alexander Fedorov (1868–1949), the poet and playwright, lived in Odessa.
42. According to a decree of 1861, Jews who acquired a university diploma were permitted to live anywhere in Russia, i.e., outside the Pale of Settlement.
43. Anatole de Monzie (1876–1947), a scholar and French politician of the Third Republic, was a friend of Zionism.
44. Podolia is the southwestern area of present-day Ukraine. Galicia was the northeastern region of the Austro-Hungarian Empire.
45. Razdelnaya was a small town to the north of Odessa, where the train station was located.
46. Naum Reichsberg (1867–1928), professor of philosophy at the University of Bern, was the author of *Sotsial'nyi vopros na Zapade* (St. Petersburg: Rabotnik, 1905).
47. Georgii Plekhanov (1856–1918) was a Russian revolutionary and Marxist theoretician. SD refers to Social Democrat; SR, to Socialist Revolutionary. In brief, Social Democrats were strictly Marxist and believed in the inevitability of the historical process, whereas Socialist Revolutionaries believed in the creative individual as an agent of history. The arguments between Lenin and Plekhanov concerned the program of the Russian Social Democrats. In September 1901 representatives gathered in Zurich. The majority despaired of reaching unity and left the congress. This led to the division between the Bolsheviks (Lenin's disciples) and the Mensheviks.
48. Hayim (Chaim) Zhitlovsky (Zhitlowski) (1865–1943) received his doctorate from Bern University in 1892. A major figure in the Jewish and socialist world of the time, Zhitlovsky was closely associated with the Union of Russian Socialist Revolutionaries. At the same time he strongly defended Jews' rights to political and cultural autonomy. He was a scholar of Yiddish and an organizer of the famous Yiddish language conference in Czernowitz in 1908. He did not support Zionism but was loosely associated with the Bund. He promulgated the view that a territorial solution to the Jewish problem could be attained.
49. Nahum Sirkin (1868–1924), the political theorist, was a founder of the theory of Socialist Zionism.
50. Abraham Lichtenstein (birth/death dates not known) became a teacher of philosophy in Palestine. Lichtenstein's wife was the sister of Chaim Weizmann's wife. Lichtenstein's dissertation, completed at the University of Bern, was titled "Lotze und Wundt: Eine vergleichende philosophische studie" (1900). Jabotinsky's experiences in Bern have been analyzed by Stanislawski in *Zionism and the Fin de Siècle,* esp. 127–32 and 144–45.

51. Hayim Rappoport (Charles Rappoport; 1865–1941) was a Russian-born French radical and communist. He started his career as a revolutionary in the faction of Narodnaya Volya, which supported terrorism. In 1887 he moved to France and became associated with many Russian revolutionaries abroad. He sided with the Mensheviks in 1903, and was a follower of Plekhanov in the period 1907–10.
52. "Gorod mira, drevnee skazanie," *Voskhod* (November 1898): 142–44.
53. Richard Wagner (1813–83), the German composer and art theoretician, was a major reformer of the opera form; he was known for his anti-Semitism, expressed especially in his article "Judaism in Music" (1850). Igor Stravinsky (1882–1971) was a Russian composer; Claude Debussy (1862–1918), a French composer and impressionist.
54. Antonio Labriola (1843–1904) was an Italian Marxist theoretician; Enrico Ferri (1856–1929), an Italian criminologist and sociologist.
55. Giuseppe Garibaldi (1807–82) was an Italian national leader; Giuseppe Mazzini (1805–72) was a journalist and politician who struggled for the unification of Italy. Jabotinsky stayed in Rome from 1898 to 1900. Some historians see Jabotinsky's Italian years as formative for his entire career. See Arye Naor, "*'Bereshit bara': Yehid ve-leum be'hashkafat Jabotinsky,*" in *Leumiut liberalit* (Tel Aviv: Jabotinsky Institute, 2013), 11–56. Giacomo Leopardi (1798–1837), Italian poet, philosopher, and philologist; Giuseppe Giusti (1809–1850), Italian poet.
56. Tommaso Salvini (1829–1915), Ernesto Rossi (1827–1896), and Adelaide Ristori (1822–1906) were famous Italian actors; Gabriele D'Annunzio (1863–1938), an Italian playwright and poet associated with Symbolism; Eleanora Duse (1858–1924) and Ermete Novelli (1851–1919), leading Italian actors of the period; Vittorio Alfieri (1749–1803), a classical Italian dramatist; Ermete Zacconi (1857–1948), an Italian stage and film actor; Henrik Johan Ibsen (1828–1906), Leo Tolstoy (1828–1910), and Gerhart Hauptmann (1862–1946), well-known European writers and playwrights of the time.
57. Borgo is a neighborhood in Rome.
58. Filippo Tommaso Marinetti (1876–1944) was the founder of Italian futurism and one of the creators of Italian fascism; he closely collaborated with Mussolini.
59. *Odesskie Novosti,* the leading daily Russian-language newspaper in Odessa, was published from 1884 to 1920, except for the period when the Bolsheviks controlled the city. In 1893 the paper expanded and began to call itself a political, literary, scientific, cultural, and commercial newspaper. After the Revolution of 1905, circulation rose to forty thousand copies sold per day.
60. The Transvaal is located to the north of the Vaal River in South Africa; the reference here is to the First Boer War, which was the setting for Jabotinsky's first play, *Krov'* (*Blood,* 1901). The "revolt of the Boxers" refers to the Boxer Rebellion in China, a violent anti-foreign and anti-Christian movement that occurred between 1898 and 1900.
61. Jean Jaurès (1859–1914) was a French socialist known for his oratory.
62. Decadents were the first generation of Symbolist poets in Russia, which included Dmitry Merezhkovsky (1865–1941) and Konstantin Balmont (1867–1942).
63. Max Nordau (1849–1923) was a Zionist leader, physician, and social critic. *Decadence* is the English translation of Nordau's book *Entartung* (1892). Jabotinsky admired Nordau greatly and emulated him in several ways; in particular Jabotinsky valorized

the idea of the "muscular Jew," and later he adopted Nordau's program for the mass immigration of Jews to Palestine.
64. Beatrice Cenci (1577–99), an Italian aristocrat, was convicted of murdering her father and subsequently beheaded.
65. "Greek Church" likely refers to the Russian Orthodox Church, sometimes called the Eastern Orthodox Church.
66. "Three revolutions" refer to those of 1905, February 1917, and October 1917. "My soul was scorched by fire" references the line from Hayim Nachman Bialik's famous poem "*Megilat ha-esh*" (1905).
67. Jabotinsky was originally a foreign correspondent for the paper, but he became a member of the editorial board and a leading editorial writer (feuilletonist).
68. *Il Codice Cavalleresco* (Florence: Di G. Barbèra, 1883).
69. Altalena, the most well-known of Jabotinsky's many pseudonyms.
70. Vladimir Vladimirovich Bariatinsky (1874–1941) was the editor of *Severnyi Kurier*; he also worked as a playwright and writer.
71. The term "literature of moods" refers to Jabotinsky's article "Anton Chekhof e Massimo Gorki: L'impressionismo nella letteratura russa," *Nuova Antologia* (Rome), 36, no. 719 (November–December 1901): 723–33.
72. Maxim Gorky (pseud. of Alexei Peshkov; 1868–1936) was a Russian realist writer. He was the hero of more than a dozen of Jabotinsky's articles.
73. "*Kokhav nedach*" and "*Metei Midbar*."
74. One needed Greek to pass the entrance exams for enrollment in a Russian university; it is likely that the Greek requirement was instituted to keep children of the lower classes from gaining entrance.
75. Izrail Moiseevich Heifetz was the editor of *Odesskie Novosti* and a theater reviewer who wrote under the pseudonym "Staryi teatral." He was also the head of the city's branch of the philanthropic organization Funds for the Mutual Help of Writers and Scholars (Kassy vzaimopomoshchi literaturov i uchenykh) and vice-chair of the city's Literary Artistic Club. Heifetz describes his first meetings with Jabotinsky in a delightful short memoir that appeared as "Altalena," in *Rassvet* 42 (1930): 19–20.
76. Jabotinsky's thumbnail sketch of the Revolution of 1905 in Odessa does little justice to the real events, in which the loss of governmental power was not centralized in the Student Assemblies but rather was dispersed among local worker committees, various political parties, and liberal interest groups in the Coalition Council. For a more exact depiction of the 1905 Revolution in Odessa, see Robert Weinberg, *The Revolution of 1905 in Odessa: Blood on the Steps* (Bloomington: Indiana University Press, 1993).
77. Odessa's Literary Artistic Club was established in 1897 and opened on January 24, 1898. Among its leaders were V. M. Doroshevich, E. I. Bukovetskii, P. A. Nilus, and B. V. Eduards. The first mention of Altalena in the society's proceedings is in 1901. Jabotinsky became a member in 1902, and was excluded at the end of 1904.
78. See Introduction, note 21, above.
79. The lecture, "The Fate of Literary Criticism," was based on Jabotinsky's article, "Vskol'z'. O literaturnoi kritike. Osoboe mnenie," *Odesskie Novosti*, December 20, 1901. The protocols mention two other lectures that Vladimir Evgen'evich delivered,

"O literaturnoi kritike" and "O kapitalizme i nekotorykh momentakh sovremennoi psikhiki." The cover page of *Odesskie Novosti*, February 19, 1902, carries the article "O literaturnoi kritike," which summarizes the meeting at the club and describes the speeches of the lecturer and his opponents, including S. Lazarovich, Kornei Chukovsky, G. Lifshits, and others. It says that "Mr. Altalena answered each and every critic individually." Kornei Chukovsky (1882–1969) is the famous children's writer and poet. In his youth he was Jabotinsky's close friend. In his memoir about his origins as a writer, Chukovsky describes Jabotinsky's help in submitting his first article for publication. See "Kak ia stal pisatelem; priznaniia starogo skazochnika," in *Zhizn' i tvorchestvo Korneia Chukovskogo* (Moscow: Detskaia literatura, 1978), 159–82. The extensive correspondence of the two men has been published as well: Elena Ivanova, *Chukovskii i Zhabotinskii: Istoriia vzaimootnoshenii v tekstakh i kommentariakh* (Moscow: Gesharim, 2005).

80. Lazar Osipovich Karmen (Korenman, 1876–1920) was a very popular Odessa journalist and a contributor to *Odesskie Novosti*. Among his central subjects was the life of Odessa's impoverished proletariat.

81. Jabotinsky's drama, *Krov'* (*Blood* [Odessa, 1901]), was published under the title *Minister Gamm (Blood)—Drama in 3 Acts: Based on the Plot of "Sangue," a Social Drama by R. Lombardo* (Odessa: Odesskie Novosti, 1901). The play was first performed by the company of N. N. Solovtsov at the Odessa City Theater, September 29, 1901. See also M. Stanislawski, "Jabotinsky as Playwright," in *Studies in Contemporary Jewry* 12, *Literary Strategies: Jewish Texts and Contexts*, ed. Ezra Mendelsohn (1996): 53, n. 7.

82. A copy of Jabotinsky's play *Ladno* can be found in Viktoriya Levitina, *... i evrei, moaya krov': Evreiskaia drama—russkaia stsena* (Moscow: Vozdushnyi transport, 1991), 241–71.

83. "Noala" ("Noela") did appear in Russian and Hebrew. It was included in the play *Ladno* and published in the volume *Me-shirei neurav shel Zeev Jabotinsky* (Tel Aviv: Dafus Gutenberg 1940), 39–46; and again in his collected works in the book *Shirim: Targumim shirei tsion, shirei hol* (Jerusalem: Eri Jabotinsky, 1947), 261–64. "Schafloch" is included in Hebrew translation in both books. The first publication of "Noala" appeared in a rare collection, *Petersburgskii sbornik* (St. Petersburg, 1904); the police prohibited sales of the volume. Hananiah Reichman (1905–82) was a well-known writer and translator.

84. Altalena, "Vskol'z': Ryzhie," *Odesskie Novosti*, April 9, 1902. This article can be found in V. Jabotinsky, *Polnoe sobranie sochinenii*, vol. 3, part 2 (Minsk: Met, 2010), 187–91.

85. A. E. Kaufman (1855–1921), the correspondent of *Odesskii Listok*. Jabotinsky was making a very impolite pun on the journalist's name: Kaufman's pseudonym was "Znakomyi" (Acquaintance); Jabotinsky called him "Nasekomoe," in other words "Znakomyi, na-sek-omyi" (an acquaintance, insect, or one who has been beaten with a whip).

86. Iosif Menassievich Bickerman (1867–1942) was the author of the article (in Russian) "O sionizme i po povodu sionizma," published in *Russkoe Bogatstvo* 7 (1902): 27–69. Jabotinsky answered Bickerman in an article, "O sionizme," *Odesskie Novosti*, September 8, 1902. Jabotinsky characterized him as an assimilationist.

87. The term "lover of Zion" refers to Hibbat Zion, the Zionist group organized in post-1882 Odessa, Imperial Russia.

88. Andrei Zhelyabov (1851–81) was a Russian revolutionary and member of the executive committee of the People's Will Party. Alexander II was Tsar Alexander Romanov (1818–81), known as the tsar liberator for his act of liberating the serfs in 1861. He was hailed among Jews for his efforts to reform and lessen anti-Jewish liabilities.
89. Because of the discrepancies between the names of the inmates in the police files and Jabotinsky's narrative, one may presume that Jabotinsky made up these names to reflect his own ideological and political positions. Honoré Gabriel Riqueti, comte de Mirabeau (1749–91), was a leader during the early stages of the French Revolution. Guiseppe Garibaldi (1807–82) was an Italian general and politician famous in the struggle for Italian independence. Fernand Labori (1860–1917) was an attorney who defended Alfred Dreyfus. Ghed's identity is unknown.
90. Deribas Street was one of the central streets of Odessa. It was named in honor of José de Ribas, the founder of Odessa and its first mayor; his house was located on the street. Jabotinsky is referring perhaps to an event that occurred before his arrest, with the unfurling of a red flag by revolutionaries, or he has mistakenly remembered a well-known event of 1905, when revolutionaries tore down portraits of the tsar and his family and put up red flags in their place.
91. Moldavanka was a poor section of Odessa that contained a dense Jewish population.
92. Avram Moiseevich Ginzburg (1878–1937) was a well-known revolutionary and Menshevik. After the October Revolution, he worked in the Ministry of Economics, where he was the assistant director. In 1928 he helped organize a counter-revolutionary group, but he was arrested in 1930; in 1931 he was condemned to ten years in prison. He died in the party purges of 1937.
93. "Bund" here refers to the General Jewish Labor Bund in Lithuania, Poland, and Russia. Characterized by a blending of socialism and nationalism, the Bund was the leading Jewish political party in Russia in the decade before 1917.
94. Arcadia was the tourist area near Odessa, located on the shore of the Black Sea. The Large Fountain ("Bol'shoi Fonton"), located on the banks of the Black Sea, was one of the largest and most popular tourist sites in Odessa.
95. Sergei Witte (1849–1915) served as Russian prime minister under Nicholas II. His book *Zemstvo and Autocracy* (*Samoderzhavie i zemstvo*) was published twice, in 1899 and in 1903. The second edition contained two prefaces, one by Pyotr Struve and a note by the author who was minister of finance at the time. This edition did not contain the original four-page introduction by Plekhanov, which caused the scandal. In the book Witte warned the tsar of the incompatibility of democratic institutions and an autocratic state.
96. "*Lecha dodi*" is a Hebrew song sung on Friday night, at the start of the Sabbath.
97. The winter of 1902.
98. The review was *Gazzetta Musicale di Milano*.
99. Solomon Davidovich (Shlomo) Zal'tsman (1872–1946), publisher and Revisionist Zionist, was Jabotinsky's close friend. With Jabotinsky, Zal'tsman helped establish the publishing house Kadima, which printed Jabotinsky's books. Zal'tsman headed the Zionist Palestine Society in Odessa and later in Moscow became a leader of the local Zionist organization. He was a delegate to the ninth, twelfth, fourteenth,

sixteenth, and twenty-first Zionist congresses. He moved to British-controlled Egypt in 1919 and later came to Palestine, where he continued his publishing activities. His memoir contains a long chapter devoted to Jabotinsky. See *Min he-avar* (Tel Aviv: Zal'tsman, 1943), 240–90.

100. Israel A. Trivus (1883–1955) was a Hebrew writer and Revisionist politician. A graduate of St. Petersburg University, he played an active role in the Jewish philanthropic organizations EKO (Jewish Colonization Society) and OPE (Society for the Promotion of Enlightenment among the Jews of Russia). He published in the Russian and Jewish press and served as a leader of the Jewish self-defense efforts in Odessa. Tsohar is the designation of Jabotinsky's Revisionist Party. Trivus also described his relationship with Jabotinsky in Odessa in *Reshitah shel ha-haganah* (Tel Aviv: Yodefet, 1950–51).

101. The pogrom in Kishinev occurred on April 6–7, 1903. It was perhaps the most well-known pogrom of tsarist times. Kishinev was the capital of Bessarabia (today Moldova).

102. A "silk young man" refers to a successful young Jew who can move in and out of different groups, easily gaining entrance to elite positions without appearing even to try.

103. Henrik Shaevich (birth and death dates unknown) was an agent of Sergei Zubatov. Beginning in 1903 he was assigned the job of monitoring and neutralizing the Jewish revolutionary movement in Odessa. Shaevich had a doctorate from the University of Berlin and was a member of the Independent Jewish Workers Party.

104. Sergei Zubatov (1864–1917) was a Russian police administrator who initiated a program to permit labor strikes that were free of political demands. See N. Panasenko, "Zhabotinskii i politicheskie partii," *Moriia: Al'manakh* (Odessa), no. 12 (2011): 6–20.

105. Georgy Gapon (1870–1906) was a Russian Orthodox priest and labor leader who led the march on the Winter Palace that became known as Bloody Sunday, on January 8, 1905 (old style).

106. Jabotinsky wrote in more detail about his thoughts on pogroms in "V traurnye dni," in his book *Fel'etony*, 25–33.

107. Jabotinsky participated in activities that provided aid to those hurt in the Kishinev pogrom. By calling Kishinev one of the "places of slaughter," Jabotinsky alludes to Hayim Nachman Bialik's poem *"Ir ha-Harega"* ("City of Slaughter"), which appeared in Jabotinsky's translation in 1904 as "Skazanie o pogrome."

108. Yakov Bernstein-Kogan (1859–1929) was an early Zionist leader in Kishinev who was involved in the establishment of a Zionist movement in Russia. At the First Zionist Congress in Basel, in 1897, he was elected to head the efforts for the creation of Zionist organizations in Russia. From 1897 to 1901 he was the head of the Correspondence Bureau, which was responsible for coordinating activity and communication among organizations throughout Russia. In 1901 he joined the Democratic Faction; he later opposed the Uganda solution. He moved to Kharkov and played an important role in the development of Zionism in the city. Menachem Ussishkin (1863–1941) was an important Russian Zionist leader in the world movement. Vladimir Tiomkin (1861–1927) was a Russian Zionist leader in the Revisionist movement. Tiomkin graduated from the Technological Institute in St. Petersburg (1886). He

participated in revolutionary circles and joined the Jewish national movement after the pogroms of 1881–82. He was involved in Odessa's philanthropic societies and also its nascent Palestinophile groups. From 1893 to 1917 he served as the state rabbi of Elisavetgrad. In 1920 he joined *Rassvet*'s editorial board, and in 1925 he was elected head of the Zionist-Revisionists of France. In 1935–38 he was one of the leaders of the New Zionist Organization. Joseph Sapir (1869–1935) was a writer and political activist. Born in Odessa, he was an important Zionist who was one of the original leaders of the nationalist circles in Vienna (Kadima). During the first decade of the twentieth century, he was a member of the greater Zionist Actions-Comité. Later he helped found the Yiddish publishing house Biblioteka-Kopeika; he wrote for *Voskhod, Evreiskaia Zhizn'*, and many other publications.

109. *Ba'alei-batim* refers to wealthy men; in Hebrew, literally, masters or owners of homes.
110. On August 14, 1903, the British colonial minister, Joseph Chamberlain (1836–1914), offered Theodor Herzl (1860–1904), the head of the Zionist movement, a program for the settlement of a territory in North Africa. El-Arish was the city in the Sinai Peninsula that became the subject of a heated debate about whether Zionists should accept a temporary site for emigration. Theodor Herzl was known as the Father of Zionism. Herzl grew up in Budapest; his family moved to Vienna when he was a young man. He studied law and became a well-known playwright and journalist for the Viennese *Neue Freie Presse*. He covered the arrest and trial of Alfred Dreyfus in Paris in 1894. In 1897 he organized the First Zionist Congress in Basel and served as chairman of the World Zionist Organization. In 1903 he traveled to Russia to meet Russian officials, despite accusations that these individuals were responsible for the Kishinev pogrom (1903). In 1903 the British government offered the World Zionist Organization a Jewish settlement in East Africa. Herzl put this offer before the Zionist Congress; the controversy became known as the Uganda Affair. Herzl authored important works, including *The Jewish State* (1896) and *The Old New Land* (1902). Although Jabotinsky revered Herzl, he nonetheless sided with the opposition. Russian opposition to Herzl is described in Israel Klausner, *Opozitsyah le-Hertsl* (Jerusalem: Ha-Ahiaever, 1960).
111. Members of the executive committee from Russia included E. Tchlenov, Z. Tiomkin, Ia. Bernshtein-Kogan, Ts. Belkovsky, V. Yakobson, Ts. Bruk, and I. L. Gol'denburg.
112. Chaim Weizmann (1874–1952) was a Zionist statesman and the first president of Israel. The term "opposition" here refers to the group that opposed the El-Arish proposal.
113. Viacheslav von Plehve (1846–1904) was minister of the interior under Nicholas II; he was considered the architect of the Kishinev pogrom. For this reason many were surprised that Theodor Herzl came to Russia and met Plehve in 1903. The terrorist arm of the Socialist Revolutionaries, which was killing tsarist officials throughout the period, was responsible for Plehve's assassination.
114. Michael Stanislawski has shown that this encounter between Jabotinsky and Herzl likely never occurred. See his *Zionism and the Fin de Siècle*, 119; see also J. B. Schechtman, *Rebel and Statesman: The Vladimir Jabotinsky Story—The Early Years* (New York: Thomas Yoseloff, 1956), 85–90.

115. Dr. Isaiah Friedman (birth/death dates not known) was Herzl's close friend.
116. It seems plausible that Jabotinsky invented the scene in which he defended Herzl's meeting with Plehve in order to appear supportive of Herzl and lessen his sharp criticism of Herzl's Uganda plan. After all, following the rejection of the plan by the congress, Herzl died. Thus this mythical support for Herzl regarding something other than Uganda permitted Jabotinsky to forge his connection to the Father of Zionism without needing to justify his behavior at the congress. Jabotinsky's reverential attitude toward Herzl at the time can be evinced in the articles written immediately after Herzl's death, especially the poem "Hespêd," which appeared in *Evreiskaia Zhizn'* 6 (June 1904): 8–10, and in "Sidia na polu," *Evreiskaia Zhizn'* 6 (June 1904): 14–21.
117. Jabotinsky's recollection of events differs from his impressions as he described them at the time. See "Nakanune kongressa: Ot nashego korrespondenta," *Odesskie Novosti*, August 15, 1903, 2–3; "Bezel'skie vpechatleniia: Kongress sionistov," *Odesskie Novosti*, August 19, 1902, 2; "Bazel'skie vpechatleniia. 'Mazrakhi,' ot nashego korrespondenta," *Odesskie Novosti*, August 20, 1903, 5; "Bazel'skie vpechatelniia. Gertsl' i Neinsager'y," *Odesskie Novosti*, August 23, 1903, 3.
118. Jabotinsky's reports from the congress appeared in *Odesskie Novosti*: "Nakanune Kongressa," August 15, 1903; "Bazel'skie vpechatleniya. I. Shestoi Kongress Sionistov," August 19, 1903; "Bazel'skie vpechatleniya. II. 'Mizrakhi,'" August 23, 1903; "Bazel'skie vpechatleniya. III. Gertsl' i Neisanger'y," August 26, 1903.
119. "Uganda" here refers to the British proposal made to Theodore Herzl for a Jewish territory in Africa (present-day Kenya). The Uganda solution split the Zionist organization at the Sixth Zionist Congress in 1904.
120. *Neinsager* and *Jasager* refer to, respectively, the opponents and supporters of the Uganda proposal. The Russian members of the Actions-Comité left the hall to protest the Uganda plan and organized a new Zionist organization, Tsiony Tsion, with M. Ussishkin and E. Tchlenov as the leaders. Tsiony Tsion were Zionists who supported immigration to Palestine exclusively.
121. Jabotinsky's attitude toward Palestine and the various territorial solutions can be seen in his book *Sionizm i Palestina* (1905), which appeared originally in *Evreiskaia Zhizn'*, vol. 2 (1904): 203–21, and vol. 1 (1905): 49–72; see also his article, "Pis'mo ob avtonomizme," *Evreiskaia Zhizn'* 7 (1904): 81–90.
122. From Psalm 137: "If I forget thee Jerusalem . . ." Here the phrase points to Herzl's declaration at the Sixth Zionist Congress that Jewish immigration to Palestine was still the organization's primary goal.
123. Joseph Chamberlain (see note 110, above) served as secretary of state for the colonies and later leader of the opposition; he offered Herzl the Uganda proposal in April 1903. Arthur James Balfour (1848–1930) was a British political leader and government official. In November 1917 he signed the historic Balfour Declaration, which transmitted to the Zionist movement the British government's intention to create a Jewish homeland in the historical home of the Jewish people, Eretz Yisrael, known at the time as Palestine.
124. Jabotinsky described his travels in the Roman ghetto in his article "'Rimskoe getto': Pis'ma iz Rima," *Odesskie Novosti*, April 3, 1899, which appeared under the pseudonym

"Egal." In fact, three articles on the ghetto were published in *Odesskie Novosti* in 1903, and then as a pamphlet, *Chuzhie! Ocherki odnogo "Shastlivogo" getto* (*Notes of a "Happy" Ghetto*) (Odessa: Levinson, 1903). Marcus Tullius Cicero (107 BCE–44 BCE) and Juvenal (55–60 CE?–died 130 CE) were Roman writers who expressed anti-Jewish attitudes in their works.

125. Primo Levi (1853–1917) was an Italian avant-garde intellectual and journalist.
126. Jabotinsky describes his experience of revisiting old friends and discovering their Jewish identity in "Ocherki odnogo Shastlivogo getto," *Odesskie Novosti*, October 12, 1903, and October 18, 1903.
127. Ahad Ha'am (pseud. of Asher Ginsberg [1856–1927]) was a Zionist thinker and writer considered the father of "spiritual Zionism." Jabotinsky sided with Herzl in the debates between political and spiritual Zionism. Nonetheless, Jabotinsky noted an affinity with Ahad Ha'am: the latter did not negate the need for a Jewish majority, and Jabotinsky also valued infiltration, the up-building of the land, or so-called facts on the ground.
128. *To the Enemies of Zion* (*Nedrugam Siona*) refers to Jabotinsky's pamphlet of 1905, published in Odessa with Zal'tsman's publishing house.
129. General Bezsonov (Vladimir Bessonov [1842–?]) was an Odessa police official. He received his education in the Second Moscow Kadet Corps; he served as chief of police in Zhitomir, Odessa, and from June 1904 to December 1905 as police chief of St. Petersburg. The top tsarist official with whom Jabotinsky met in 1904 was Dmitry Neidgardt (1861–1942; see note 253, below), Odessa's city governor (*gradonachal'nik*) from 1903 to 1905. The Count Shuvalov whom Jabotinsky mistakenly mentions here is likely Pavel Pavlovich Shuvalov (1859–1905), who served as the top official of Odessa from 1898 to 1903. Jabotinsky admits to making a mistake regarding who was the head of the city when he was arrested.
130. Nikolai Sorin (1880–1933) was the owner and editor of *Rassvet* (*Evreiskaia Zhizn'*); according to Joseph Schechtman, Jabotinsky lived in St. Petersburg in 1904, legally registered as Sorin's "domestic servant." Schechtman, *Rebel and Statesman*, 92.
131. Jews without a special dispensation were not permitted to live outside the Jewish Pale of Settlement. In 1891 thousands of Jews were arrested in the cold of winter and forced to leave Moscow. Jews who were caught living illegally in the Russian capitals were given twenty-four hours to leave and received a special stamp in their passports. His cousin had a diploma and therefore the right to live outside the Pale of Settlement. Nikolai Sorin had the right to live in St. Petersburg probably as a member of the First Merchant Guild. Guild members paid a steep tax and had such privileges.
132. Jabotinsky's article appeared in the first issue of the new journal: "Na voprosy dnia: fel'eton," *Evreiskaia Zhizn'* 1 (January 1904): 203–11.
133. *Rassvet* was the Russian-language Zionist journal that was originally founded in 1904 as *Evreiskaia Zhizn'*; the volume began to appear once again but now in Paris starting in 1923. In tsarist times the paper appeared primarily under the title *Evreiskaia Zhizn'*. Jabotinsky became the journal's editor in 1924. A source for information on *Rassvet* in the pre–World War I period is Yehuda Slutzky, *Ha'itonut ha'yihudit-rusit be'mea ha'esrim (1900–1918)* (Tel Aviv: Ha'aguda le'haker toldot ha'yihudim, 1978), 203–67.

134. The elder Aleksei Suvorin (1834–1912) published *Novoe Vremya* (1878–1917), a conservative-nationalist newspaper that promoted the values of statism and Russian nationalism. The paper was also notably anti-Semitic and popular with the public. The younger Alexei Suvorin (1862–1937) was the middle son of the archconservative publisher of the same name. The younger Suvorin established *Rus'*, a liberal Russian paper (1903–8) in which Jabotinsky widely published. *Oko, XX Veka*, and *Molva* were substitute publications for *Rus'* that appeared when *Rus'* was closed by the government.
135. *Rus'* was published as a monthly paper.
136. Moisei Markovich Margolin (1862–1939) was a contributor to the liberal Jewish periodical *Voskhod* and an author of the influential book *Osnovnye techeniia v istorii evreiskogo naroda: Etiud po filosofii isotrii evreev* (St. Petersburg: Severnaia Skoropechatnaia, 1900). He was also an editor of the famous Jewish encyclopedia that was published in St. Petersburg by Brockhaus and Efron. Jabotinsky and Margolin differed ideologically in the period after 1905: Jabotinsky hoped for organization according to national lines, whereas Margolin predicted "differentiation by parties." Jonathan Frankel, *Prophecy and Politics: Socialism, Nationalism, and the Russian Jews, 1862–1917* (London: Cambridge University Press, 1981), 168–69.
137. Ilya Efron (1847–1917) was founder of the Russian publishing house Brockhaus-Efron. He was involved in publishing a famous encyclopedia of Jewish life (1907–13). See *Evreiskaia entsiklopediia: Svod znanii o evreistve i ego kul'ture v proshlom i nastoiashchem*, ed. L. Katsenel'son, 17 vols. (St. Petersburg: Brockhaus-Efron, 1907–13).
138. Colonel Eliezer Margolin (1875–1944) was an officer in the Jewish Legion during World War I.
139. Shlomo Gepstein (1892–1961) worked for *Rassvet* in Russia and went to Palestine in 1924, where he became a leading Revisionist. Alexander Goldstein (1884–1942), born in Minsk, was an active participant in *Rassvet* (1904–18); he became one of the heads of Keren Ha-Yesod. Goldstein's memoirs include a description of the Petersburg period in Jabotinsky's life. See *"Pirke zikhronot,"* in *He-avar* 14 (1967): 3–87. Arye Babkov (1881–1948), also a contributor to *Rassvet*, made *aliyah* in 1920 and was one of the founders of Zionist Revisionism. Arnold Seideman (1880–1927) was a leader of the Central Committee of Russian Zionists from 1919. Max Soloveichik (Soliali; 1883–1957), a bible scholar originally from Kovno, was the head of the Jewish community in Lithuania from 1919 to 1921; he made *aliyah* in 1933 and served as an Israeli government minister. Moshe Zeitlin (1872–1907) was killed in a car accident on his way to the Seventh Zionist Congress.
140. Julius Brutzkus (1870–1951) was a Jewish historian and politician who later joined the Zionist Revisionists.
141. Avram Idel'son (1865–1921) was the founder of Synthetic Zionism; he also served as editor of *Rassvet* (*Evreiskaia Zhizn'*). He joined the Moscow Palestinophiles during his university days and then adopted political Zionism when it was established. He contributed to the newspaper *Budushchnost'* and the Petersburg Hebrew-language paper *Ha'zman*. In 1905 he took over as editor of *Rassvet* (*Evreiskaia Zhizn'*). He

became a member of the large *Actions-Comité* at the time of the Seventh Zionist Congress. See Brian Horowitz, "What Is 'Russian' in Russian Zionism?" 54–71.

142. Samuel Grusenberg (1855–1909) was a medical doctor and journalist. He served as an editor of *Voskhod* and later established the pro-Zionist newspaper *Budushchnost'*, which was published from 1902 to 1904.

143. Israel Rosov (1869–1948) was a Russian Zionist and, later, Revisionist; he was a close friend of Jabotinsky. Rosov was an engineer in the Russian oil industry; a contributor to *Rassvet*, he made *aliyah* in 1919 and was among the original group of Zionist Revisionists.

144. *Galut* refers to the exile of Jews from Israel, but the word carries a religious connotation as well. Jews had lived in ancient Israel, but were scattered around the world after their defeat by the Romans. The *galut* will end with the in-gathering of Jews once again in the Holy Land.

145. Isaac Goldberg (1860–1935) was an important Zionist and philanthropist in Kiev. Betsal'el Yaffe (1868–1925) was a native of Grodno and a leader in Belorussia. The life of young Zionists in pre–World War I Grodno has been described by Betsal'el's brother, Leib Jaffe, in the latter's memoir *Katvim, igorot ve-yomanim* (Jerusalem: Sifriya Tsionut, 1964), 1–75. Hillel Zlatopolsky (1868–1932) was a banker and Zionist leader who supported Hebrew-language publications. On Zionism in Russia, see Yitzhak Maor, *Ha'tnuah ha'tsionit be'rusiyah: Mereshita ve'ad yameinu* (Jerusalem: Magnes/Ha'sifriyah ha'tsionit, 1986).

146. The monthly Zionist journal *Rassvet* (known also as *Evreiskaia Zhizn'*) appeared from 1904 to 1919. Seven years would mean that Jabotinsky stopped publishing in *Rassvet* in 1911 or 1912. His articles appeared in *Rassvet* in 1913.

147. "Externs" refers to university students who were unable to attend classes but were working on their own toward their diplomas. In socioeconomic terms he is speaking of the young Jewish intelligentsia. Vilna is the capital of Lithuania.

148. *Lita* is the Hebrew name for Lithuania.

149. Shaul Tchernichovsky (1875–1943), Hebrew poet; Ya'akov Cohen (1881–1960), Hebrew playwright, writer; Zalman Shneur (1887–1959), Hebrew poet.

150. Landvarovo is a town in the Vilna District of Lithuania, the administrative center of the Landvarov region. It is located fourteen miles northwest of Vilna. Helsingfors is the Swedish name for the Finnish city, Helsinki, which had a modicum of political autonomy within the Russian Empire.

151. Herzl won a vote to send an exploratory party to Uganda, but at the Seventh Congress (1905), another vote withdrew support for the plan.

152. The period of meetings is known in Russian history as "the Banquet Campaign." Throughout 1904 liberals and professionals, including doctors, lawyers, and teachers, held lectures and discussions under the guise of public banquets. Jabotinsky's participation in it indicates his association with the liberal (Zemstvo and Union of Liberation) opposition. Jabotinsky was close with the *Rassvet* group, which expressed a liberal perspective that favored a revolution but opposed extreme radicalism. Jewish liberals at this time supported the Constitutional Democratic Party (Kadets) and

wished for the establishment of a Duma, a democratic governing body based on free elections, and such principles as freedom of the press and equality for the national minorities. *Liberation* was also the name of the famous émigré journal edited by Pyotr Struve (1902–5).

153. *Nasha Zhizn'* was a liberal daily newspaper published in St. Petersburg from November 1904 to July 1906.
154. It does not appear that Jabotinsky's article was buried. In fact it appeared as "Nabroski bez zaglaviia," *Nasha Zhizn'* (December 1904). Even the words about laughter were published: "After leaving the prison I stayed in Odessa for a day and visited many people. I can assure you that on that day there was not a single house in the whole city in which a hearty and bilious laugh was not heard in reaction to my heroism."
155. Ekaterina Dmitrievna Kusskova (1869–1958), a Russian politician, editor, and publisher, was involved at this time in the Union of Liberation movement. With *Nasha Zhizn'*, which she edited, Kusskova helped spread the idea of revolution among Russia's workers and intellectuals.
156. "[V]iolation of all the traditional principles of Russian liberalism" refers to a polemic that Jabotinsky began in 1903. It already appears in his first article for the weekly *Iuzhnye Zapiski* 17 (1903), in which he blamed the Jewish intelligentsia for addressing Jews as "they" and never as "we." From that time, this theme became one of his main polemical tropes against his opponents among the Russian Jews.
157. *Russkie Vedomosti* refers to the famous liberal daily newspaper. It began publishing in 1863 and was closed in 1918 by the Bolsheviks. Jabotinsky left Russia in late 1914 to serve as a correspondent for *Russkie Vedomosti*. He published dozens of articles between 1914 and 1918. These letters follow his travels in Europe, through North Africa and Palestine, and then in England and Ireland. For example, his reportage on September 16, 1914, was titled "Po opustoshennoi Bel'gii" ("In Devasted Belgium"). The article printed on January 6, 1915, is titled "V Severnoi Afrike" ("In North Africa"). On June 19, 1916, Jabotinsky published an article titled "Irlandskii teatr: O novoj Irlandii" ("Irish Theater: Regarding New Ireland"). Jabotinsky wrote about the home fronts, including issues that indirectly related to his work on behalf of the Jewish Legion, such as the rules about military service in England. See "Military Obligation in England" ("Vosennaya povinnost' v Anglii"), March 24, 1916.
158. It is not entirely true that the readers were "no longer alive." In fact, in 1936 not only were many of the readers alive, having emigrated from Soviet Russia, but some were also writing for *Rassvet*.
159. Maxim Vinaver (1863–1926) and Henrik Sliozberg (1863–1927) were famous Jewish lawyers and leaders of the Kadets (Constitutional Democratic Party). "Katsaps of the Mosaic faith" is a term that mocks the Jewish Kadets and their strategy of subordinating Jewish interests to the achievement of liberal principles, such as equality for all the national minorities. Jabotinsky wrote about Vinaver sarcastically in "Medved' iz berlogi" ("Bear from His Lair"), *Rassvet* 3 (March 15, 1909): 4–7. The article appeared in both editions of *Fel'etony* (1913 and 1922).
160. Jabotinsky's point in saying that there are "more than a hundred nations" in Russia is to underscore the fact that Russia was not a nation-state but rather a multinational

state; therefore its repressive laws and institutions were self-destructive and potentially could end in revolution. It is important to note that the 1897 census did not contain the category of nationality, although there were such categories as native language, religious confession, and social estate. Different groups interpreted the census information differently. For some the census merely reflected the human diversity of the imperial community; for others more sensitive to the political language of nationalism, these indicators were useful to construct nations. The census results offered these statistics: 5,211,085 identified themselves as belonging to the Judaic faith; 5,063,156 claimed Yiddish as their mother tongue. Jabotinsky was one of these who viewed such statistics as underscoring the existence of distinct nations within Russia.

161. In addition to equal rights, the Bund, as a member of the Russian Social Democratic Labor Party (it rejoined in 1906), dedicated itself to conferring national cultural autonomy on the Jewish worker, including Jewish cultural rights.

162. "Cultural autonomy" refers to the right of national minorities in the Austro-Hungarian Empire to have schools in their native languages and pursue other cultural activities. Rudolf Springer was a pseudonym of Karl Renner (1870–1950), the Austrian theorist of nationality policy. Jabotinsky wrote an introduction to Springer's book in Russian translation, *Gosudarstvo i natsiia* (1906). It is also important to recall that Jabotinsky was an expert on autonomism and federalism; he wrote two articles on these topics in the Russian newspaper *Radikal* in 1905. Shimon (Semyon) Dubnov (1860–1941) was the most famous Russian-Jewish historian, journalist, and theorist of diaspora nationalism of his time. In this context see his *Letters on Old and New Judaism* (1907). He advocated a theory of autonomism involving cultural autonomy for the Jews of Russia, which would include the establishment of their own schools, lectures in Jewish languages, and internal political organizations. In additional to his activity as a theorist, Dubnov tried his hand at practical politics. He helped organize the Folkspartei in 1906 and was a party leader. As a historian Dubnov was not merely a scholar: he created a modern narrative and ideology of Russian-Jewish history.

163. See V. Jabotinsky, *Bund i tsionizm* (Odessa: Kadima, 1906).

164. The first publication of the Russian translation of the poem had the title "Skaznie o Nemirove." It appeared in Jabotinsky's translation, along with his introduction, in *Evreiskaia Zhizn'*, November 11, 1904, 160–62. See also Kh. N. Bialik, *Pesni i poemy: Avtorizovannyi perevod s evreiskogo i vvedenie Vl. Zhabotinsky* (St. Petersburg: S. D. Zal'tsman, 1911).

165. Adam Mickiewicz (1798–1855) was a Polish national poet and the author of *Pan Tadeusz*.

166. *Moskal* is a Polish derogatory term for "Russian."

167. Jabotinsky is referring to the Helsingfors Conference of 1906.

168. *Neshama ha-yetera* refers to a person's second soul, which he or she receives on Shabbat.

169. Jan Kirschrot (1879–1912), an engineer and Polish Zionist, was editor of *Życie Żidówske* from 1906 to 1907; Noah Davidson (1877–1928), trained as an eye doctor, was a Polish Zionist.

170. The Bialystok pogrom took place in the city of Bialystok, June 14–16, 1906.
171. Apolinari (Meir) Hartglass (1883–1953), a lawyer, parliamentarian, and leading Polish Zionist, also served as an editor of *Życie Żidówske*. He later was appointed director general of the Israeli Ministry of Interior. His memoirs were published as *Na pograniczu dwóch światów* (Warsaw: Oficyzna Wydawnicza Rytm, 1996).
172. Eliza Orzeszkowa (1841–1910) was a leading Polish writer and Positivist. She was known for her liberal attitudes, Polish patriotism, and opposition to anti-Semitism.
173. Roman Dmowski (1864–1939) was a Polish leader of the right-wing Endecja Party (National Democracy Movement). Jabotinsky later entered into a polemic with Dmowski especially over Jabotinsky's volume *Poliaki i evrei: Materialy o pol'sko— evreiskom spore po povodu zakonoproekta o gorodskom samoupravlenii v Pol'she* (Odessa: M.S. Kozman, 1911).
174. This paragraph marks an abrupt change of subject matter. Jabotinsky begins talking about the Helsingfors Conference, although a little later he introduces an entire chapter entitled "Helsingfors."
175. "Takiya or SERP" refers to the Jewish Socialist Workers Party in Tsarist Poland. The Vozrozhdenie (Revival) group was founded in 1906 and became the Jewish Socialist Workers Party, an organization that considered a Jewish parliament to be the precondition for solving Jews' political problems. Its leader was Chaim Zhitlovsky, who supported territorialism. See Matityahu Mintz, "Fereynikte," in *The YIVO Encyclopedia of Jews in Eastern Europe*, 1: 501. It is possible that Jabotinsky here means the followers of Ber Borochov (1881–1917), the Zionist theorist who founded the Poale Tsion Party, which united the ideas of socialism and Zionism. See also Jonathan Frankel, *Prophecy and Politics: Socialism, Nationalism, and the Russian Jews, 1862–1917* (New York: Cambridge University Press, 1984), 275–76. See also the recent book by Kay Scheigmann-Greve, *Chaim Zhitlovsky: Philosoph, Sozialrevolutionar und Theoretiker einer sakularen nationaljidischen Identität* (Potsdam: Werhahn Verlag, 2012).
176. "Complete" rights was stronger than "equal" rights because it signified the desire for political change rather than merely additional rights.
177. The conference was organized by the Jewish People's Group in November 1909 and featured an initiative to modernize and democratize the Jewish community structure in Russia. See Christoph Gassenschmidt, *Jewish Liberal Politics in Tsarist Russia, 1900–1914* (New York: New York University Press, 1995), 85–94.
178. *Die Dergreicher* were supporters of the Union for the Attainment of Full Rights for the Jewish People in Russia (*Soiuz dlia dostizheniia polnopraviia evreev*), a coalition of Jewish Kadets and various nationalists and Zionists in 1905–6.
179. The "Russo-Japanese War" refers to the conflict of 1904, in which Russia was defeated. In 1905 a series of strikes and armed conflicts between Russian subjects and the government ended with the capitulation of the tsar and the establishment of a legislative Duma. The State Duma was the legislative body established in 1906; there were ultimately four Dumas before the fall of tsarism. In the October pogroms of 1905, 800 Jews lost their lives, and Jewish material losses exceeded 70 million rubles.

180. Solianyi Gorodok was a complex of buildings in St. Petersburg that borders the Fontanka River, Solianyi Lane, and Pestel' and Gangutskaya Streets. Its name derives from the salt warehouses that were city territory in the nineteenth century.
181. Jabotinsky described the role of the Russian people in a revolution before October 1905, predicting that Jewish blood would flow as a result. See "Evreiskoe slovo," *Khronika Evreiskoi Zhizni* 6 (February 6, 1905): 9–11 (signed "Zimri"). At an earlier meeting where Jabotinsky offered these ideas, Menachem Ussishkin refuted the remarks and even tried to stop Jabotinsky from speaking.
182. The elections took place for the most part in February and March of 1906, but somewhat later in the outlying regions so that, of the 524 deputies, around 480 were in place at the start and additional deputies joined as time went on. The leftist parties and those of the extreme right boycotted the Duma elections. The leftist parties believed the Duma did not possess any real power, and the extreme right opposed the idea of parliamentary democracy. Among the leftist parties that boycotted were the Mensheviks and the Socialist Revolutionaries. Vladimir Lenin later admitted that the boycott had been a mistake.
183. Jabotinsky is referring to one of the congresses of the Union for the Attainment of Full Rights for the Jewish People in Russia, which gathered in 1906 in St. Petersburg. Although the Zionists complained about the Liberals' commitment to a struggle, first and foremost, for Jewish interests, the union nonetheless held at this time. Twelve Jews were elected to the First Duma, which lasted from April 27, 1906, until July 8, 1906.
184. Jabotinsky's report at the congress of the Union for the Attainment of Full Rights for the Jewish People in Russia was published in *Khronika Evreiskoi Zhizni* (May 19, 1906).
185. Moisei Yakovlevich Ostrogorsky (1854–1921) was a constitutional democrat of Jewish descent. Ostrogorsky was highly esteemed for his magisterial work, *La democratie et l'organisation des partis politiques* (Paris, 1903). The "Vinaver group" refers to the Constitutional Democratic Party (Kadets).
186. Jabotinsky is likely speaking about the first congress of the Jewish People's Group, which took place in St. Petersburg on January 17, 1907. The Jewish People's Group, which represented the Liberals, emerged after the breakup of the Union for the Attainment of Full Rights and divisions developed between Liberals and Zionists and Liberals and other Jewish nationalists. The demands, by Zionists and diaspora nationalists, for a Jewish cultural program led members of the Jewish People's Group to adopt some of these ideas, including a national program that emphasized "developing the national culture of Russian Jewry" as well as a struggle for civil equality and economic opportunity. Gassenschmidt, *Jewish Liberal Politics in Tsarist Russia*, 53.
187. Zakhary Grigor'evich Frenkel (1869–1970) was a Jewish member of the State Duma.
188. Earlier, in 1906, the Jewish People's Group was known as "the Attainers," a name that was used pejoratively. According to many at the time, a more appropriate term would be "struggle." "Attainment" had a passive connotation—"struggle" was in tune with the revolution. The name "Attainers" was embarrassing. Jews needed to struggle and fight to obtain rights; they would not merely be attained, as though given from

heaven. Nonetheless, the union was intended to act as a kind of Jewish bloc in the Duma and to include all twelve Jewish representatives in the First Duma. Jabotinsky and his colleagues at *Rassvet* left the union because of a perception that the Russian parties on the left and center, the Trudoviki and Kadets, were not prepared to make the acquisition of equal rights for Jews an exclusive priority.

189. Daniil Pasmanik (1869–1930) was a medical doctor and an important Zionist theoretician and contributor to *Rassvet*. During World War I he worked in a field hospital, providing medical care to Russian troops. In 1917 he became a member of the Kadet leadership and joined the so-called White Army during the Russian Civil War.

190. Gaetano Donizetti (1797–1848), Italian composer; Vincenzo Bellini (1801–35), Italian composer of operas.

191. Boris Goldberg (1865–1922); Leib Jaffe (1876–1948). Dr. Joseph Lurie (1871–1937) was the editor of the Poale Tsion group's official Yiddish-language weekly, *Dos yiddisher Folk*.

192. Mizrachi was a political party made up of Jews who were religiously Orthodox Jewish and Zionist. The movement was founded in Vilna in 1902. Its name is an acronym of Merkaz Ruhani (Religious Center).

193. It is interesting to compare Jabotinsky's memory here with other events he "witnessed." In this case his depiction, decades later, corresponds almost word for word with the transcript of the event. See Jabotinsky's article from 1903: "Mizrakhi," *Odesskie Novosti*, August 20, 1903.

194. "Minorities" here refers to the liberal ideas about minorities' rights stipulated at the Helsingfors Conference.

195. Daniil Pasmanik left Russia after the October Revolution and joined the White forces that attempted to overthrow the Bolshevik government.

196. *Evreiskaia Mysl'* was a weekly Jewish-Zionist journal in the Russian language that was published in Odessa with some irregularity from 1906 to 1907. The head editors were Menachem Ussishkin and Israel Trivus; the journal reflected the views of the Odessa Palestine Committee.

197. Count Alexander Tyshkevich was a Polish magnate. The Helsingfors Conference took place on December 4–10, 1906 (new calendar). Among other things, the conference demanded national rights for Russia's national minorities and also promoted *Gegenwartsarbeit*, the idea of political and educational activity in the Diaspora. Jabotinsky wrote about the Helsingfors Conference in many publications, but see his article, "Hel'singforskaia programma," *Rassvet* 25, nos. 15–16 (April 13, 1930): 4–5; and no. 17 (April 27, 1930): 7–8.

198. The dispersal of the First Duma occurred on July 8, 1906.

199. Alexandria is a village in the province of Volyn, in northwestern Ukraine. Rovno is a city at the center of Rovno province, in Ukraine. There was a Lovers of Zion group in the city as early as 1884. In Jabotinsky's time Rovno was home to various Zionist and other political parties, including the Bund. In 1909 the Jewish population of Rovno was 18,631 (55.8 percent of the population). Requirements for running for office included ownership of property.

200. This was a mistake later acknowledged by Jabotinsky. It was the third congress of Russian Zionists. The conference of November 21–27 (December 4–10), 1906, in today's

Helsinki, dealt with a plan for Zionist activity after the Revolution of 1905. The conference discussed the condition of Jews in the Russian Empire and the tasks of world Jewry following the death of Theodor Herzl. The debates reflected struggles within the Zionist organization in connection with Uganda and the new situation in Russia. The conference formulated the idea of "Synthetic Zionism," a synthesis of political and practical work (the practical aspect meaning settlement in Palestine). The turning point was the resolution regarding political and cultural activity in the Diaspora.

201. An article in *Moscovskie Vedomosti* from November 20, 1906, noted: "The correspondent of the newspaper *Svoboda i Zhizn'* Jabotinsky, who had just arrived in Petersburg, was arrested at the editorial board of *Evreiskii Narod*. He is one of the best-known candidates to the State Duma from the Jewish population of the northwestern region." *Peterburgskaia Gazeta* from November 21, 1906, reported that "Jabotinsky today was freed at 1 PM. He was arrested with five comrades who had stopped here on their way to Helsingfors, as delegates to the Zionist Congress. The congress opens tomorrow at 12 noon."

202. Given what has been said about Sliozberg in the preceding pages, one might be surprised to learn that, in the Russian community living outside of Russia, Jabotinsky wrote a laudatory essay about Sliozberg that appeared as an introduction to the latter's memoirs. See Jabotinsky, "G. B. Sliozberg," in G. B. Sliozberg's *Dela minuvshikh dnei: Zapiski russkogo evreia*, 2 vols. (Paris: Izd. Komiteta po chestvovaniiu 70-I letnego iubileia G. B. Sliozberga, 1933), 1: ix–xiv. Part of the article also appeared in *Rassvet* 29, no. 5 (29, 1933): 3.

203. These are the Revisionist Party and the youth group, respectively. Ha-Tsohar (Revisionism) was the branch of Zionism that Jabotinsky established. Its main tenets included the principles that Jews must be a majority of the population in the land; that the Jewish state be created on both sides of the Jordan River; and that Jews have the means to defend themselves by forming an armed force (legionism). Betar was the Revisionist youth group. Its name is derived as an acronym of "Brit Yosef Trumpeldor" and refers to the place-name of Bar Kochba's final defeat in 1935. Founded in Riga in 1923, Betar promoted the idea of pioneering in Palestine and of creating and training a Jewish legion or armed force.

204. "Conquest of positions" refers to the strategy of infiltration in Palestine by which Jews would achieve a Jewish homeland, staking out settlements and creating a Jewish society and economy through practical efforts.

205. The Revisionist program designated both sides of the Jordan River—i.e., Transjordan—for the Jewish state.

206. Yitzhak Gruenbaum (1879–1970) was a noted leader of Polish Zionism; Koło refers to the Polish political party that sought Jewish autonomy in the Diaspora.

207. Hayim Grinberg (or Greenberg [1889–1953]), theorist of Labor Zionism, was head of Poale Zion in the United States. Sholem (Ben-Baruch) Schwartz (1887–1965) was a journalist and editor of the *Palestine Daily Bulletin*. He was born in Russia and moved to Palestine in 1920. He is the author of such works as *The Arab Problem, The Poetry of Tchernichovsky,* and *Herzl in His Diaries*.

208. Solomon Poliakov-Litovtsev (1875–1945) was a political thinker and cultural critic.

209. "Sionist. Sredi evreev," *Rus'* 33, no. 2 (1907): 4. Pavel Milyukov (1859–1943), an economist and historian, was leader of the Constitutional Democratic Party; Maksim Kovalevsky (1851–1916) was a famous sociologist; Alexander Kerensky (1881–1970), a lawyer and head of the Russian government after the February Revolution of 1917, was deposed by the Bolsheviks in October 1917.
210. Mark Ratner (1871–1917), a lawyer, was a political theorist of Jewish socialism and territorialism. Maxim Slavinsky (1868–1945) studied law at St. Petersburg University. He was a correspondent for *Zhizn'* and *Severnyi Kur'er*, and secretary of the famous journal *Vestnik Evropy* in 1911. Slavinsky served as minister of foreign affairs in the Symon Petliura government in 1921. He made a pact with Jabotinsky to allow armed Jews to follow the Ukrainian forces and prevent pogroms in the upcoming White offensive, which never took place. Jabotinsky was roundly criticized for this "pact with the devil." Symon Petliura (1879–1926) was a journalist and the head of the Ukrainian People's Republic following the Russian Revolution of October 1917. Petliura was killed in Paris in 1926 by Samuil Shvartsband. During Shvartsband's trial for murder, and the subsequent scandal and discussion over Petliura's guilt for the pogroms in Ukraine at the time of the Russian Civil War, Jabotinsky wrote the article "Petliura i pogromy," which appeared in *Poslednie Novosti* [Paris], October 11, 1927. Jabotinsky did not exonerate Petliura but argued that "objective conditions" were a stronger motivating force than "personal anti-Semitism." See "Petliura i pogromy," *Lekhaim* (May 2014).
211. The Black Hundreds was an ultra-nationalist mass movement that was institutionalized during the first Russian revolution. It combined elements of populism, temperance movement ideology, monarchism, anti-Semitism, and anti-revolutionarism. It practiced what it called "black terror," in opposition to the revolutionary "red terror."
212. A *minyan* is a group of ten Jewish men (today also women) who make up a quorum to hold religious ceremonies. The *huppa* is a cloth held by four poles which serves as a canopy for a Jewish wedding.
213. These are the words that by Jewish tradition bind a man and woman in matrimony.
214. Alexander Poliakov (1879–1971) was Jabotinsky's old friend; also a journalist, he emigrated in 1920, and from 1922 he worked in Paris as the secretary for the editorial board of the newspaper *Poslednie Novosti*, edited by Paul Milyukov. In 1940 Poliakov moved to the United States and worked for *Novoe Russkoe Slovo*. Moshe Ginsberg (Matvei Markovich [Meerovich]) was Jabotinsky's school friend. Ginsberg attended Novorossiiskii University but was expelled for revolutionary activity in 1902; he was reinstated in 1903 and graduated in 1905. Little is known about him besides that he became a well-regarded surgeon in Moscow. See Evgeniia Ivanova, *Chukovskii i Zhabotinskii: Istoriia vzaimootnoshenii v tekstakh i kommentariiakh*, 11, 13, 15.
215. Since Jabotinsky had made the declaration of marriage in front of a witness and given Anya the gold coin, he was in fact married according to Jewish law.
216. The Austro-Hungarian Empire was governed through a constitutional monarchy within which some political parties represented national minorities. See Jabotinsky's

writings on the nationality question, "Samoupravlenie natsional'nogo men'shinstva," *Vestnik Evropy* (September 1913): 117–38; (October 1913): 131–58.

217. Jabotinsky suggested that modern Hebrew be written in Latin script. See Vladimir Jabotinsky, *Taryag Milim: 613 (Hebrew) Words—Introduction into Spoken Hebrew (in Latin Characters)* (New York: Jabotinsky Foundation, 1949).

218. The Turkish revolution of 1908 reversed the 1878 suspension of the Ottoman parliament. The revolution was carried out by an "unlikely union of reform-minded pluralists, Turkish nationalists, Western-oriented secularists, [and] minorities such as Ottoman Armenians and Greeks." "Young Turk Revolution" in Wikipedia, en.wikipedia.org/wiki/Young_Turk_Revolution, accessed on April 5, 2015. Jabotinsky wrote a number of articles for Russian papers from Turkey: "Besporiadki v Konstantinopole," *Rassvet* 3, no. 15 (April 12, 1909): 3–6; "Pis'ma iz Turtsii," *Odesskie Novosti*, August 20, 1909; "Sionizm i Turtsiia: Nakanune 9 sionistskogo kongressa," *Odesskie Novosti* (date unclear), 1909. He also wrote for the French press in Constantinople: "Le congress des juifs ottomans," *L'Aurore* 1, no. 15 (October 3, 1909): 1–2, and "De la langue," *L'Aurore* 1, no. 17 (October 17, 1909): 2.

219. Djavid Bey (1875–1926) was an Ottoman economist and statesman. Shabbetai Tzvi (1626–76) claimed to be the Jewish messiah; a number of Jews followed Shabbetai Tzvi to Istanbul and remained in Turkey after his death. Enver Pasha (1881–1922) was the leader of the Young Turk Revolution.

220. The "Zionist bank" refers to the Anglo-Levantine Banking Company. (Its official name was the Jewish Colonial Trust Limited.) Victor Jacobson (1869–1935) was leader of Hibbat Zion and later a Zionist diplomat.

221. Alliance Israélite Universelle. This institution funded secular Jewish schools in the Ottoman Empire and also a school in Tel Aviv. See Aron Rodrigue, *French Jews, Turkish Jews: The Alliance Israélite Universelle and the Politics of Jewish Schooling in Turkey, 1860–1925* (Bloomington: Indiana University Press, 1990).

222. Padishahs were the great leaders of the Persian world. At the time neither Jabotinsky nor anyone else had predicted that the revolutionaries' stubborn insistence on assimilation would lead to the breakup of the empire. Later, during World War I, Jabotinsky realized the Ottoman Empire would not survive the war.

223. Jaffa is the Arab port city that borders what is today modern Tel Aviv. Meir Dizengoff (1861–1936), the Zionist politician and first mayor of Tel Aviv, grew up in Odessa. Some scholars, such as Joachim Schlör, have underscored the resemblance between Tel Aviv and Odessa. See his *Tel Aviv: From Dream to City* (London: Reaktion Books, 1999).

224. Arabic for "Hello, how are you?"

225. *Leshon ha-kodesh* refers to the Hebrew language.

226. David Wolfsohn (1856–1914) was the second president of the World Zionist Organization.

227. This translation was published in *Nashi vechera: Literaturno-khudozhestvennyi sbornik*, 1st ed. (Odessa: Typ. Aktsionernogo Iuzhno-Russkogo Obshchestva pechatnogo dela, 1903). It also appeared in the collection *Chtets-deklamator*, vol. 2 (Kiev, 1907).

228. Dmitry Ilovaysky (1832–1920) was a Russian historian with a pro-government orientation. Ilovaysky became a radical monarchist after 1905. "Pythagoras's trousers" refers to a school verse about Pythagoras's theorem: "Pifagorovy shtany na vse storony ravny" ("Pythagoras's pants are equal on all their sides").
229. A political commissar held an officer's rank and was responsible for Communist ideological orthodoxy.
230. Djelal Nuri-Bey (1882–1938), a well-known journalist in Istanbul. A depiction of Jabotinsky's participation in the "building up" of a Zionist press in Constantinople can be found in Joseph B. Schechtman, *Rebel and Statesman*, 156–58. According to Schechtman, Jabotinsky gave fiery Zionist speeches, but they were reported in the local press as having an entirely opposite meaning from what Jabotinsky actually said.
231. Sami Hochberg was owner and editor of *Le Jeune Turc*, a French-language Zionist journal in Istanbul.
232. Isaac Nofech (1879–?) was a lawyer and Zionist in Russia in the period before World War I.
233. Nazim Bey (1870–1926), trained as a doctor, was a leader of the Young Turks who became a rabid nationalist; he called for the indiscriminate killing of Christians in the Ottoman Empire. He argued for the need to carry out a genocide against the Armenian nation. He was executed in 1926 for attempting to assassinate Mustafa Ataturk.
234. Tómas de Torquemada (1420–98), Spanish Dominican friar and first Grand Inquisitor.
235. Jacobus Kahn (1872–1945) was an important Dutch Zionist leader. Max Bodenheimer (1865–1940) was a Zionist leader in Germany in the years before World War I.
236. Jacobus Kahn's book that frustrated Jabotinsky is titled *Erez Israel, das jüdische Land* (Köln: Jüdischer Verlag, 1909).
237. Dr. David Marcus (birth/death dates not known) was a member of the Ashkenazi Jewish community in Constantinople. Maccabi teachers taught in pro-Zionist schools and received subsidies from Zionist funds.
238. Shimshon Rosenbaum (1860–1934), born in Pinsk, became a Zionist leader in Lithuania and served as a minister in the first Lithuanian government after the country gained independence. He was close to Jabotinsky in the *Rassvet* group.
239. During the years 1910–1914, Jabotinsky was occupied with, among other things, the blood-libel trial of Mendel Beilis (1911–13). It is interesting that this incident, like other episodes, was excluded from his Zionist autobiography here. But it was not fully expunged. In 1933 Jabotinsky referred to the accusations against the Revisionist suspects in the murder of Haim Arlosorov as a "new Beilis epic" ("novaia beilisiada").
240. Eri-Theodore Jabotinsky (1910–69), Vladimir Jabotinsky's son, arrived in Eretz Yisrael in 1919. He later lived in France, where he received a degree in engineering in Paris. He played important roles in the Revisionist movement and Aliyah Bet. He ultimately worked as a professor of mathematics at the Technion in Haifa and wrote articles on politics.

241. Yaroslavl, an old university town, is located two hundred miles northeast of Moscow.
242. For information about the Society for the Promotion of Culture among the Jews of Russia, see Brian Horowitz, *Jewish Philanthropy and Enlightenment* (Seattle: University of Washington Press, 2009).
243. Ahad Ha'am moved to England in 1907 and then to Tel Aviv in 1922. The phrase regarding the land growing quiet appears to be a free quotation from Leviticus 26:34.
244. "Two-fifths" refers to the demand by the opposing Odessa branch of the Society for the Promotion of Culture among the Jews of Russia regarding the number of hours spent on Jewish subjects in schools that received a subsidy from the society.
245. Like many Russians, Jabotinsky admired the *szlachta*, the Polish nobility, for its civilized and European manners. Russian progressives in particular criticized the Russian government's control over Poland. Józef Piłsudski (1867–1935) was leader of the Polish Socialist Party and later Poland's chief of state in independent Poland from 1918 to 1922. In May 1926 he led a coup d'état and served as government head until his death. Jabotinsky trusted Piłsudski—in contrast to Dmowski—not to incite passions against Jews as a way of gaining popularity.
246. The *Rassvet* group remained consistent in its personnel and political approach. The journal's ideological viewpoint was largely open, although the journal opposed assimilation, discussed practical questions of colonization in Palestine, and polemicized with the Bund and other groups. However, the editors permitted non-Zionists such as Dubnov to publish in its pages.
247. The Third Duma opened in 1907 and closed in 1912.
248. In the Russian the translator rendered the word as "I am a Jew who speaks Hebrew." Vladimir (Ze'ev) Jabotinsky, *Povest' moikh dnei* (Jerusalem: Sifria Aliya, 1985), 96.
249. Jabotinsky's article appeared as "Pis'mo o natsional'nostiakh i oblastiakh: Evreistvo i ego nastroeniia," *Russkaia Mysl'* (Moscow), January 1, 1911, 95–114. A discussion of Struve and Zionism can be found in Taro Tsurumi, "The Russian Origins of Zionism: Interactions with the Empire as the Background of the Zionist World View," *Kyoto Bulletin of Islamic Area Studies* 3, no. 1 (2009): 261–71.
250. Jabotinsky is perhaps referring to A. I. Kastelianski, *Formy natsional'nogo dvizheniia v sovremennykh gosudarstvakh: Avstro-Vengriia, Rossiia, Germaniia* (St. Petersburg: Obshchestvennaia pol'za, 1910).
251. Arthur Van Gehuchten (1861–1914) was a Belgian doctor and anatomist who taught biology at Cambridge University.
252. This marks the end of the first part of the Hebrew version of *Story of My Life*, which was published in the 1946–47 edition of Jabotinsky's collected works, *Ketavim*.
253. Dmitry Neidgardt (1861–1942), as mentioned in note 129, was Odessa's city governor (*gradonachal'nik*) from 1903 to 1905. He is notable particularly because his tenure coincided with the beginning of the revolutionary events in Odessa: the revolt of the battleship *Potemkin* and the Jewish pogrom of 1905 in Odessa.
254. Nachman Syrkin (1868–1924) was a famous theorist of Zionism and founder of Labor Zionism. Moses Nahum Sirkin (1878–1918) was a friend of Jabotinsky; as a journalist in Kiev, he wrote for *Rassvet* and was the author of *Ha-opozitsiya ha-tsionut* (Kiev, 1913).

255. "Goroskop," *Odesskie Novosti*, January 1, 1912, 3. The article was republished a number of times.
256. *Der Fraynd* was the first Yiddish daily in Russia; it began publishing in 1903.
257. Kaluga is a region ninety-five miles southwest of Moscow.
258. "S Bogom" means "God be with you."
259. Efim Tchlenov (1863–1918) was an important Russian Zionist leader and author of books on Russian Zionism; Arthur Hantke (1869–1955) was a Zionist leader and head of Keren Hayesod.
260. "Sambatyon" refers to the river beyond which the ten tribes of Israel were sent; in other words, far way and irrevocably unattainable.
261. Knut Hamsun (1859–1952), the Norwegian author, was awarded the Nobel Prize in Literature in 1920; Selma Lagerlöf (1858–1940) was a Swedish writer and the first woman to win the Nobel Prize in Literature.
262. Sven Hedin (1865–1952), a Swedish explorer, wrote a number of books in the first quarter of the twentieth century that were suspicious of an expansionist Russia. He was also an apologist for German military might during World War I. For example, see *With the German Armies in the West*, trans. H. G. de Walterstorff (London: Lane, 1915).
263. Nicholas II (1868–1918), last tsar of the Russian Empire, ruled from 1894 to 1917. During his reign two revolutions were fomented: one in 1905 and a second in February 1917. Nicholas had many problems with Jews, whom he apparently personally disliked. He continued and in several ways expanded the anti-Semitic policies of his father, Alexander III. During his reign immigration of Jews to the United States flourished. Nicholas criminalized Zionist activities. However, as a result of the October Proclamation (1905), Jews acquired limited suffrage to elect representatives to a State Duma. Nicholas and his family were assassinated by Bolsheviks in 1918.
264. "Transjordan front" refers to the battles between British and Turkish forces in 1918. Colonel John Henry Patterson (1867–1947) was the Irish-born commander of the Zion Mule Corps in Gallipoli (1915) and of the Jewish Legion at the end of World War I. Patterson was famous as a lion hunter in Africa. His book, *The Man-eaters of Tsavo and Other East African Adventures* (1907), was a bestseller in its time. Patterson wrote an introduction to Jabotinsky's *Story of the Jewish Legion* and is himself the author of *With the Zionists in Gallipoli* (1916) and *With the Judeans in the Palestine Campaign* (1922).
265. Vasco de da Gama (1469–1524) was a Portuguese explorer.
266. Franz Joseph I (1830–1916) was emperor of Austria and king of Hungary.
267. Woodrow Wilson (1856–1924), the twenty-eighth president of the United States.
268. Alexandre Millerand (1859–1943) was a French socialist politician and president of France from 1920 to 1924.
269. Frédéric Mistral (1830–1914) was a French writer and lexicographer of the Occitan language; he wrote the poem *Mirèio* in 1859.
270. "Song of Magali" refers to part of Mistral's poem *Mirèio*.
271. Julius Berger (1884–1948) was editor of the Zionist journal *Die Welt*.
272. Oskar Marmorek (1863–1909) was an Austro-Hungarian architect and Zionist.

INDEX

Abbati, degli Abbati, Armanda, 8, 57, 64, 127n21
Achimeir, Abba, 6
Ahad Ha'am, 11, 31, 71, 75, 102, 143n127, 155n243
Alexander I, Tsar Alexander Romanov, 134n34
Alexander II, Tsar Alexander Romanov, 61, 134n27, 139n88
Alexandrovsk, 37, 38, 60, 132n11
Aliyah, 7, 15, 104
Allenby, Edmund (General), 19
Altalena, 13, 54, 57, 58, 74, 135n39, 137n69–77, 138n79, 138n84. *See also* Jabotinsky, Vladimir
Anti-Semitism, 7, 11, 12, 43, 52, 70
Arabs, 9, 14, 95
Arlosorov, Haim, 6, 127n19, 154n239
Ashkenazi, 96, 98, 100, 154n237
Assimilation, 14, 27–30, 70, 99
Austria, 38, 81, 94, 107, 116, 123
Autobiography, 1, 3, 6, 10, 17, 18, 26, 31, 33

Babkov, Arye, 74, 144n139
Balfour Declaration, 9, 19, 20, 70
Bar-Mitzvah, 7, 41
Bartholomew's Night, 49
Basel, Switzerland, 13, 53, 67, 70, 103
Beilis, Mendel, 6, 15, 128n34, 154n239
Ben-Gurion, David, 2, 6, 17, 129n51
Berberova, Nina, 25
Berdichev, 35
Berger, Julius, 123, 156n271
Berlin, 25, 37, 39, 74, 94, 105, 106, 110, 117, 123
Bern, Switzerland, 7, 46–49, 54, 107
Bernstein-Kogan, Yakov, 66, 140n108

Bezsonov (Bessonov), Vladimir, 72, 143n129
Betar, 2, 8, 10, 11, 22, 90, 113
Betarist, 10, 22
Bey, Djavid, 95, 153n219
Bey, Nazim, 98, 154n233
Bialik, Hayim Nachman, 13, 25, 54, 55, 66, 71, 76, 80, 101, 102, 128n39, 130n77, 137n66, 140n107, 147n164
Bialystok, 80, 81
Bible, 36
Bickerman, Iosif, 60, 138n86
Bilu, 11, 128n35
Binational State, 14
Black Hundreds, 11, 92
Black Sea, 6, 38
Blood Libel, 6, 11, 15
Bodenheimer, Max, 99, 154n235
Bolshevism, Bolshevik Russia, Bolsheviks, 16, 26
Book of Job, 28
Borochov, Ber, 82, 86, 148n175
Britain, 9
British Army, 20
British government, 8
Brit Shalom, 14
Brit Yosef Trumpeldor. *See* Betar
Brutzkus, Julius, 15, 74, 144n140
Bund (General Jewish Labor Bund in Lithuania, Poland, and Russia), 62, 79, 80, 88
Bunin, Ivan, 17, 25

Caucasus, 21
Catholic Church, 7, 53
Cenci, Beatrice, 53, 137n64
Chekhov, Anton, 5, 54, 134n27, 135n39, 137n71

INDEX

Cherikov Affair, 26
Chikhachev, Nicholai, 38, 133n15
Chukovsky, Kornei, 58, 128n37, 138n79
Civil rights, 13, 14, 79–83
Cohen, Ya'akov, 76, 145n149
Congress Poland, 11. See also Poland
Constantinople, 95–101, 104. See also Istanbul
Cosmopolitanism, 7, 8
Crimean War, 111

D'Annunzio, Gabriele, 50, 136n56
Dante, Alighieri, 2, 25, 27
Davidson, Noa, 80, 90, 147n69
Debussy, Claude, 50, 136n53
Decadence, 8, 29, 30
De La Gama, Vasco, 116, 156n265
Democracy, Democratic, 9, 15, 42
Der Fraynd, 109, 156n256
Der Morgen Journal, 3, 126n11
Diaspora, 14–17, 49, 82, 104
Dichtung und Wahrheit, 27, 29
Dickens, Charles, 44
Die Dergreicher, 83, 85. See also Union for the Attainment of Full Rights for the Jewish People in Russia
Discipline, 8, 11, 51
Dizengoff, Meir, 96
Dmowski, Roman, 16, 81, 102, 148n173, 155n245
Dnieper, 12, 37, 38, 60, 132n11, 133n13
Donizetti, Gaetano, 86, 150n190
Dreyfus, Alfred, 62, 139n89, 141n110
Dubnov, Shimon (Semyon), 79, 105, 147n162, 155n246
Dumas, Père, 15, 44, 134n30, 148n179
Duse, Eleanora, 50, 136n56

Eastern Europe, 2, 17, 23
Efron, Ilya, 74, 144n137
Egypt, 11, 67, 112
El-Arish, 67
Elliot, George, 44
Emigration, 11, 16
Endecja, 16, 102
Ethiopian, 10, 45
Evreiskaia Mysl', 88
Evreiskaia Zhizn', 13, 73, 88

Fascism, 8, 51
Fedorov, Alexander, 46, 135n41
Ferri, Enrico, 50, 52, 136n54
Fictional autobiography, 5, 27
Fin de Siècle, 3, 8, 12
Finland, 11, 73, 89, 90, 110, 111
Finland Station, 89
France, 22, 28, 49, 62, 70, 79, 84, 94, 112–19, 123
Franz Joseph I, Emperor of Austria, 117, 156n266
Friedman, Isaiah, 69, 142n115

Galicia, 48, 49, 52
Galilee, 96
Gallipoli, 22
Galperin, Jeanne (Johanna), 10, 45, 93, 134n36
Galut, 13, 75, 80–87, 90, 103
Gapon, Georgy, 66, 79, 144n105
Garibaldi, Giuseppe, 50, 61, 62, 129n52, 136n55, 139n89
Gegenwartsarbeit, 13
Gehuchten, Arthur Van, 106, 155n251
Geneva, 28, 62
Gepstein, Shlomo, 74, 144n139
German, 4, 6, 35, 37, 39, 49, 70, 79, 95, 105–11, 116, 119, 120–23
Giusti, Giuseppe, 50, 136n55
Goldberg, Isaac, 75, 76, 86, 88, 109, 110, 145n145
Goldstein, Alexander, 74, 144n139
Goncharov, Ivan, 44, 129n52, 134n32
Gordon, A. D., 22
Gordon, Yehudah Leib, 41, 45, 133n21
Gorky, Maxim, 5, 17, 54, 137n72
Gourd of Jonah, 39
Goy, 21, 72, 70
Greater Israel, 3
Greek Church, 7, 53
Greeks, 12, 95, 98
Grinberg, Hayim, 91, 151n207
Grossman, Meir, 5, 131n90
Gruenbaum, Yitzhak, 90, 151n206
Grusenberg, Samuel, 75, 145n142

Hadar, 22
Halastra, 75, 79, 76, 85, 84
Ha-Melits, 38
Hamsun, Knut, 112, 156n261

158

INDEX

Hantke, Arthur, 110, 156n259
Harte, Bret, 44, 134n30
Hartglass, Apolinari, 18, 80, 81, 148n171
Hasidism, 132n3
Ha-Tsohar (Zionist Revisionist Party), 24, 90
Hauptmann, Gerhart, 50, 136n56
Haynt, 3
Hebrew (Hebraic) culture, 15, 27, 47, 76, 102, 103
Hebrew language, 3, 15, 41, 46, 76, 94, 102–5, 121
Hebrew schools, 15, 105
Hedin, Sven, 114, 156n262
Heifetz, Izrail Moiseevich, 55–58, 102, 137n75
Helsingfors (Helsinki), 13, 14, 86–92, 107, 110
Helsingfors program, 76, 82, 88, 90
Herut Party, 2
Herzl, Theodor, 8, 14, 17, 22–24, 30, 68, 69, 83, 90, 105, 131n71, 141n110, 142n115, 143n127, 145n151, 151n200
Hibbat Zion, 11, 90, 98
Hitler, Adolph, 6
Hochberg, Sami, 98–100, 154n231
Horowitz, Brian, 128n41n44, 145n141, 155n242
Hungary, 38, 52, 94, 132n6, 156n266

Ibsen, Henrik Johan, 50, 136n56
Idel'son, Avram, 13, 18, 75, 86, 88, 90, 106, 128n41, 144n141
Ilovaysky, Dmitry, 97, 154n228
Irgun (Irgun Zvai Leumi), 2
Israel (Eretz Yisrael), 2, 3, 31, 57, 85, 93, 95, 98, 104, 113
Istanbul, 1, 5, 114, 154n230, 153n219
Italian, 3, 8, 13, 51–64, 84–86, 93–98, 116, 117, 121

Jabotinsky, Eri, vii, viii, 125n1, 126n11, 134n36, 138n83, 154n240
Jabotinsky Institute, vii, ix, 4
Jabotinsky, Miron (Mitya), 36
Jabotinsky, Tamar 36, 132n7
Jabotinsky, Vladimir Ze'ev, vii, ix, 4, 126n2, 127n21, 128n33, 129n49, 131n88, 131n89, 155n248
Jabotinsky, Vladimir Ze'ev, works: *Blood (Krov')*, 136n60, 138n81; *Collected Works (Ketavim)*, vii, 155n252; *Exile and Assimilation (Golah ve-hitbolelut)*, viii, 3, 125n3; *Five, The (Piatero)*, vii, 2, 27, 131n87; *Samson the Nazarite (Samson Nazorei)*, 2, 3, 25–27, 131n83; *Stories (Razskazy)*, 25, 131n82; *Story of the Jewish Legion*, viii, vii, ix, 3, 19, 20, 22, 27, 31, 125n1, 126n9, 130n57, 156n264; *Story of My Life (Sippur yamai)*, vii, 2, 3, 18, 125n2, 126n14; *Turkey and the War*, 20; *What Do Revisionists Want*, 24
Jabotinsky, Yevgeny, 12, 38, 41
Jabotinsky, Ze'ev, ix
Jacobson, Victor, 95–97, 153n220
Jaffa, 96
Jaffe, Leib, 86, 145n145, 150n191
Japan, Japanese, 21, 84, 108
Jaurès, Jean, 52, 136n61
Jerusalem (Yerushalayim), 24, 49, 50, 70, 76
Jewish education, 6, 7, 42, 131n1, 133n26
Jewish Legion, vii–ix, 3, 6, 19–22, 27, 31, 74, 110
Jewish majority, 9, 14, 24, 48, 79, 81
Jewish National Fund, 21
Jewish Parliament, 15
Jewish people, 6, 19, 21, 49, 70, 83
Jewish People's Group, 148n177, 149n186
Jewish self-defense, 13, 15, 25, 26, 65, 66, 79
Jewish Socialist Workers Party, 148n175
Jewish Socialist Workers Party in Tsarist Poland, 82
Jewish State, 6, 9, 14, 17, 31
Jordan River, 9, 24,
Judaism, 7, 14, 29, 41, 42
Judennot, 11, 82
Juvenal, 70

Kahn, Jacobus, 99, 100, 154n235
Karmen, Lazar Osipovich, 58, 138n80
Kastelianski, A. I., 105, 155n250
Katowice, 5
Katsis, Leonid, vii, 125n6, 131n86
Katz, Samuel (Shmuel), ix, 126n9
Katznelson, Berl, 11
Kerensky, Alexander, 92, 152n209
Kharkov, 37, 140n108
Khodasevich, Vladislav, 25
Kibbutz, 22
Kiev, 12, 37, 75, 77, 105
Kipling, Rudyard, 40, 133n18
Kirschrot, Jan, 80, 90, 147n169
Kishinev, 13, 25, 64–68

INDEX

Kook, Rav (Abraham Yitzhak ha-Cohen), 6
Korolenko, Vladimir, 17–19, 45, 129n53, 130n54, 135n39
Kovalevsky, Maksim, 92, 152n209
Kusskova, Ekaterina Smitrievna, 77, 146n155

Labori, Fernand, 61, 139n89
Labor Party (Avoda), 2
Labor Zionism, 6
Labriola, Antonio, 50, 52, 59, 136n54
Lebedintsev, Vsevolod, 8, 12, 18, 43, 56, 64, 134n28
Lenin, Vladimir (Ulianov), 49, 52, 134n37, 135n47, 149n182
Leopardi, Giacomo, 50, 136n55
Lermontov, Mikhail, 44, 134n29
Levant, 14, 20
Levi, Primo, 70, 143n125
Levin, Shmarya, 17, 128n36, 129n51
Liberalism, 8, 9, 15, 50, 78
Liberals, 8, 15
Lichtenstein, Abraham, 49, 135n50
Likud Party, 2
Lita, 76
London, 20, 22, 119, 78, 95, 119–23
"Lover of Zion," 60. *See also* Hibbat Zion
Lurie, Joseph, 86, 150n191
Lviv (Lvov), 12

Maggid of Dubno, 35
Manchester Guardian, 109
Mapai, 2, 6, 8
Marcus, David, 100, 154n237
Margolin, Moisei Markovich, 74, 144n136
Marinetti, Filippo Tommaso, 51, 136n58
Marllamé, Stéphane, 25
Marmorek, Oskar, 123, 156n272
Marx, Karl, 48, 56
Marxism, Marxist, 13, 52, 62, 80
May Laws, 11
Mazzini, Guiseppe, 50, 136n55
Merezhkovsky, Dmitry, 25, 136n62
Mickiewicz, Adam, 16, 44, 80, 134n33, 147n165
Millerand, Alexandra, 121, 156n268
Milyukov, Pavel, 92, 152n209
Minorities, 9, 12, 14, 15, 86, 90, 105
Minority rights, 9, 14, 15

Mistral, Frédéric, 121, 156n269
Mizrachi (Merkaz Ruhani), 86, 150n192
Moldavanka, 61, 65
Monzie, de Monzie, Anatole, 46, 47, 135n43
Moscow, 11, 12, 66, 74–78, 101, 109, 110, 123
Moskal, 16, 80
Muscular Jew, 23

Nabokov, Vladimir, 17, 25, 131n80
Naiditsch, Isaac, 15
Nakhimovsky, Alice, 28, 29, 131n90
Nasha Zhizn', 77
Nationalism, 7, 8, 29
National rights, 9, 13–15, 76, 79–83
Nation-State, 14
Nazi, 6
Neidgardt, Dmitry, 107, 143n129, 155n253
New Zionist Organization (NZO), 6
Nicholas I, Romanov, Tsar of Russia, 21, 108
Nicholas II, Romanov, Tsar of Russia, 114, 139n95, 141n113, 156n263
Nietzsche, Friedrich, 8, 43, 54
Nofech, Isaac, 98, 154n232
Nikopol, 38, 39, 63
Nordau, Max, 11, 17, 22, 23, 31, 52, 123, 126n13, 130n67, 132n1, 136n63, 137n63
Nordau Plan, 23
Northern Messenger (Severnyi Vestnik), 135n39
Novelli, Ermete, 50, 136n56
Novoe Vremya, 74, 144n134
Nuri-Bey, Djejal, 97, 100, 154n230

October Revolution, 134n37, 137n66, 133n18, 139n92, 152n209, 160n195
Odessa, 1, 2, 3, 6, 12, 25, 28, 30, 36, 39, 52, 55, 59, 60, 70, 74, 77, 96, 99, 103, 110
Odesskie Novosti, 13, 51
Odesskii Listok, 46
Olim, 23
Orzeszkowa, Eliza, 16, 81, 148n172
Ostrogorsky, Moisei, 85, 149n185

Padishah, 96
Pale of Settlement, 11, 15, 28, 46, 84, 89, 92
Palestine, 6, 9, 14, 16, 19–24, 30, 49, 67, 74, 80, 97–99, 104–6, 110
Paris, 19, 53, 73, 74, 98, 119–23

INDEX

Paris Peace Conference, 19
Pasha, Enver, 95, 153n219
Pasmanik, Daniil, 85, 86, 150n189
Pasternak, Boris, 17
Patterson, John Henry (Colonel), 117, 22, 115, 156n264
Pinsker, Leon, 11, 30
Plehve, Viaceslav von, 68, 79, 141n113, 142n116
Plekhanov, Georgy, 49, 62, 135n47, 136n51, 139n95
Podolia, 48, 77
Poe, Edgar Allen, 25, 45, 97, 101, 134n33
Pogroms, 1, 11–15, 25, 60–66, 82, 84, 155
Poland, 11, 16, 80, 81, 90, 102
Poliakov-Litovtsev, Solomon, 92, 151n208
Polish government, 16, 23
Polish Jews, Polish Jewry, 16, 17
Polish Zionists, 16, 17, 80
Polonsky, Yakov, 40, 133n17
Port Arthur, 21, 28
Pravda, 45
Pushkin, Alexander, 25, 44, 127n30, 134n29

Radicalism, Radicals, 1, 77
Rappoport, Hayim, 49, 136n51
Rassvet, 13, 15, 98, 74, 97, 98, 103–9
Ratner, Mark, 92, 152n210
Ravnitzky, Yehoshua, ix, 7, 41, 42, 49, 60, 70, 133n20
Razdelnaya, 48. *See also* Odessa
Red Terror, 15
Reichsberg, Naum, 48, 135n46
Reid, Mayne, 44, 134n30
Renner, Karl, 147n162
Revisionism (Revisionist Zionism), 2, 6, 8, 15, 20, 24, 90
Richelieu Lyceum, 10, 45
Ristori, Adelaide, 50, 136n56
Romania, 94
Romanticism, 16, 80
Rome, viii, 1, 5, 7, 12, 26, 39, 46, 50–58, 70, 93, 106, 116, 117
ROPIT, 12, 37–39
Rosenbaum, Shimshon, 100, 154n238
Rosov, Israel, 75, 77, 108, 145n143
Rossi, Ernesto, 50, 136n56
Rostand, Edmond, 44, 134n33

Rus', 74, 77, 78, 92
Russia, 7–15, 25, 31, 37, 48, 49, 56, 65, 68, 76–81, 83, 97–101, 105, 108, 111
Russian colony, 48, 49, 50, 54. *See also* Russian Emigration
Russian emigration, 11
Russian language, 3, 13, 16, 35, 41, 121
Russian literature, 17, 57
Russian State Duma, 15, 104
Russian Symbolists, 25
Russia's Silver Age, 1, 30
Russkie Vedomosti, 78, 109
Russo-Japanese War, 21, 84

Salonika (Salonica), 95–98
Salvini, Tommaso, 50, 136n56
Schiller, Friedrich, 35, 132n5
Schwartz, Sholem, 91, 151n207
Scott, Walter, 44, 134n30
Second Aliyah, 15, 104
Seideman, Arnold, 15, 74, 97, 144n139
Self-fashioning, 4, 5, 17
Semites, 10, 36
Sephardic, ix, 98
SERP. *See* Jewish Socialist Workers Party in Tsarist Poland
Settlements (Jewish Settlements), 96, 104
Shaevich, Henrik, 65, 66, 140n103
Shakespeare, William, 25, 27, 44, 50
Shem, 10, 36
Shneur, Zalman, 76, 145n149
Shuvalov, Pyotr, 72, 73, 107, 143n129
Sirkin, (Moses) Nahum, 49, 91, 107, 135n49, 155n254
Slavinsky, Maxim, 92, 152n210
Sliozberg, Henrik, 79, 83, 89, 103, 146n159, 151n202
Social Democrat (SD), 49, 84
Socialism, Socialists, 1, 15, 16, 23, 49–56, 61
Socialist Revolutionary (SR), 8, 49, 57, 84
Soloveichik, Max, 74, 144n139
Sorin, Nikolai, 15, 73, 74, 143n130
Spielhagen, Friedrich, 44, 134n31
Springer, Rudolf, 79, 147n162. *See also* Renner, Karl
Stanislawski, Michael, 5, 22, 126n13, 129n53, 130n70, 131n1, 135n50, 138n81, 141n114
Stavsky, Abraham, 6

INDEX

Stoessel, Anatoly (General), 21, 130n60
Stolypin, Pyotr, 15
St. Petersburg, v, 1, 12, 28, 45, 49, 53, 60, 66, 71–79, 83, 84, 88, 89, 92, 95, 97, 101–3, 109, 114, 119
Stravinsky, Igor, 50, 136n53
Struve, Pyotr, 15, 105, 129n50, 139n95, 146n152, 155n249
Suvorin, Alexei, 74, 77, 78, 144n134
Switzerland, 7, 47, 94
Synthetic Zionism, 13
Syrkin, Nachman, 107, 155n254

Takiya. *See* Jewish Socialist Workers Party in Tsarist Poland
Tatars, 86, 90
Tchernichovsky, Shaul, 76, 145n149, 151n207
Tchlenov, Efim, 15, 110, 141n111, 142n120, 156n259
Teffi (Nadezhda Lokhvitskaya), 25
Tel Aviv, vii, ix, 3, 4, 6, 96
Tel Hai, 21, 22
Tiomkin, Vladimir, 15, 66, 140n108, 141n111
Tolstoy, Leo, 13, 17, 50, 134n27, 136n56
Transjordan, 115, 151n205, 156n264
Trivus, Israel, 15, 18, 65, 91, 140n100, 150n196
Trumpeldor, Joseph, 20–23, 151n203
Tsiony Tsion, 77, 142n120
Tsvetaeva, Marina, 25
Turkey, 20, 95–100, 123
Turks, 12, 95, 96, 99, 100, 105
Tyshkevich, Alexander, 88, 150n197

Uganda Proposal, 69, 70, 77
Ukraine, 7, 12, 35–38, 60, 80
Ukrainians, 12, 38, 86, 92, 105, 108
Union for the Attainment of Full Rights for the Jewish People in Russia, 83, 84
United States, 91, 117
Ussishkin, Menachem, 15, 66, 93, 97, 105, 140n108, 142n120, 149n181, 150n19

Vienna, 1, 38, 39, 48, 94–99, 101–5, 116
Vilna (Vilno, Vilnius), 28, 66, 71, 75, 79, 86, 88, 97, 99, 103
Vinaver, Maxim, 79, 83–85, 146n159, 149n185
Voskhod, 45, 49, 79, 80
Vozrozhdenie Group, 148n175

Wagner, Richard, 50, 86, 136n53
Warsaw, 3, 16, 28, 80, 81, 88, 91, 98, 102
Weizmann, Chaim, 1, 8, 10, 11, 15, 17, 20, 23, 68, 69, 105, 106, 123, 129n51, 135n50, 141n112
Wilhelm I, Kaiser of Germany, 39, 133n16
Wilson, Woodrow, 117, 156n267
Witte, Sergei, 3, 62, 63, 139n95
Wolfsohn, David, 5, 15, 97–100, 127n17, 153n226
World War One, viii, 1, 3, 15, 20, 31, 51, 74, 101
World Zionist Organization (WZO), 5, 6, 97

Yaffe, Betsal'el, 75, 145n145
Yiddish, 3, 4, 6, 35, 41, 48, 49, 62, 65, 76, 80, 86, 96, 109
Young Turks, 95, 99

Zacconi, Ermete, 50, 136n56
Zak, Meir, 35
Zal'tsman, Shlomo, viii, 18, 64, 67, 71, 102, 139n99
Zeitlin, Moshe, 74, 144n139
Zhelyabov, Andrei, 61, 139n88
Zhitlovsky, Hayim, 49, 135n48, 148n175
Zionism, 1–15, 19–24, 27–31, 46, 49–52, 60, 66–70, 74, 75, 79–87, 90, 98–104, 107
Zionist Congress, 5, 11, 13, 23, 67, 77, 83, 86, 90, 103
Zionist Movement, 6, 19, 22, 24, 67, 74, 75, 90
Zion Mule Corps, 22
Zlatopolsky, Hillel, 75, 105, 145n145
Zola, Emile, 44
Zschokke, Johann Heinrich Daniel, 35, 132n5
Życie Żidówske, 147n169, 148n171

www.ingramcontent.com/pod-product-compliance
Lightning Source LLC
Chambersburg PA
CBHW051746230426
43670CB00012B/2184